THE AUGUSTINIAN PERSON

THE AUGUSTINIAN PERSON

PETER BURNELL

THE CATHOLIC UNIVERSITY OF AMERICA PRESS

Washington, D.C.

The paper used in this publication meets the minimum
requirements of American National Standards for Information
Science—Permanence of Paper for Printed Library Materials,
ANSI Z39.48-1984.

∞

LIBRARY OF CONGRESS CATALOGING-IN-PUBLICATION DATA
Burnell, Peter, 1945–
The Augustinian person / Peter Burnell.— 1st ed.
p. cm.
Includes bibliographical references and index.
ISBN-13: 978-0-8132-1418-4 (pbk. : alk. paper)
ISBN-10: 0-8132-1418-1 (pbk. : alk. paper)
1. Man (Christian theology)—History of doctrines—Early church, ca. 30–600.
2. Augustine, Saint, Bishop of Hippo.   I. Title.
BT701.3.B87 2005
233′.092—dc22
2004018080

TO *Herbert Batt, Todd Breyfogle, Kevin Corrigan,*
Jene Porter, and Robert Sider

CONTENTS

PREFACE

The purpose of this book is to make plain Augustine's often implicit notions of person and human nature. The reader will notice that this enterprise entails correcting numerous twentieth-century criticisms of Augustine's thought. It would be a serious misunderstanding to conclude from this that the book is intended merely to defend him against his critics. As will emerge, especially in the final chapter, some of Augustine's positions—his insistence, for example, on the damnation of every baby who dies unbaptized, or his acceptance of judicial torture into the list of genuine public duties—leave him open to criticism, as he tacitly admits. The point, then, is not that Augustine should not be criticized but first, that many modern criticisms of his thought are gravely misdirected and need to be redirected to the right places and second, that the errors concerned, uncorrected, obscure his anthropology.

None of the material here has been published before, with a small exception: about a page of argumentation in chapter 3 has appeared, almost as it does here, in my essay "Is the Augustinian Heaven Inhuman? The Arguments of Martin Heidegger and Hannah Arendt," in *History, Apocalypse, and the Secular Imagination: New Essays on Augustine's "City of God,"* ed. Mark Vessey, Karla Pollmann, and Allan D. Fitzgerald, O.S.A. (Bowling Green, Ohio: Philosophy Documentation Center, 1999), published concurrently in *Augustinian Studies* 30, 2 (1999).

The translations in this book are my own unless otherwise noted. The notes are used only for references, with the occasional addition of a short comment specifying the point of a reference.

The five dedicatees are people whose help has been fundamental; Herb Batt, Kevin Corrigan, and Robert Sider all read the manuscript at different stages of cultivation and prevailed on me to make important changes (though I am uncomfortably aware that the remaining flaws are instances of my resistance or neglect of their advice); Todd Breyfogle and Jene Porter gave plentiful help and encouragement in associated matters. I owe them all a lot and thank them very much for their great kindness and generosity.

Thanks also to the University of Saskatchewan for allowing me to devote two half-year sabbatical leaves to work on the manuscript; to Susan Needham, former managing editor at the Catholic University of America Press, for her perceptive comments; to Beverly Towstiak for her considerable editorial help; to the two readers who evaluated the manuscript (one of whom identified himself as Gerald Bonner) for their incisive observations; to Carla Barber for one valuable suggestion; and to Pat Magosse for her highly intelligent criticisms.

ABBREVIATIONS

The following abbreviations are used in parenthetical references in the text for Augustine's works. Also listed here are the full Latin titles, their English translations, and the date of composition of each work.

Ad Oros.	*Ad Orosium contra Priscillianistas* *To Orosius against the Priscillianists* [415]
Ad Simpl.	*Ad Simplicianum* *To Simplicianus* [396]
C. duas ep. Pel.	*Contra Duas Epistulas Pelagianorum* *Against Two Letters of the Pelagians* [ca. 420]
C. Faust.	*Contra Faustum Manichaeum* *Against Faustus the Manichee* [ca. 398–ca. 400]
C. Iul.	*Contra Iulianum* *Against Julian* [ca. 421]
C. Iul. op. imp.	*Contra Iulianum Opus Imperfectum* *Unfinished Work against Julian* [428–430]
C. serm. Ar.	*Contra Sermonem Arianorum* *A Sermon of the Arians* [ca. 418]
CD	*De Civitate Dei* *City of God* [413–427]
Conf.	*Confessiones* *Confessions* [397–401]
DC	*De Doctrina Christiana* *On Christian Teaching* [ca. 395 and 426]

De ag. Chr.	*De Agone Christiano* *On the Christian Struggle* [396–397]
De an. et eius or.	*De Anima et eius Origine* *On the Soul and Its Origin* [ca. 419–ca. 421]
De bapt. c. Don.	*De Baptismo contra Donatistas* *On Baptism against the Donatists* [400–401]
De corr. et gr.	*De Correptione et Gratia* *On Reproof and Grace* [ca. 426–ca. 427]
De div. qu. 83.	*De Diversis Quaestionibus 83* *Eighty-Three Diverse Questions* [ca. 388–396]
De gr. Chr. et pecc. or.	*De Gratia Christi et de Peccato Originali* *On the Grace of Christ and Original Sin* [418]
De gr. et lib. arb.	*De Gratia et Libero Arbitrio* *On Grace and Free Will* [426–427]
De lib. arb.	*De Libero Arbitrio* *On Free Will* [387–395]
De nat. et grat.	*De Natura et Gratia* *On Nature and Grace* [415]
De nupt. et conc.	*De Nuptiis et Concupiscentia* *On Marriage and Concupiscence* [419–420]
De pecc. mer.	*De Peccatorum Meritis et Remissione et de Baptismo* *Parvulorum* *On the Merits and Remission of Sins* [411–412]
De perf. iust.	*De Perfectione Iustitiae Hominis* *On the Perfection of Human Righteousness* [ca. 414]
De sp. et litt.	*De Spiritu et Littera* *On the Spirit and the Letter* [412]
De Trin.	*De Trinitate* *On the Trinity* [399–ca. 420]
En. in Ps.	*Enarrationes in Psalmos* *Elucidations on the Psalms* [392–ca. 418]

Ench.	*Enchiridion ad Laurentium de fide spe et caritate* A Handbook on Faith, Hope, and Charity [ca. 421–423]
Ep.	*Epistulae* Letters
Exp. quar. prop. *ex ep. Rom*	*Expositio quarundam Propositionum ex Epistula* *Apostoli ad Romanos* Exposition of Certain Propositions from the Epistle to the Romans [394–395]
Fid. et Symb.	*De Fide et Symbolo* On Faith and the Creed [398]
GL	*De Genesi ad Litteram* Literal Commentary on Genesis [ca. 400–414]
Mus.	*De Musica* On Music [ca. 387]
Retract.	*Retractationes* Retractations [426 or 427]
Serm.	*Sermones* Sermons
Tr. in 1 ep. Ioh.	*Tractatus in Epistulam Iohannis ad Parthos* Tractates on St. John's First Epistle [407]
Tr. in Ioh. Ev.	*Tractatus in Iohannis Evangelium* Tractates on St. John's Gospel [ca. 408–ca. 420]

INTRODUCTION

One of the crucial observations in Charles Taylor's *Sources of the Self* is that Augustine thought of God as "behind the eye" as well as (platonically) before it:[1] God is not only the human mind's ultimate object but the foundation even of its subjectivity. An indication of this is that the most characteristically Augustinian proof of God's existence is based on radical mental self-observation: even as we experience knowing something, we rely on an absolute source of truth as guarantee that we are in fact knowing; so in realizing that we know something we imply the existence of God (*De div. qu. 83.* 54; *De lib. arb.* 2.3.7–2.15.40; *Conf.* 7.10.16, 10.8.12–10.28.39).[2] But other aspects of human nature have a similar importance for him. He saw the human soul as opening not only onto God but, through the body, onto matter. Given that the soul is so made by creation, and we are created in God's image, his theology is much concerned with the relationship of body and soul.[3] Moreover, to Henri Marrou's disgust, Augustine interprets "all Creation still groans and mourns, expecting the revelation of the sons of God" as meaning precisely that human beings in this world so groan, mourn, and expect—not that the holy angels, or beasts, or vegetables and rocks, do. The point, Augustine argues, is that only human nature contains God's entire Creation, by representing each of its degrees from intellect to physical object (Rom 8.19, 22;

1. Charles Taylor, *Sources of the Self: The Making of the Modern Identity* (Cambridge, Mass.: Harvard University Press, 1989), 136.

2. Taylor, 132; Eugène Portalié, S.J., *A Guide to the Thought of Saint Augustine*, trans. Ralph J. Bastian, S.J. (London: Burns and Oates, 1960), 126.

3. See John M. Rist, *Augustine: Ancient Thought Baptized* (Cambridge: Cambridge University Press, 1994), 92–95.

I

De div. qu. 83. 67.2–5; Exp. quar. prop. in ex ep. Rom. 53; Ad Oros. 8.11).[4] So St. Paul's long-awaited universal salvation is, for Augustine, human salvation. Furthermore, as we shall see, Augustine expounds his understanding of the Incarnation in terms of human society. His theology, then, is anthropological.

Conversely, his approach to human nature and experience is theological. In the *Confessions* he begins to explore the enigma of his own heart by repeatedly asking what relationship is possible between himself and God. The main theological controversies that punctuated his life established and reaffirmed this approach. The dispute with the Manichaeans gave a theological context, in his mind, to the relationship of soul and body, the nature of human motivation, and human morality. The dispute with the Donatists forced him to give theological consideration to human society. The dispute with the Pelagians led him to conclude that the human relationship with God determines the human condition in its every aspect. Thus his theology determined what were the important questions of his anthropology.

These questions, when put in a general form, are the central ones for any theologian claiming to elucidate the human relationship with God: How is human nature constituted? In what sense are both God and human beings persons? Given our nature and personality, what are the fundamental conditions in which all people live and act? In those conditions, what acts and states of mind primarily befit a human individual and connect human morality with divine goodness? In what modes are human individuals socially related to one another, and what is the relationship of human society with God? And finally (the question subsuming all the others): What, outright, is the relationship between human beings and God?

4. Henri-Irénée Marrou, *Saint Augustin et l'augustinisme* (Paris: Editions du Seuil, 1955), 73–74. For later statements of a view similar to Marrou's, see Paula Fredriksen, "Beyond the Body/Soul Dichotomy: Augustine on Paul against the Manichees and the Pelagians," *Recherches augustiniennes* 23 (1988): 113. For a reply to Marrou (mentioned but not dealt with by Fredriksen), see Thomas E. Clarke, S.J., "St. Augustine and Cosmic Redemption," *Theological Studies* 19 (1958): 133–64, esp. 163–64.

Recast in their specifically Augustinian forms, these questions are: What is the relationship between soul and body? Since the soul is the core of a human being and the mind is the primary characteristic of the soul, what is the structure of the human mind, by which we exceed the other animals and (like God) exist as persons? Given the fundamental constitution of humanity, what determines our present condition, how do sin and grace operate in it, and in what other conditions can human life be lived? If charity, in any possible human condition, is the essence of virtue, what is its relationship with other virtues and other forms of love, and given that it is a specifically human virtue, in what sense do both God and human beings act as persons by exercising it? Given that charity must be exercised toward other human beings, what are the specifically social principles by which we can have citizenship in God, and what is the relationship of such a society with other forms of human society? These questions all form parts of a further, larger one: In what sense are human beings made in the image of God and even, in the end, made divine?

That these six subjects are the central ones in Augustine's anthropology is confirmed by their tendency to overtake others that he considers important. The moral principles specific to the family, for example, he treats as components of civil morality, for it is in civil society that, according to him, social ethics impinge on theology directly (CD 19.16). Again, friendship is an obviously important area of experience for Augustine; it is grief at a friend's death that first lays open to him the fathomlessness of his own soul (Conf. 4.4.9). But when he makes it a subject of discourse he treats it, in the Confessions, as part of our fourth question (What is the rightful place of one's love for mortal beings in relation to one's love for God?) and later, in both the Confessions and the City of God, as part of our second question (What is the relation between emotion and understanding?) (Conf. 4.7.12; CD 9.5). Again, in his early works he is much concerned with aesthetics, but as R. J. O'Connell points out, Augustine's theory of art inexorably opens onto the wider areas—notably his conception

of human nature—from which that theory springs; thus his speculations on the meaning of art are ancillary to his primary, anthropological task.[5]

The order followed in this book alternates between questions of
human nature and of personality, and as will be seen the two approaches yield different results. The first chapter is on the fundamentals of Augustine's notion of human nature, the second on his notion
of person. Going beyond those fundamentals will necessitate a direct
study of his concept of the human condition, since so much of his
mature theology is pervaded by questions of sin and its effects; the
third chapter, which is on this subject, has human nature as its main
application. Chapter 4, which is on virtue—on the divine and human
response to sin—addresses his idea of person in that context; his notion of charity will be fundamental here. Chapter 5 again reverts to
human nature, since as we shall see, according to Augustine orientation upon others—a primary characteristic of persons—also determines the natural character of human society. In chapter 6 both
strands of thought are further developed.

On each of the main issues, despite Augustine's changes of mind,
there is either a single work or a group of works in which, it is commonly agreed, his thought reaches a definitive culmination. His
thinking on the relationship of soul and body is most fully elaborated
in *De Genesi ad Litteram,* his *Literal Commentary on Genesis;* on the human mind and its faculties and the person, human and divine, in *De
Trinitate;* on grace and the human condition in the anti-Pelagian
works, where that theory has its highest development; on the nature
of charity in the *Tractates on St. John's First Epistle* (which copyists
called *De Caritate*);[6] and on human society in the *City of God.* As to
how he conceived human beings to be made in God's image, because

5. Robert J. O'Connell, S.J., *Art and the Christian Intelligence in St. Augustine* (Cambridge, Mass.: Harvard University Press, 1978), 3–4, 19.

6. See Dany Dideberg, S.J., "Caritas: Prolégomènes à une étude de la théologie augustinienne de la charité," in *Signum Pietatis: Festgabe für Cornelius Petrus Mayer,* ed.
Adolar Zumkeller (Würzburg: Augustinus-Verlag, 1989), 373.

this issue subsumes the preceding ones, the works just mentioned are all crucial, *De Trinitate* being, however, the one most plainly and specifically concerned with the subject. There will be no attempt here to restrict discussion to these works, but it will be taken for granted that they contain much of Augustine's crucial, developed thought on each subject respectively.

To give focus to this discussion it will be useful to consider some modern criticisms of Augustine—indeed, it will be necessary, since much modern scholarship on these areas of his thought has taken the form of criticism. With this in mind we may look ahead to each main chapter in more detail.

The subject of the first chapter is: What, for Augustine, fundamentally constitutes a human being? On his supposedly dualistic notion of body and soul it has been argued that although he was influenced by Porphyry's idea of a "unity without confusion of the constituents" (ἀσύγχυτος ἕνωσις), Porphyry's idea was the more subtle, distinguishing, as Augustine's did not, between a permanent and a temporary mixture.[7] But the discussion of angelic bodies in book 3 of *De Trinitate* shows Augustine to be quite aware of this distinction (*De Trin.* 3.1.5–6). The question, then, is why he omits it from his anthropology.

Others have argued, more radically, that Augustine's dualism in this area is simply too stark to allow him to see a human being as a genuine unity, and that by going to the extreme of positing separate creations of body and soul he distorts both Christian belief and the meaning of the biblical account of Creation.[8] More generally, if we have two natures rather than one, there is nothing to prevent one kind of behavior from befitting one of our natures and a quite different, even opposite, kind of behavior from befitting the other.

7. See Gerard O'Daly, *Augustine's Philosophy of Mind* (London: Duckworth, 1987), 43.

8. P. Agaësse and A. Solignac, *La genèse au sens littéral: 1–7 and 8–12: Bibliothèque augustinienne: Oeuvres de saint Augustin en douze livres* (Paris: Desclée de Brouwer, 1972), 2:540.

Another criticism connected with his supposed dualism of body and soul arises in one of P. Ricoeur's objections to the Augustinian doctrine of original sin. The doctrine, according to Ricoeur, is incompatible with the dualism (the correctness of which Ricoeur accepts); for if Augustine's famous distinction between the natural and the voluntary implies two separate human operations, a physical and a moral, then the idea of hereditary sin is a category mistake, heredity being in the realm of nature and the doctrine of original sin being intended to preserve the principle that sin is not nature, but will. "Speculations, principally Augustinian, about original sin" are, says Ricoeur, "a later rationalization that mixes ethical categories with biological ones."[9] This criticism has recently been reiterated by C. Kirwan.[10] Another dimension of the same problem emerges in J. M. Rist's contention that for Augustine the crucial distinction relevant to the transmission of original sin is rather between what is individual and what is common, and that in this context his sharp disjunction of soul from body is misleading.[11] Augustine himself shows signs of being aware of the problem. When he hesitantly rejects both traducianism and creationism as explanations for the origin of individual souls he does so in dealing with the issue of heredity in sin. His attraction to traducianism (the idea that we inherit our souls from Adam) is particularly strong because it helps to make the idea of hereditary original sin intelligible. That it also tends to a materialistic conception of the soul abhorrent to him indicates the depth of his dilemma and the force of Ricoeur's objection in particular. It is difficult to see how that objection can be countered if the assumption about Augustine's dualism is correct. The logical validity of this part of Augustine's theology thus depends on what conception he has of

9. Paul Ricoeur, *The Symbolism of Evil*, trans. Emerson Buchanan (Boston: Beacon Press, 1969), 83–84, 239. Cf. Paul Ricoeur, "Original Sin: A Study in Meaning," in *The Conflict of Interpretations* (Evanston, Ill.: Northwestern University Press, 1974), 269–86, esp. 286.

10. Christopher Kirwan, *Augustine* (London: Routledge, 1989), 141–42.

11. Rist, 126–28.

the relationship between body and soul. If he has a fundamentally coherent anthropology it must entail an implicit solution to this problem.

Moreover, since Adam and Eve were both created rather than generated, two further features of the basic human constitution confronted Augustine: difference of sex and individuality. These are important in two controversial areas of his thought: his view of women and his doctrine that some people, not all, are predestined to salvation. Regarding the former, his best-known idea (from the *Literal Commentary on Genesis*) is that womanhood can be defined in terms of its auxiliary function: woman, as distinct from man, was created for reproduction (*GL* 9.5.9). Does that idea implicitly demean women's humanity by regarding men as spiritually superior? S. Soennecken has pointed out that for Augustine a man and a woman, equally having a rational soul, are equally in the image of God. On this crucial point, she observes, Augustine rejected the comparatively misogynistic judgments of his own and earlier times;[12] but although he asserted not only that, but also that Eve received God's orders directly, as Adam did, and that her soul was created from nothing, not derived from Adam's, nevertheless Augustine called her the *mediatrix* of sin because of a moral vulnerability rooted in a female's natural inferiority. This, Soennecken argues, is an incongruous relapse into conventional ancient prejudice on the subject. Also Soennecken finds the functionary account of Eve's creation inconsonant precisely because it is functionary, because it still holds a woman to be, though of course fully human spiritually, still purely functional in her purpose as a woman.[13]

Against this must be set a later passage, from the end of the *City of*

12. Silvia Soennecken, "Die Rolle der Frau in Augustins *De Genesi ad Litteram*," in *Signum Pietatis: Festgabe für Cornelius Petrus Mayer*, ed. Adolar Zumkeller (Würzburg: Augustinus-Verlag, 1989), 289–300.

13. See also Kari Elisabeth Børresen, *Subordination and Equivalence: The Nature and Rôle of Woman in Augustine and Thomas Aquinas* (Kampen: Kok Pharos, 1995), 30–31, 34–35.

God, in which Augustine says that in heaven there will still be sexes, but not reproduction (*CD* 22.24). Though possibly, as Rist suggests, the two passages simply are inconsistent, the later passage in any case takes the problem to a deeper level.[14] Again, the relationship of body and soul is at the heart of the question. Augustine says that in heaven resurrected bodies will be spiritual in the sense that souls now fully immortal will animate them and be the source of their entire character (*CD* 22.21). If, as is commonly assumed, Augustine regarded sexual difference as exclusively physical, not spiritual at all, this perfect heavenly economy leaves no logical room for that difference.[15] Here, then, there is arguably another inconsistency connected with his notion of the relationship of body and soul.

Second, the notion that Adam and Eve were created separately implies that human beings were created as individuals: individuality is therefore fundamental to us; it did not arise secondarily (by generation, for example). This is especially important in connection with Augustine's doctrine of grace, above all his notorious conviction that even when tiny infants die some are saved, some not. This idea is not only baffling in itself; it raises a question about the extent to which we are born with our individuality already established. Augustine's theological position is that the divine choice is made gratuitously, not in response to independent virtues or vices in individuals (*De gr. Chr. et pecc. or.* 1.26.27; *C. Iul.* 4.8.44). Either, therefore, it is arbitrary as regards the human beings chosen (as Rist asserts) or Augustine must have left room for an innate spiritual individuality by which, even though innocently, each human being is somehow limited.

The second main area of Augustine's anthropology is that of the mind's structure, the basis of human personality; and the subject of chapter 2 is his notion of that structure and indeed his entire notion of person in its primary features. Here the best-known problems arise from what is supposed to be his notion of the will. He is said, for example, to have been the first to specify the will as a distinct fac-

14. Rist, 120.   15. Ibid., 115.

ulty.[16] In the 1940s this idea, together with the underlying one that the human mind is an assemblage of separately operating faculties, was attacked by Gilbert Ryle as a misrepresentation of human mental processes.[17] A volition is not a distinct deed of the mind, Ryle argued, but an aspect of mental activity. The Jansenists of the seventeenth century, though completely opposed in principle to a view of reality such as Ryle's, had at least interpreted Augustine as he did: their theory of irresistible grace (purportedly derived from Augustine) depended on just such a sharp distinction between desire and will (God providing some people, for example, with the desire for heaven but not with the will to achieve it).[18] The distinction appears, with extreme sharpness, in Pascal's remarkable statement that the choices we make in life will not harm us spiritually, provided that they are made against our desires.[19]

It is not completely established, however, that Augustine disjoined the mental faculties so thoroughly. J. Wetzel, while agreeing with the Jansenists that Augustinian grace works irresistibly, argues that it does so not by wrenching one mental faculty away from another but by working through the normal human impulses of intellect and emotion; and only in that way can it both be irresistible and preserve the freedom of the human will.[20] On the other hand Wetzel remarks that Augustine treats the mental faculties as separable and often separate, even if not as ultimately working separately; for in the earlier stages of grace, he argues, Augustine thought of God as having prepared the human will to receive grace "before even the advent of new desires for the good." Moreover, he says, according to Augustine's anti-Pelagian theology, one begins, under irresistible divine in-

16. Albrecht Dihle, *The Theory of the Will in Classical Antiquity* (Berkeley: University of California Press, 1982), 123–29.

17. Gilbert Ryle, *The Concept of Mind* (New York: Barnes and Noble, 1949), 62–82.

18. C. Jansenius, *Augustinus* (Rouen: J. Berthelin, 1643), 3.3.1.

19. Blaise Pascal, *Pensées* (Paris: Bibliothèque de la Pléiade, no. 267, n.d.), 895.

20. James Wetzel, *Augustine and the Limits of Virtue* (Cambridge: Cambridge University Press, 1992), 216.

fluence, to will the good before having any knowledge of doing so. And this notion, he says, "drives a wedge between knowing and willing," a wedge that at a later stage is removed.[21] This implies that Augustine regards the mental faculties as inseparable in normal human activity but separable at a deeper, unconscious level in a way known and initially exploited by God; but it does not necessarily clear Augustine of Ryle's charge that the notion of a pure "volition" is an absurdity. The will is still conceived of in Wetzel's account as initially informed (though unconsciously) aside from feelings and understanding. This account of Augustine's psychology is still open to Ryle's interpretation—that that pyschology posits pure acts of the will. But whether it actually does so is still not quite clear. Rist, for example, contests the assertion that for Augustine grace is irresistible but eventually accepts that "Augustine does not pursue these problems with sufficient precision."[22] The underlying problem, then, is that Augustine's precise conception of human mental motivation is in doubt.

Moreover, Augustine's notion of the human mind's structure has an importance beyond his theology of grace, for he regarded that structure as the divine image present in a human being. Modern scholars have various ideas of what he meant by this. The view of J. Laplace and J. Daniélou is that for Augustine it is in the intellect that human beings specifically resemble God (whereas for Gregory of Nyssa, they argue, the resemblance consists in moral freedom).[23] But as G. Bonner points out, Augustine, too, in a Christological and eschatological context, describes the human image of God volitionally: the core of a human being, which is progressively perfected by Christ, is freedom of will, being first the freedom not to sin, then the freedom even from the ability to sin.[24] Here it is the image of the di-

21. Ibid., 194, 192.

22. Rist, 133-35.

23. Jean Laplace, S.J., and Jean Daniélou, S.J., *La création de l'homme (Grégoire de Nysse)* (Paris: Editions du Cerf, 1943), 94.

24. Gerald Bonner, "Augustine's Doctrine of Man: Image of God and Sinner," *Augustinianum* 24 (1984): 510.

vine freedom of will that is the human attribute eventually brought to perfection in heaven. Augustine, in other words, designates the divine image in both ways—by the intellect and by the will (in almost exactly contemporary passages, written about 426). Moreover, even when (near the end of the *City of God*) he talks of "the spark of reason, in which man has been made to God's image," the contrast is not between reason and any other mental faculty but between mind and body (*CD* 22.24). But although in any case the disjunction between these two designations of the divine image is not a necessary one, the relationship between them requires clarification.

Furthermore, since Augustine, in *De Trinitate,* takes the position that the mind's structure forms the person, his notion of person itself is directly at issue here. That notion has been criticized, most notably by A. C. Lloyd, as self-contradictory—as inconsistently combining the categories of substance and relation.[25] This criticism in effect impugns Augustine's theology at its core.

The two primary aspects of Augustine's anthropology so far mentioned have already proved to be not fully separable from his notion of the human condition; and this subject, as we shall see, also pervades his moral theology and his social and political philosophy. Its complexities require it to be treated as its own, main area of Augustine's theory of humanity. Much of what he regarded as characteristically human was a matter of our fallen state, not of our originally created nature. It is desirable to have as clear an understanding as possible of his thought on the subject.

But this area of his thought, though highly developed, is also highly contested. Every one of its specifically Augustinian ideas has been treated with serious reservation by at least some modern commentators. These judgments (many of them commonplaces of Augustinian criticism) are: that he gave a garbled account of the original human transgression, implying that all Adam's descendants prenatally partic-

25. A. C. Lloyd, "On Augustine's Concept of a Person," in *Augustine: A Collection of Critical Essays,* ed. R. A. Markus (Garden City, N.Y.: Anchor, 1972), 199–203.

ipated in that act (N. P. Williams, J. N. D. Kelly, C. Kirwan); that he held each of us, in the consequently "condemned lump," to incur not only original sin but also (though this was theologically unnecessary) original guilt as a separate liability (J. N. D. Kelly); that in contrast with Irenaeus's humane notion that sin is essentially a stage in our development, Augustine propounded a far harsher doctrine largely his own—sin as a complete catastrophe, disruptive of the divine plan for human beings (J. Hick); that he derailed the moral tradition of Western Christianity with another innovation—his insistence that even after baptism (by which original sin and original guilt are taken away) there persists yet a third liability in the form of concupiscence, the internal turbulence of fallen human nature (P. Brown); that this notion of post-baptismal concupiscence is, albeit unintentionally, empty of moral content (J. Wetzel); that in his doctrine of concupiscence Augustine failed to distinguish between irrational desire, hostile to reason and to order in the soul, and merely nonrational desire, innocent in itself (J. Burnaby); that to the idea that damnation consists in eternal separation between holy God and sinful human beings he added the superfluous idea that God inflicts further, positive vengeance (J. Burnaby); that his doctrine of predestinatory grace was an implicit denial of human free will (P. Ricoeur, C. Kirwan); that his conviction that those who die unbaptized are necessarily damned shows an archaic and inflexible sacramental theology (J. M. Rist); that in his doctrine of grace not only are the saved implied to be chosen from the *massa damnata* arbitrarily, but the eventual impeccability of those chosen makes inexplicable, and philosophically unacceptable, the notion that God created us capable of sin in the first place (J. M. Rist); and that the very notion of heavenly impeccability is an unwarranted violation of the economy of human nature even by Augustine's own lights (M. Heidegger).[26]

26. Norman Powell Williams, *The Ideas of the Fall and of Original Sin: A Historical and Critical Study* (London: Longmans, Green, 1927), 372; J. N. D. Kelly, *Early Christian Doctrines*, 4th ed. (London: Adam and Charles Black, 1968), 364; Kirwan, 71, 76, 128, 132, 134–36, 138–42; John Hick, *Evil and the God of Love*, rev. ed. (San Francisco: Harper and

If these criticisms are justified, the conclusion must be that Augustine did not have a coherent idea of the human condition. As we shall see, some support for a number of them can be found in Augustine's thought. Some of them, however, contradict each other: for example, his doctrine of post-baptismal concupiscence might be criticized either for seriously damaging the Christian moral tradition or for being morally inconsequential, but not, consistently, for both. Though it is possible that in some such instances Augustine himself is inconsistent, the possibility must also be considered that at least some of these interpretations are misreadings. Which, then, of the theological shortcomings, if any, are really Augustine's, and in what degree? And if some of the modern interpretations have been misreadings, does their correction yield a coherent Augustinian account of the human condition? A final, specifically theological, question (underlying some of the criticisms just noted) is whether Augustine's notion of the human condition is so fragmented as to preclude the doctrine that Christ assumed the human condition in a more than superficial sense.

Since Augustine treats original sin and concupiscence as damage to our nature, the orientation of chapter 3 will be on human nature.

The fourth chapter is about Augustine's conception of morality. Here again, his notion of our fallen condition is important, but problematic. He takes the view that although sin is opposed to virtue, the fact of sin is also a precondition for virtue, in particular for charity, which for him is the master virtue, the core of morality, and the main difficulties in his thought on this subject come from his describing charity in reference to suffering and sin rather than in paradisal or heavenly terms and yet asserting its divinity even more starkly than St. John the Evangelist had. But can love defined as a desire for happiness be love in the same sense as the love that the Persons of the

---

Row, 1977), 214; Peter Brown, *Religion and Society in the Age of Saint Augustine* (London: Faber and Faber, 1977), 183–207; Wetzel, 175–86; John Burnaby, *Amor Dei: A Study in the Religion of St. Augustine,* rev. ed. (Norwich: Canterbury Press, 1991), 59, 208–9; Ricoeur, *Symbolism,* 84, 151–57; Rist, 278, 285; Theodore Kisiel, *The Genesis of Heidegger's "Being and Time"* (Berkeley: University of California Press, 1993), 205.

Holy Trinity have for each other, or that God has for us, or that the saints in heaven have for each other? Moreover, if God's love expressed Incarnationally is compassion, in what sense could a human being's love for God be of the same nature?

In this area, too, a number of modern writers argue that there are confusions in Augustine's thinking. In particular, the distinction between love defined as a desire and love as disinterested and transcendent in character has struck, though differently, one commentator after another. A. Nygren, for example, regarded the two as ultimately irreconcilable, despite Augustine's attempted synthesis of them; M. C. D'Arcy as complementary but distinct both in themselves and in Augustine's thought; H. Arendt as successfully combined though not perfectly integrated by Augustine; J. Burnaby (in his great reply to Nygren) as integrated, but in a way that still ultimately implies a difference in kind between divine charity and human charity.[27] The central question is whether Augustine provides a principle of charity that organically integrates the various features of that virtue specified in his thought. But the deeper purpose of the chapter is to show, developed and elaborated, the Augustinian notion of person (rudimentarily laid out in chapter 2).

The fifth chapter is about Augustine's conception of human society. As a consequence of the moral primacy of charity, he thought the center of morality to be one's relationships with others.[28] But the form of society those relationships naturally take, whether in circumstances of sin or not, are a further theologically crucial area of his anthropology. The *City of God* is by far his most elaborate account of this subject. In effect it is also his *De Incarnatione* in respect of human nature; it narrates the history of civil life as the history both of the

27. Anders Nygren, *Agape and Eros,* trans. Philip S. Watson (London: SPCK, 1953), 452, 553–55; M. C. D'Arcy, S.J., *The Mind and Heart of Love: Lion and Unicorn: A Study in Eros and Agape,* 2nd ed. (London: Faber and Faber, 1954), 75; Hannah Arendt, *Love and Saint Augustine,* ed. Joanna Vecchiarelli Scott and Judith Chelius Stark (Chicago: University of Chicago Press, 1996), 98–112; Burnaby, 311.

28. See, e.g., Dideberg, 369.

restoration of our nature and, where that life is not informed by the Incarnation, of its perdition; in his view citizenship, despite the importance for him of other modes of relationship, is the ultimate form of human society, and the only eternal one.

The problems in this area, as with his notion of charity, have to do with the interpenetration of nature and sin. In the *City of God* he constantly either asserts or implies that civil government is religious in its ultimate concerns and practical in its immediate ones. Yet although he frequently mentions that political institutions can be changed, he does not say what the correct form of government is. Moreover, he admits that for practical reasons civil government in this world necessitates coercion, which nevertheless he regards as in a sense unnatural. These observations have led some modern commentators to conclude that in this world practical civil duties are, in Augustine's view, divorced from religion.[29] It is difficult to see how they can be, if he sees civil life as having an ultimately religious purpose. This conjunction of ideas is therefore highly problematic. Yet if there was any tension between those two concerns of political life, "Augustine," as R. A. Markus says, "seems not to have been aware of it."[30] Furthermore, the harsh governmental policies that he countenanced, even on the part of Christian civil authorities (judicial torture, the coercing of schismatics back into the Church), have led one contemporary historian of ideas to conclude that Augustine gave what he knew to be immorality a spurious place in his political theory.[31] Finally, it has been argued that Augustine made a stark distinction in kind between all politically constituted societies of this world and the divinely consti-

29. J. Ratzinger, *Volk und Haus Gottes in Augustins Lehren von der Kirche* (Munich: Münchener theol. stud. 11/7, 1954), 313–314; R. A. Markus, *Saeculum: History and Society in the Theology of St. Augustine*, rev. ed. (Cambridge: Cambridge University Press, 1988), 70–71; Herbert A. Deane, *The Political and Social Ideas of Saint Augustine* (New York: Columbia University Press, 1963), 224.

30. Markus, 148.

31. John Milbank, *Theology and Social Theory: Beyond Secular Reason* (Oxford: Blackwell's, 1990), 417–420.

tuted society of heaven—in other words, that heaven for him is not really a human civil society, a *civitas,* at all.[32] This would mean that the fundamental idea of the *City of God,* that of heavenly citizenship, is a mere metaphor, not an analogy (in the full sense of the word) as Augustine implicitly asserts it to be throughout that work. The purpose of chapter 5, then, is to establish, if possible, what Augustine thinks the essence of citizenship is.

Chapter 6 is directly concerned with the larger question (of which all the others are aspects) of Augustine's notion of the divine image in human beings. Here an important general observation has been made by scholars interested in specifying the differences between Eastern and Western Christianity. That observation's main point (though it takes various detailed forms) is that for Augustine our being the image of God is a matter of extrinsic approximation, mere similarity, whereas the Greek Fathers—or Gregory of Nyssa, at least —follow Plotinus in thinking that the soul of a human individual reflects God intrinsically and uniquely; and though some inferior part of each individual has become separated from that divine image, the image itself, the core of that individual, has not; Augustine's notion of the Fall is, by this view, more radical but less organic: although each human individual has always existed in perfection as conceived in the divine mind, we ourselves have nevertheless fallen en masse from our full contiguity with that perfection, and our regeneration, where it happens, will simply be restoration of that contiguity—reinstatement of a lost similarity with that unchanging exemplar.[33] The question, however, is not whether Augustine and Gregory Nyssen differ in their relation to Plotinus on this point (for they obviously do), but whether modern scholars have made the contrast accurately, and

32. Arendt, 111.

33. Vladimir Lossky, *Orthodox Theology: An Introduction,* trans. Ian and Ihita Kesarcodi-Watson (Crestwood, N.Y.: St. Vladimir's Seminary Press, 1978), 57, 130f. Cf. Louis Dupré, *Passage to Modernity: An Essay in the Hermeneutics of Nature and Culture* (New Haven, Conn.: Yale University Press, 1993), 32–33.

in particular whether they have characterized Augustine's position in enough depth. Our other issues (aspects of this one) already indicate a greater subtlety in Augustine's thought than such simple comparisons allow. On this issue specifically *De Trinitate*, for example, cannot fairly be summarized and shelved so quickly: as we shall see, it distinguishes between human nature as the image of God and the human person as the image of God, and comes to different conclusions about each.

Chapter 7 is an epilogue specifying certain questions that Augustine has left open. These concern whether his doctrine of Heaven adequately addresses the problem of evil as he has raised it, and what forms civil society will appropriately take in this world. The questions concerned have been asked (directly or indirectly) by Isaiah Berlin, Albert Camus, and E. L. Fortin.

This study is concerned throughout with questions of unity: first, with whether Augustine conceives of humanity as one species or of body and soul as two different ones; then with other questions of unity analogically subtended by the first—whether he conceives of the human mind as essentially one; whether, although evil strictly does not have a nature, Augustine has a notion of human alienation from God wide enough to contain both Christ and sinners, so that one can say that without sin Christ genuinely experienced the human condition; and whether in his view human society has one nature, so that the family, for example, and friendship, are subsumed in the Eternal City and not left over as irreclaimable residue. And beyond human nature, on the subject of personality, our main question again ultimately concerns unity: does Augustine succeed in establishing a single notion, such that both God and human beings are persons in the same sense?

THE SOUL AND BODY

It has been argued that although Augustine on occasion divides human nature into three parts—spirit (or mind), soul, and body—this division is a mere ecclesiastical relic in his thought; and that his more fundamental division of our nature is into two—soul and body.[1] But in fact both the trichotomy and the dichotomy are fundamental to his thought on the subject throughout his career.[2] Moreover, there is no disjunction between them: they are simply versions of the same conception of human nature. We consist of body and soul, but the soul has two main aspects, the mental and the animative, so we can also be said to consist of body, soul, and mind (*Tr. in Ioh. Ev.* 26.2; *CD* 12.24). It is no contradiction of the latter formulation to say that the most basic question of Augustine's anthropology is how he conceives of the relationship between soul and body.

On this most basic question it would leave a false impression to restrict oneself to a single approach. Augustine himself does not do so. In the *Literal Commentary on Genesis,* for example, when he considers the origin of the soul in terms of its place in the universal hierarchy, he takes the preexistence of the human soul as the hypothesis more probable than any other (*GL* 7.24.35, 10.3.4); a few chapters later, when he discusses the origin of the soul with reference to the transmission

1. Hubertus R. Drobner, *Person-Exegese und Christologie bei Augustinus: Zur Herkunft der Formel "una Persona"* (Leiden: E. J. Brill, 1986), 114–15 n. 165.

2. For the trichotomy see *Fid. et Symb.* 4.8, 10.23; *Conf.* 10.6.10–10.7.11; *Tr. in Ioh. Ev.* 26.2; *De Trin.* 12.7.12, 15.7.11; *CD* 12.24. For the dichotomy see *Mus.* 6.5.13; *Ep.* 3.4, 137.3.11; *Conf.* 10.6.9; *Ench.* 10.13; and again *Tr. in Ioh. Ev.* 26.2; *CD* 12.24.

of original sin, that "more probable" hypothesis recedes into the background and the rival theories are taken more seriously (GL 10.11.18–10.26.45). Thus his presentation of the fundamentals of human nature changes, though not necessarily beyond consistency, when a different phase of human existence provides the context. The central question in the first (the major) part of this chapter is how, if at all, Augustine's idea of the relationship between soul and body allows him to think of a human being as one substance. (Here Robert J. O'Connell's assertion that for Augustine all human souls are in a fallen condition by sheer virtue of having bodies will be especially in question.)[3] For this discussion Augustine's notion of the different phases of human existence (Creation, this world, and Eternity) provides a series of contexts. And although he notoriously remained undecided as to whether we all inherit our souls from Adam by generation, a study of his treatment of that question will nevertheless be crucial to the argument of this chapter. Our two special problems (the nature of sexual differentiation and that of individuality) will be discussed separately at the end of the chapter.

For this area of Augustine's thought the Neoplatonic background is especially important. Agaësse and Solignac point out that he follows Plotinus not only in regarding the body as the soul's instrument (a point also repeatedly emphasized by Gilson) but also in placing the soul above the body in a hierarchy of which God is the supreme term: "the soul exceeds every physical creature," says Augustine, "just as God exceeds every creature—by nobility of nature" (GL 7.19.25).[4] But this similarity with Plotinus highlights the main problem entailed in a duality of body and soul. Just as for Plotinus the One is absolutely unknowable, as no other real being is, so for Augustine the difference between God and Creation is absolutely a difference in kind; but to conceive analogously (as they both do) of the

<hr/>

3. Robert J. O'Connell, S.J., *The Origin of the Soul in St. Augustine's Later Works* (New York: Fordham University Press, 1987), 273.

4. Agaësse and Solignac, 1:702; Etienne Gilson, *The Christian Philosophy of St. Augustine,* trans. L. G. M. Lynch (New York: Random House, 1960), 167, 208.

soul's relationship with the body is arguably to make an analogously sharp division through human nature—to deny implicitly that there is one human nature. For Plotinus himself the soul does not, in its true reality, participate in the life of a physical human being but gives rise to such a being out of a combination of something entirely physical, though expressly qualified for the combination, with "a certain light, so to speak, distinct from the soul itself [παρ' αὐτην], but of which the soul itself is the source [δοθέντος]."[5] The similarity, and difference, between this and Augustine's notion that the mind is in part "assigned to lower duties" by having to attend to physical experience must be our initial concern in this chapter (De Trin. 12.3.3).

On this central issue it must be borne in mind that Plotinus does not have, as Augustine does, the notion of a general Fall affecting the entirety of each human soul (as distinct from a Plotinian descent by proliferation downward, away from the true soul toward involvement in the physical world). In De Genesi ad Litteram, however, although Augustine has much to say about the Fall, he has not quite developed there the fulness of his anti-Pelagian preoccupation with it, and is primarily interested in exploring the specific excellences of humanity as originally created. His fundamental division of the created order is into the spiritual and the corporeal (GL 8.20.39). Metaphysically, therefore, he is without question a dualist (both on this point and in the distinction between God and creatures). Because the human mind is essentially intelligible rather than material, he classifies the human and angelic natures together, all other creatures being primarily physical.

This association of the human mind with the primary intellectual creation (the angels) is very close. God creates the physical beings, unlike the intelligible ones, first in the angelic mind (in the timeless six days of Creation), then in themselves (in time). The angelic creation itself is exempt from any such preexistence in a higher created

5. Ennead 1.1.7.

mind, being both divinely poured forth and converted to fulfilment on the first timeless day. Hence, says Augustine, in its case there is no "and it was so" (denoting prior creation in a higher created mind) with repetition of "and God made" (denoting creation in time) as there is in the case of lesser beings. Human beings, he says, are similarly exempt in the text of Genesis (GL 2.8.16, 3.20.30–32). Like the angels, we do not require the intervention of other creatures in our creation. Thus the human and angelic natures together constitute the intelligible level of created being. On the other hand, their association stops short of identity; the primal "light" itself is the fulfilled—that is, holy—angelic nature alone: it does not include the human mental nature. (Some scholars have suggested that the *lux* includes the human mind, but Augustine simply says that it is *omnes sancti angeli atque virtutes*, "all the holy angels and virtues.") (GL 2.8.16).[6]

The difference between the two natures is of particular metaphysical importance for Augustine, for his notion of angels has a certain negative significance for the problem of how spirit and matter can be connected. Although, as we have just seen, the pure created intelligence in a way mediates between the divine Word and the lower creatures at the Creation, it must not be imagined as doing so by transforming intelligible principles into physical effects: its sphere is exclusively the intelligible (GL 1.9.17).[7] This in effect transfers the problem of spirit and matter to humanity; for though it has been argued that Augustine assumed angels to be both intellectual and physical (with more subtle and rarefied bodies than ours), Augustine's mature opinion (not certainty) is that angels do not intrinsically have bodies:[8] for purposes of apparition they either borrow physical substances or transform "their own" bodies at will—bodies to which

---

6. For the view rejected here, see Agaësse and Solignac, 1:587.

7. See Agaësse and Solignac, 1:104–5 n. 14.

8. For the suggestion that Augustine thought angels to be physical, see Edmund Hill, O.P., trans., *Augustine: "The Trinity": The Works of Saint Augustine: A Translation for the 21st Century*, ed. John E Rotelle, O.S.A. (Brooklyn: New City Press, 1991), 125 n. 31.

they are not subjected but which they rule (*De Trin.* 2.7.12). But even in the latter speculation the bodies would not be really their own (part of the angelic nature in the sense in which a human body is part of the human): either the angels "inspire" the shining bodies in the heavens (Augustine explains later) or they do not have bodies at all (*De Trin.* 8.2.3). The latter idea, he adds, is "a very difficult one for carnal comprehension." This suggests rather the difficulty of grasping a spiritual truth than the obscurity of an unlikely or false idea.

Moreover, except where the question arises in explicit form, his assumption is that whereas angels are spiritual creatures without bodies, human beings are spiritual creatures with bodies. When, for example, he considers (at the beginning of *De Genesi ad Litteram*) whether the original, angelic light is spiritual or corporeal, he assumes a strong disjunction: *utrum spiritale quid an corporale?* (*GL* 1.3.7). Conversely, when he discusses the problem of a conjointly spiritual and physical substance, it is human nature that is at issue (*GL* 7.24.35– 7.28.43, 8.21.40–8.22.43). R. J. O'Connell rightly points out that on the subject of the soul's origin, "how the soul became incarnate" is the form in which that problem always presents itself to Augustine's mind.[9] This being the most fundamental distinction in the created order, how can human nature be both spiritual and physical?

Metaphysically there could be no question, for Augustine, of conflating the spiritual and the physical. He had inherited this distinction in orders of being both from Scripture and from classical philosophy, and was conscious of both lines of inheritance.[10] The soul, whatever commerce it may have with the physical nature, is not itself physical (in the sense of being a mixture of the orders of being)(e.g., *De Trin.* 11.2.5; cf. *GL* 7.15.21). The primacy of fire over the other elements in the physical world, and the priority of the unmoved over the moved in the causing of physical movement, are signs of the soul's primacy

9. O'Connell, *Origin*, 243.

10. For quotations of Scriptural precedents, see *De Trin.* 14.16.22. For quotations of classical precedents, see *De Trin.* 15.7.11. Cf. O'Daly, 54, 56–58.

but are not solutions to the conundrum of its intimacy with so different a nature as the body (GL 3.4.7–3.5.7, 8.21.41). The particular interest of human nature in this regard is that its inclusion of both orders
of being is inescapable. Given that those orders cannot be conflated,
what, if anything, about human nature as created prevents soul and
body from merely being two—and humanity from being consequently a conjunction of two natures (with the resulting wild moral incon-
gruities) rather than a nature of its own?

The point of primary importance for Augustine is that in respect
of the body the soul has not only a rightful priority but absolute primacy—not a matter of degree. His reasons for holding this conviction are worth studying in some detail.

In *De Genesi ad Litteram* he concludes that whereas the soul of each
person has always existed, the body has not. He is, however, far from
certain on this conception of human nature: he merely concludes
that this is the hypothesis that appears "more acceptable to informed
human reason" than the alternatives (GL 7.24.35). His reasons, therefore, are more important than his conclusion: they are fundamental
assumptions about the relationship of soul and body at the Creation.
In some sense everything, he maintains, was made in the six "days" of
Creation. The human soul, if it was not itself actual from the beginning, must have existed from the beginning as a providentially
planned cause *(ratio causalis)* in some actual creature. The two possible ones are the "primal light" (the angelic creation) and "earth-and-
sea" (the foundational physical creation from which, in some sense at
least, the body undoubtedly comes). Augustine considers the first
possibility carefully. It would, he says, make the angelic creation in
some sense the father of the human soul (GL 7.23.34); but that would
establish two separate origins of ancestry for human beings, the body
being from the earth (then later bodies from earlier ones), the soul
from the angels (then later souls from earlier souls). This idea, he
says, is not only difficult but absurd. He does not explicitly state his
reason for this opinion. It has been suggested that later in the work

he gives that reason: that the hypothesis of a radically double origin is without scriptural basis (*GL* 10.5.8).[11] This is not an adequate explanation. An absence of scriptural basis might leave a hypothesis unsupported, but it would not make it either difficult or absurd. Here, in book 7, then, Augustine's argument is unreformedly enthymematic: he takes the tacit position that a human entity, if it is the result of two always separate lines of causation, is two entities, and he simply assumes this to be an intolerable conclusion.

The other possibility, that the physical creation could be the origin of the human soul, would be a solution to that particular problem—both soul and body would then have the same causal basis. But Augustine rejects that hypothesis out of hand as even more absurd. This a fortiori argument also is enthymematic: it simply assumes that one is not justified in making the causes of soul and of body converge by lowering the soul to the body's level. They must somehow converge at origin, as his earlier argument has asserted, but their distinctness must be preserved to the extent of one's not saying that the soul is a body. The soul, then, is not a different being from the body, *tout court,* for a human being is not merely two beings in tandem. Nor, on the other hand, can the soul be regarded as being on the same level as the body, as having, without qualification, the same parentage, as it were; for that would impugn its distinctly spiritual character. Augustine's solution is to conclude that both the soul and the body were in God's primary creation: the soul already in its reality, but the body only in its "causal plan" *(ratio causalis)*—not yet actual. In the passage concerned this favored hypothesis is applied to Adam alone.[12] Later in the work it is extended to all human beings (*GL* 10.3.4).

This notion of the soul as having existed for all time (though only God is eternal) has been criticized as internally self-contradictory, each soul being both temporal and nontemporal (because kept existent but unchanging until the moment of embodiment) and also

11. See Agaësse and Solignac, 1:715.
12. Ibid., 2:540.

both nonspatial and destined to vivify a spatial body.[13] The former criticism, at any rate, is applicable to Augustine's notion specifically. Its essential point is that the notion both asserts each human soul to exist as a substance before embodiment and fails to explain what mode of existence this could possibly amount to.

Augustine's theory of the human soul's two "existences" follows from his distinction between God's *conditio* (initial foundation) and his *administratio* (creative governance) of the universe. The hypothesis Augustine favors is that souls, having all been created at the initial foundation, become successively embodied in the course of the administration, but become so neither in conscious obedience to divine orders nor in a spontaneous, intentional act by each (though Augustine discusses both these possibilities), but by a natural willingness utterly intrinsic to every human soul, "because for this the soul is made" (*GL* 7.27.38); this, then, is what a human soul duly does, in order to be a human being.

O'Connell has argued that here Augustine "unmistakably deems" the soul's pre-corporeal existence to have been superior to the one it eventually has in the body, its embodiment thus being a movement "from bliss to misery."[14] Certainly, as O'Connell says, the subject of a happy preexistence of unembodied human souls is given a kind of prominence at one point in the *Literal Commentary*. But Augustine argues that the idea of the soul's either spontaneously choosing to leave or being divinely instructed to leave a purely spiritual life and to animate a body is a dubious one, since in either case the soul would be leaving a superior life for an inferior one—and what would be the point of such an enterprise? Or, if the soul left that superior life for good reason, how would it not be already operating as a moral being? Augustine's point, however, is not that the soul in fact did live such a superior life, but that if it did, its descent will have to have tak-

13. Ibid.
14. O'Connell, *Origin*, 221–22.

en one of two forms theologically impossible for preexistent human souls—sin, by the spontaneous choice of an inferior path, or virtue, by obedience to a divine command. The third alternative, which Augustine chooses (the soul's spontaneous affinity for what naturally suits it), precludes both those conclusions by implicitly denying that in coming to animate a body the soul has left some properly better life. Each human soul, then, is part of the *conditio,* but cannot act until its body goes beyond being a mere providentially created causal reason and becomes actual in the divine *administratio.* Thus the body's realization is also the second (the administrational) realization of the soul. In that way the human creation, which cannot be positively described in both its phases in terms of the body, can be so described in terms of the soul, for the two divine modes of creation involve two degrees of existence for the soul.

This primacy of the soul is, as far as it goes, a principle of unity in human nature; but it leaves as yet unclear precisely what original relationship the soul has with the body.

Though, like all physical living beings, each human body exists before the passage of time, but only as an immaterial "causal reason" (the dynamic principle of its development, divinely installed in the material "elements of the universe"), nevertheless once time begins to pass, all such causal reasons, except those of the first physical beings, have also a further prior existence, beyond the mere elements of the universe, in the ancestors in each species. The result is that once human beings had begun to exist, formed from the mud of the earth, they then bore within them, immaterial but somehow localized, the physical causal reasons—now "seminal reasons"—of those who would be conceived later (GL 6.6.11, 6.10.17).[15]

What, before conception, has each seminal reason to do with the soul that is its opposite number? Augustine considers the question once, albeit rather obliquely. What, he asks, can the divine Incarna-

---

15. For the causes' preseminal existence "in the elements of the universe," see *GL* 7.24.35. Cf. 5.4.11.

tion, that great exception in the history of human heredity, tell us about the relationship of body and soul? (*GL* 10.20.35–10.21.37). We know, he says, from a passage in the Epistle to the Hebrews that when Abraham paid the tithe to Melchizedek Levi was in his loins, Christ was not (Heb 7.4–10). So Levi, but not Christ, is to be numbered, by heredity, among the payers of that tithe. The "traducianists" used that text to prove the heredity of souls: for we know that physically Christ was in Abraham's loins; therefore his absence must have been only psychical; but Christ's case, say the traducianists, is the exception: he was absent in the same respect as Levi was present; therefore the soul of Levi (the one whose case is typical), as well as his body, was present in Abraham's loins; and therefore souls are normally hereditary.

In his rebuttal of this argument Augustine implies assumptions of his own about the fundamental human constitution. He points out that Christ's absence from the loins of Abraham was not restricted to his soul, for the *ratio causalis* of his body also was absent, as that of Levi was not, because, exceptionally, it had never taken preliminary form as a *ratio seminalis,* since Christ was never to be begotten by a man. Only if, as normally, one is to be so begotten has the causal reason of one's body taken seminal form from Adam on. In this argument the crucial distinction regarding absence from Abraham's loins is not between body and soul, but between an actual human body (or any part of one) and its immaterial causal reason, whether seminal or not. In Christ's case, unique in human history, the physical causal reason did not take seminal form but came from outside the prior history of the human race to be joined to an actual corporeal substance (that of his mother). The mistake in the traducianists' argument, then, is to attach the human soul to the human seed by failing to distinguish between the causal reason of the body and the body as materially constituted. That would in effect make the soul material. "Who could maintain," says Augustine, "that the soul has both the manifest matter of the seed and the hidden reason of the seed?" (*GL*

10.21.37). This implies that the causal reason of the body is distinct from the physical universe but not from the soul. It is, then, in some sense an aspect of the soul. But we know that the physical causal reasons also resided, at the beginning, in the material "elements of the universe." In the first instance they cannot have done so as localized in parts of the existent physical universe, for that is where the distinction lies between a *ratio causalis* as originally constituted and a *ratio causalis* as a *ratio seminalis*. Thus a human physical causal reason in the first instance has two dimensions: as an aspect of the soul and as a virtuality in the material basis of the universe; for before it is realized it associates the soul, from which it is not distinct, with the material world, from which it is distinct, but does so virtually. When it is realized (at conception) it associates them actually. (Its intermediate, seminal, phase, which did not apply in the cases of Adam and Eve, must also be one of virtual presence, though somehow localized, for it is still in the general class of causal reasons.) Thus at the original *conditio* a human being was created as a unity, the principle of which was the soul, for the *ratio causalis* of the body is not distinct from the soul; rather it is distinct from the material substance that the physical causal reason eventually takes up and makes its own in the subsequent divine *administratio*.

Before we turn to that *administratio*, a further point should be made about Augustine's conception of the aspects of the soul as created. He guards against any suggestion either that we have two souls, a mental one and an animal one, or that the human soul is divided into mental and animatory parts. In the course of showing that the soul is not a physical being he says in effect that it animates the body by the same faculty with which it exercises its will: "The soul in wonderful ways is mixed with the body, to vivify it, by the same incorporeal volitional power [*eodem incorporeo nutu*] with which it also gives commands to the body by a certain concentration [*quadam intentione*], not by physical force" (GL 8.21.42). The two distinctions concerned in this passage are between *intentio* (conscious act of willing) and *moles* (physical force), and between *intentio* (specifically conscious

act of willing) and *nutus* (volitional power in general, whether exercised consciously or unconsciously). *Nutus* is intrinsically mental in
meaning if it is used in reference to the soul. That in this context it is
also volitional is shown by the expression *nutus voluntatis,* which he
has just used to refer to the psychical faculty by which we move our
bodies. He now says that it is "by one and the same *nutus*" that the
soul both animates our bodies and enables us to move them consciously. The only difference is that in the latter case there is conscious concentration in that action. The difference between physical
animation and mental will does not, therefore, correspond to any division in human nature. The same inward ability has both effects.

Augustine's parallel delineation of human consciousness in *De
Trinitate* ultimately confirms this account of human nature. Having
begun book 12 with a distinction between the interior and the exteri-
or (that is, the mental and the physical) dimensions of a human being, Augustine extends the distinction to different modes of consciousness: we in a sense share with other animals the consciousness
of physical things; yet in other animals the consciousness even of
physical things is not, after all, like ours, for our physical consciousness entails taking note of things, and we can do that only in a specifically human way:

There is that in us which is concerned with corporal action and temporal
matters in such a way as not to be something we have in common with the
beasts. It is rational, but has, as it were, been drawn off [*tamquam ductum*],
delegated [*deputatum*] from that rational substance of our mind by which we
are connected with the intelligible and unchanging truth that is above us, so
that it may deal with and govern matters that are below us. . . . it is not the
case that parts of the human soul held in common by us with the beasts af-
ford our minds, with which we consult the higher truth within us, the sort of
help that is adequate and appropriate to human nature for dealing with physical matters (*De Trin.* 12.3.3).

The human soul, then, is one and is entirely mental. Although Augustine talks about "parts" of the human soul in this passage, he does
so in order to deny that terminology's strict applicability. Elsewhere

he is quite happy to speak platonically about "parts of the soul" (e.g., *CD* 14.19). Here, however, where the question addressed is specifically whether such a division of the human soul into mental and animal parts really exists, he states that if one is talking about full, conscious awareness, it does not. For the performance of the various animal functions, Augustine says, our indivisible mental nature is somehow, and to an extent, diverted, not divided into parts (*De Trin.* 12.4.4). But his assertion that our conscious awareness of physical things and our understanding are ultimately identical (both acts of the mind) has entailed distinguishing, for contrast, between our entire faculty of mentality, which we simply do not share with the beasts, and the senses, restrictedly defined, which in a way we do share with them (*De Trin.* 12.1.1). This passage, then, if considered by itself, could still be taken to indicate a division into kinds within human nature—between our specifically human forms of consciousness and our decisively lower, bestial one. But this is not Augustine's position, for in book 10 he has precluded that possibility also: he asserts that even the faculty by which sensory images become impressed upon the soul (a faculty that he admits we share with the beasts) is impressed with those images as a result of the mind's providing something of itself for that purpose (*De Trin.* 10.5.7). In this way we do not, after all, have sensory perception as other animals have it; we have ours, rather, in a (remotely) mental way. So not even in this respect is a human being a duality: human consciousness ultimately is on all levels mental.

When one turns from the foundation of human nature to human nature as manifested under the divine administration, the problem of dualism forcibly reemerges in a different form: if soul and body are one primarily, at the first foundation, why do we (and so painfully) experience them in this world as two, even as conflicting? Augustine's answer is not easy to specify, above all because in such a context he on occasion blurs the distinction between our physical nature and our fallen condition. He on the one hand starkly contrasts our natural state in the Garden with our stricken state after expulsion (while insisting, of course, that we were physical from the start) (see especially *CD* 14.12–26); on the other hand in *De Trinitate*, when he directly discusses our experience of a duality between soul and body, he includes observations that could apply to any extended physical experience on earth:

> Precisely because of the very principle of our foundation as human beings [*illo ipso ordine conditionis nostrae*], as a result of which we have been rendered mortal and carnal, we deal with visible things more easily and more familiarly than with intelligible, even though the former are exterior to us, the latter interior, and we sense the former, physically, but understand the latter, mentally, and being in our fundamental selves souls we [*nosque ipsi animi*] are not sensory (physical, that is), but intelligible by nature, for we are life; nevertheless, as I say, we have become so used to physical experience [*tanta facta est in corporibus consuetudo*], our concentration [*intentio*] has so projected itself upon physical things, gliding outwards in that strange way it has, that when it is withdrawn from the uncertainty of physical things, so as to be fixed, with much more stable and certain awareness, on what is spiritual, it flees back to the physical and seeks rest precisely where it contracted its weakness. We have to make allowance for this sickness [*aegritudini*] (*De Trin.* 11.1.1)

Would Adam and Eve not have gained a familiarity with physical experience even without the Fall? Yet such familiarity, without any mention of that immense catastrophe, is at the end of the passage called a sickness. In this case again, R. J. O'Connell interprets the passage as meaning that our intellectually confusing familiarity with the senses is a disorder arising from our wrongful, even sinful, state of embodiment. He rightly points out that if the passage indeed means this, it is discrepant with *De Trinitate* generally, but he takes it to be in effect a fragment, "a shard . . . from a much earlier stratum of Augustine's thought" (he mentions *De Libero Arbitrio*), according to which the human "condition of ignorance and moral impotence" is the result not of an act committed by our already physical first parents, but of a "sinful choice" made by human souls to enter bodies in the first place."[16]

16. O'Connell, *Origin,* 258–60, 39. Cf. Hill, 318 n. 2. The passage from *De lib. arb.* cited by O'Connell is 3.20.58.

Again, however, even in *De Libero Arbitrio* it is not well established that such "semi-Origenism" was really Augustine's meaning. In the relevant passage Augustine indeed considers the possibility that human souls became embodied by their own choice *(sua sponte)* and that our ignorance and folly may have followed this "act of personal volition" *(propriam voluntatem);* but the Latin says nothing about sinfulness, and Augustine's speculation that, where blame is concerned, God takes issue not with our ignorance and moral difficulty but with our failure to struggle against those weaknesses, suggests a natural human ineptitude connected with being physical and requiring contention, but not culpable either in itself or in its cause. That passage, then, indicates a more subtle relationship between human nature and its condition than O'Connell attributes to it.

As to our passage from *De Trinitate,* O'Connell argues that its language does not make sense except as a description of the results of the soul's culpable descent into the body. He is right to insist that *effecti* must be construed as "turned into," not "created as," but his interpretation of *ordine conditionis nostrae* as "by the ordainment of our condition" is unlikely to be correct. Although his implicit textual emendation of *conditionis* ("foundation," "original establishment") to *condicionis* ("condition") is not implausible in itself, in the roughly contemporary *Literal Commentary* Augustine frequently combines *ordo* and *condere,* or their respective derivatives, to denote the systematic orderliness of creation: *cum creaturarum conditarum ordinem recolimus,* "when we consider the orderly sequence with which created beings were established in existence . . ." (*GL* 5.2.4; cf. 5.5.15, 5.19.37, 7.28.42). Our passage, then, is concerned with consequences of our having the nature with which we were created, and the resultantly paradoxical character of what is said there must be allowed its full effect. Augustine describes our intellectual "sickness" neither as a result of our fallenness (or at least not exclusively that) nor as an intrinsic characteristic of our corporeality, but as contracted as a result of our corporeality. His concern is not to apply a distinction between natural and fallen experience but to indicate that our experience of corpo-reality, in all the conditions available for its exercise in human experi-ence so far, has had a universally untoward intellectual result. It is of course also Augustine's position that given not earthly, or even par-adisal, but heavenly conditions, that experience would be quite differ-ent (*De Trin.* 1.13.31, 12.4.4). The Garden of Eden and this fallen world alike have failed to provide such conditions; moreover, with the Fall human life ceased even to be directed toward such an order (e.g., *CD* 13.13, 13.15, 14.1). Thus although, as will be seen later, when Augustine speculates on the final consummation he tells us something of what is ultimately proper to soul and body, a full explication of that subject cannot be given by anyone in this world, and is always deferred until that consummation itself.[17]

Meanwhile, however, our present, stricken life in the world vio-lently challenges even the notion that body and soul form one na-ture. In his mature writings Augustine frequently returns to the bibli-cal texts that most starkly present this problem: "The corruptible body weighs the soul down" (Wis 9.15: e.g., *GL* 4.6.13, 4.32.49; *De Trin.* 2.17.28, 3.4.10, 3.10.21, 4.3.5, 8.2.3; *CD* 12.16, 13.16, 14.3); "The flesh is concupiscent against the spirit, the spirit against the flesh" (Gal 5.17: e.g., *GL* 10.12.20, 12.7.18; *CD* 13.13, 15.5, 19.4, 22.23).

The mere fact that concupiscence makes one feel as if one's body and soul were separate and even working against each other is no great intellectual problem for him. He repeatedly insists that this ex-perience is not in fact caused by the duality of body and soul: human nature is more subtle than that. In book 14 of the *City of God* he points out that the corruptible flesh was not in its origin concupis-cent against the soul. The soul was the initial source of trouble, in Adam's free act of the will. In this damaged world, on the other hand, the disruptive influence has in a sense been reversed: some-thing about the corruption of the body distorts our desires. But he

17. See Rist, 145–47.

regards this form of corruption as punishment rather than crime (*CD* 14.2–3; cf. *GL* 10.12.20–21). In neither case is the trouble traceable to a fundamental conflict between soul and body. What we experience as if it were a disobedience of the body to the soul (first moral weakness, finally death) is in fact an internal disobedience in the soul (*CD* 14.15). This real disorder gives us the illusion that the trouble emerges along a line of division between soul and body.

That observation does not, however, solve the deeper intellectual problem of duality posed by concupiscence; nor does Augustine pretend that it does: concupiscence is more than a mere troublesome feature of human life in this world; it is also a radical spiritual disruption that, through its sexual manifestation in our parents—even devout, baptized parents—causes us to inherit the original sin that separates us, potentially eternally, from God (*De gr. Chr. et pecc. or.* 2.39.44; *De nupt. et conc.* 1.17.19, 1.18.20, 2.5.15). It is this potentially eternal spiritual effect of what is for our parents a troublesome feature of experience that again brings the basics of human life into question and causes Augustine to reexamine them in this new light. In text after text he returns to the question (never resolved by him) of how, given this heredity of original sin, each human soul comes to animate its body (*Ep.* 143 passim, 166 passim, 190 passim; *GL* 10.10.17–10.26.45; *C. duas ep. Pel.* 3.10.26; *Retract.* 2.82).

The four possibilities he takes seriously (propagation of souls from Adam's soul, prior creation of all souls at the beginning of time, immediately created souls, and spontaneous embodiment of immediately created souls) resolve into two that are significant as regards the transmission of original sin: propagation of other souls from Adam's (traducianism, which consistently places original sin in the soul and provides a clear solution to the problem of its transmission from Adam's soul to others') and the notion that each soul is, in one way or another, separately created rather than humanly generated (creationism, which perforce holds that the soul—created good by God—somehow contracts original sin from the body) (*GL* 10.10.17–10.26.45;

cf. *Ep.* 166.27). On human nature seen in this perspective Augustine does not come to even a tentative, "more probable" conclusion. This very inconclusiveness, with its implicit insistence that traducianism in some form may be right, is enough to acquit Augustine of the simple charge that his notion of original sin is a category mistake. Categorically he is, strictly speaking, uncommitted to any one view of the soul's origin.

Speculatively, however, he on occasion goes a long way toward developing a comprehensive anthropology. In such texts his implicit presuppositions are especially important. In some his concerns are strictly doctrinal (that one must not, for example, think of God as punishing innocent infants eternally or as causing souls to be guilty). But a discussion of the soul's origin in *De Genesi ad Litteram* has an argument largely anthropological in character (*GL* 10.14.24–25). Addressing the question how, if we are guilty by heredity from Adam, one could possibly deny that each person's soul is inherited also, he says that a "creationist" has a possible answer: that the soul is, "as it were, weighed down" by a spiritual and moral oblivion coming from the turbulent body that each inherits from Adam (turbulent as fallen, not as physical). This is a creationist argument that approaches traducianism: Augustine has just pointed out that the body is not concupiscent without the soul (*GL* 10.13.22); now he speaks of an inherited body that is "earthly, mortal, and, above all, propagated from the flesh of sin." Thus even if we do not actually inherit our souls from Adam, the soul is related to the body in such a way that the truth must nevertheless be close to that; for we must inherit bodily matter so profoundly affected by the sinful souls of our forebears, going back to Adam, that it infects our souls with sin, the infection even being potentially eternal. Even granted, then, that the soul is predominant and the seat of all human experience and character, this power of the earlier person's body to affect the later person's soul implies that the earlier person's soul, too, is concerned in the transaction, indirectly but decisively.

We inherit bodies, why not souls? we tend to ignore this possibility.

Though consciously made to be close to traducianism, this argument is nevertheless still a form of creationism. What creationism must avoid, and does in this form, is both the idea that the body can be concupiscent by itself, without a soul's making it so (two human concupiscences then being implied), and (the error of the Manichaeans) the idea that a human being has two souls, a concupiscent one and an inconcupiscent one. The problem of concupiscence must not, then, be allowed to dictate either of these extreme forms of dualism; for that is the characteristic danger of creationism not nuanced as Augustine proposes. The characteristic danger of traducianism, as has already been noted, is the tendency to regard the soul as physical as a result of treating it as genetic (*GL* 10.24.40).

The distinction between anthropological dualism and metaphysical dualism is crucial here. For traducianism to be acceptable it must be metaphysically dualistic, in the sense of not confusing a spiritual nature with the materiality of a body; for whatever the relationship of body and soul, the human soul is unquestionably of the spiritual order. In Augustine's view (in this discussion) the weakness of traducianism is not that it has found a way of seeing body and soul as a unity (that is its strength), but that ultimately it does so materialistically. The strength of creationism, on the other hand, is not its tendency to anthropological dualism, to seeing a human being as two natures (that is its weakness), but its insistence on distinguishing the spiritual from the physical. What Augustine's argumentation shows, therefore, is that he is seeking to construct an anthropology that both makes the human soul and body somehow one nature and is unequivocal about the exclusively spiritual character of the soul.

Even where, in other passages, there is an obvious and stark duality of body and soul, that proves to be only superficially the case. In Epistle 137 (written at roughly the same time as the passage from *De Genesi ad Litteram* just discussed), there is an analogy between the union of body and soul achieved by human procreation and the hypostatic union of the human and the divine substances in Christ:

As, in the unity of a person, the soul is united with the body, so in the unity
of a Person God is united with a human being. In the case of the former person there is a combination [*mixtura*] of soul and body. In the case of the latter Person there is a combination of God with a human being. . . . The former happens every day to bring about human procreation. The latter
happened once to bring about human liberation (*Ep.* 137.3.11).

This passage, formally at least, presents the human body and soul as
thoroughly distinct substances. On that basis one would logically
have to describe Christ as one Person, three substances. Elsewhere
Augustine indeed speaks in exactly such terms: "Human nature was
able to be joined [*coniungi*] to God so that there might come about
one Person from two substances, and by that means [*per hoc*] one Person from three: God, soul, and flesh" (*De Trin.* 13.17.22). In that formulation, however, it is very clear that the conjunction of two substances (God and soul) is the primary one, for through that comes
the ultimate conjunction of three. And similarly in the epistle just
mentioned Augustine says, "When the Word of God was combined
[*permixtum est*] with a soul having a body He simultaneously took up
both soul and body." This means that the primacy of soul over body
is such that the miraculous conjunction of the divine nature with a
human soul entailed its conjunction with a human body. So, far from
indicating the thoroughgoing dualism apparent in the passage at first
sight, Augustine here indicates a unitary conception of the human
person—not merely "the soul primarily, the body secondarily," but
"the soul and, by virtue of that, the body."

His assertion here that a union of two incorporeal substances is
intellectually easier to accept than a union of one incorporeal and
one corporeal substance directs our attention to the metaphysical distinction of spirit from matter. Thus that indispensable distinction is as
carefully maintained in Augustine's conception of the "administrational" phase of Creation as it was in his conception of the primary
Creation, together with a unitary anthropology that here, as before,
is constituted by the primacy of the soul.

But the doctrine of the Incarnation, the crucial turning point in God's *administratio,* arguably poses another threat to Augustine's notion of the unity of human nature. The internal disobedience to self, primarily a disturbance within the soul, resulting from the Fall, causes not only moral feebleness and emotional turbulence but death (*CD* 14.15). Yet Christ, though free from that inherited disturbance of the soul, underwent death. The possibility that this doctrine implicitly reasserts a thoroughgoing division between body and soul is considered by Augustine in *De Trinitate* (*De Trin.* 13.17.22–13.18.23; cf. 4.3.6). The Incarnation, he says, was not merely a participation in human nature but also a participation in our frail condition (though not in sin) even to death. Why so great a descent? Augustine mentions many reasons. It is clear from what he says, however, that in some sense Christ, whose intention was to heal us from the inside outward, took on not our disordered psychical conflict but its effect (mortality). That is why the mortality was temporary in his case: immortality, the outward result of a fundamental inward order already a fact in him from the beginning of his earthly life, was delayed for the duration of that earthly life. So there was nothing adventitious about Christ's immortality: given the inward order of that particular human soul, Augustine's task is to explain Christ's mortality. For Augustine, then, the doctrine of the Incarnation, far from reintroducing a dualistic anthropology, reasserts the notion that a human being is a substantial unity.

The next stage in the *administratio* is the subsequent action of grace in this world. The regeneration of a human being from the spiritual oblivion inherited from Adam is in the first instance gradual: the soul, says Augustine, "wakes up little by little into the light of intelligence" (*GL* 10.14.24). (The point is emphasized: Augustine uses *paulatim* twice in one sentence.) The essence of this awakening is the progressive reassertion of the spiritual, intellective aspect of human nature. Ultimately one will be Adam "only according to the flesh" if one perseveres after initial awakening. And by such perseverance one will be purified in the flesh, too, not by a physical cleansing, of course, but simply through the soul's acting rightly as a soul, making decent choices, assuming decent dispositions.

Grace in its phase of process does, however, present Augustine with a problem in respect of human nature. Both from Scripture and from other reported experience he accepts that the human soul can be transported from the body and have experiences in that transported state, either by ecstatic visions or by death (though before the resurrection of the dead). In his long discussion of this matter his initial conclusion is that these experiences are intellectual visions (the highest kind)—in particular, that the souls of the just, thus freed (normally by death) from the two lower kinds of vision (the imaginative and the corporeal), can contemplate God (*GL* 12.28.56–12.36.69). But the great problem raised for him by this Platonic line of thought is that it takes the idea of the soul's complete primacy (which short of this point is the principle of its unity with the body) to such an extreme that the body is in danger of being dismissed as an accidental addition to the soul, unnecessary to its characteristic activity. Here the problem arises in the form: "Why do the spirits of the dead need to receive their bodies in the resurrection if the same supreme happiness can be provided for them even without bodies?" (*GL* 12.35.68). His answer, which he admits is speculative and incomplete, is a withdrawal from the dualism suggested by the question. A disembodied soul does not, he says, have a vision equalling that of the angels, and possibly the reason is that it has become disembodied. Only when it is definitively, finally embodied will its heavenly vision equal that of the angels. Until then, its very yearning for embodiment is what clouds its vision. In that sense, then, a soul can never be definitively disembodied, for a disembodied soul is one frustrated in its physical aspect.

Second, what of body and soul in heaven, the consummation of the divine *administratio*? Taking his distinctions from the book of Revelation, Augustine repeatedly formulates his eschatology as two resurrections and two deaths: resurrection by baptismal regeneration, death by departing this life, resurrection of the body, and the death that is damnation (*De Trin.* 4.3.5–6; *CD* 20.9). Those who have participated properly (that is, with penitence and perseverance) in the first resurrection will avoid the second death (which is of both soul and body). That first resurrection is therefore the crucial one. It leads, after delay, to the perfect regeneration of soul and body—of the latter, then, by virtue of the former, for in those who are saved the body's immortality is constituted by the soul's. Conversely, the final stage of the soul's fulfilment is, or at least entails, its physical fulfilment:

> Its [the body's] is delayed until the end. For then "we shall be similar to him, since we shall see him as he is." For the moment, however, as long as "the body that is corrupted weighs the soul down," as long as "human life on earth is a trial, from beginning to end," "no one living will be justified in his sight." (*De Trin.* 4.3.5–6)

The completion of the soul's regeneration takes place by way of the bodily resurrection. In a horrific parody of that, the souls of the damned have, without the body, already been deprived of God, as in a sense all are, by the first death. Their deprivation of God is completed only at the second death, where, with their bodies, they are definitively separated from the Goodness for which they have no love. Here the lack of the soul's resurrection (the first) leads to the second death (of both body and soul). On the other hand, like the final salvation in the former case, the final death takes place by way of a kind of physical resurrection. Even in this world, says Augustine elsewhere, one can with intellectual effort be aware that the pain we experience in some sense dualistically, as physical rather than mental, is really an experience in the soul (*CD* 14.15; cf. *GL* 12.24.51). Finally, both in the ultimate salvation and in the almost unthinkable horror that would be damnation, the perfect primacy of the soul is completely rediscovered, the body playing its part as an essential aspect of the soul in its ultimate condition. Nevertheless, this rediscovery is more perfectly evinced in eternal salvation. If, says Augustine in *De Trinitate,* the

mind could ever be utterly concentrated on God, its constitution as
God's image would be completely fulfilled (*De Trin.* 12.4.4). (While
there are temporal distractions, he says, the mind acts as the image of
God only partially—only insofar as it exercises the contemplative side
of its being.)

There is no question here of a longed-for separation of soul and
body. One does not become fulfilled in one's humanity by jettisoning
so essential an aspect of it (cf. *CD* 13.17). What Augustine envisages as
the final, heavenly consummation is a condition where the soul subsumes the body entirely, the body no longer being even a temporarily
nonmental, partial concern of the mind, but playing its ultimately
proper part in the mind's contemplation.

At the end of the *City of God,* in his detailed picture of human nature's happy fulfilment, Augustine unquestionably is at pains to establish that the resurrection of the body takes place in the fullest possible way (*CD* 22.19–20). But although he speculates elaborately so as to
be able to take literally the text "not a hair of your head shall perish"
(old hair and fingernail cuttings collected and reused in the resurrected body; cannibalized flesh, treated as borrowed by its eater, restored
to its original body), he makes one significant concession: if someone
were to insist that in the resurrected body there is not the increase in
size that such speculations must assume, there is no need to argue ag-
gressively against such a view. The essential point, he says, on which
one must insist, is the perfect beauty of the resurrected body. This
means that not all the matter that made up a person's body in this life
must be taken as constituting it indispensably. Thus although a body
is undoubtedly a material thing, there is still a distinction (and not a
merely formal one) between a body and the material out of which it
is made. A particular piece of what has been its material, and is no
longer, can be lacking to it without jeopardizing the perfect, ultimate,
physical fulfilment of a human being. *hair, nails, limbs (?), organs (?)*

Earlier in the work Augustine has already elaborated both this distinction and the larger subject of the relationship between the body

and the soul of a resurrected human being: "The body, which is made of earth, would not return to earth except by its own death" (*CD* 13.15); and two chapters later: "Plato admits that God can bring it about that beings made out of elements would be rendered back into them." And here too he proceeds to distinguish between what the human body is and what it is made of. Six chapters later he again reiterates the distinction in a comprehensive picture of human nature, put in a definitive, eschatological context:

> For just as [human] bodies that have a living soul but not yet a life-providing spirit are called animate bodies yet nevertheless are not souls but really are bodies, so those bodies [that will have in them a life-providing spirit] are called spiritual bodies. We must be very careful not to believe that they will simply be spirits; no, they will be bodies having the substance of flesh, but because of the life-providing spirit they will experience no fleshly slowness or decay. Then the human being will not be earthly but heavenly; not because the body will cease to be what it is: something made out of earth; but because by a heavenly gift it will be a kind of body suitable to the inhabiting of Heaven; and not by the loss of its original nature, but by a change in the quality of that nature. . . . Then, therefore, the body will be related to the life-providing spirit as it now is to the living soul (*CD* 13.23).

At the resurrection, then, when human nature will be transformed into an immortal nature, the transformation will be in the inner quality of the human being. Both body and soul will be changed, but the change will be constituted by a divinely wrought modification of the soul. For the moment the important point is not this passage's sublime credal thought, but the philosophical assumption that the soul determines the nature of the body; for here the real duality is not between the human body and the human soul, but between the human body and the dust of the earth. This emerges with special clarity in the transformation of relationship among all three that Augustine describes here. When God makes the soul a spirit (which in the context means a soul endlessly capable of imparting life), the human being comes to be endowed with a spiritual body, no longer a body merely animal in respect of the soul's capacity to animate. What was dust of

the earth will only then cease permanently to be that and be definitively and irrevocably made human. Thus the naturally perfect unity
of a human being, adumbrated at its foundational stage in *De Genesi
ad Litteram,* is now anticipated by Augustine in its eventual fulfilment:
the consummation of the soul.

A human being, then, is, in Augustine's view, neither merely physical (that is, a body including a physical soul) nor a human soul with
an ultimately nonhuman body, nor again two human substances, a
human soul and a separately human body. Human nature combines
what are metaphysically the two most radically different kinds of
substance: the intelligible and the material. The quality peculiar to
man is of being an intelligible nature that in becoming actualized in
all respects makes human some of the dust of earth (or rather is
brought to do so by God). Initially it does so only inchoately. Simultaneously contemplating and animating, this ultimately mental nature
deals with the corporeal dimension of its own being by a divergence
of attention. Sin has sent that problematic divergence of attention
out of control. As a result the soul ceases to contemplate God, and finally fails in the activity of physical animation also. It has thus failed
first in the one direction, then, as an eventual result, in the other, producing an extreme, morbid duality of condition—a pseudo-distinc-
tion between soul and body—in the human person. When the soul is
regenerated by divine grace it already in this life begins to contemplate God again, but still in the end fails altogether to animate. The
great pause, which this indicates, between the two stages of the resurrection sharply emphasizes the duality in condition just mentioned. Ultimately, with an infinite suffusion of grace, the soul will
both contemplate and animate without any divergence of activity
whatever, as it was always intended to do.

Thus humanity was never two natures but a single nature, joining
the two metaphysical orders of being. Before any passage of time, at
the primal Creation, the unity of nature was already established, but
the joining of the two orders of being was potential (the bodily hu-

dill b/t these 2 ?

man aspect being only virtual). The primacy of the soul in human nature will be fulfilled in eternity, where the physical dimension of the contemplative mind will finally be fully actualized.

Since, however, Augustine has not created a philosophical system, certain consequences of his view of human nature have proved problematic: in particular the two natural divisions among human beings: into sexes and into individuals.

Regarding the former, the two most crucial assumptions frequently attributed to him are that he regarded the difference between men and women as exclusively physical, and that he thought the only purpose of the woman's differentiation from the man to be her reproductive function.

So, first, if, as Augustine also maintained, it is mentally, not physically, that a human being is in the image of God, and the difference between men and women is only physical, how can Augustine say that because of her sex Eve was mentally inferior to Adam? (e.g., *CD* 14.11; *GL* 11.42.58–60).[18] The problem of duality between body and soul reemerges in this context. Numerous texts dating from different periods of Augustine's life are cited to show that in his view "apart from our bodies, we are neither male nor female."[19] The most famous of these texts, from the *City of God,* is sometimes quoted as *sexus in carne est* ("a sexual difference is a physical difference"). But the full form of the statement, which yields a different meaning, is *qui sexus evidens utique in carne est:* "and this sexual difference is at any rate evident in the flesh" (*CD* 14.22). Augustine is arguing against those who do not regard human beings as originally sexual. The human flesh itself, he replies, shows sexual differentiation to be basic. This does not, however, imply that that differentiation is restricted to the flesh. Similarly, in *De Genesi ad Litteram* the statement "sexual dif-

18. See Soennecken, 290–97.

19. See Rist, 115 n. 71. (The texts discussed here are those cited by him in support of this interpretation.)

ferentiation itself cannot exist except in bodies" *(sexus ipse masculi et feminae nisi in corporibus esse non potest)* asserts that the body is a necessary condition of sex, not its exclusive place of operation *(GL* 6.7.12); for he has made the same point, with similar phraseology, in an earlier passage: those who deny that Adam and Eve had bodies from the beginning of their lives "have not," he says, "adverted to the fact that the difference between male and female could not have come about except according to the body" *(nec adtenderunt masculum et feminam non nisi secundum corpus fieri potuisse) (GL* 3.22.34).

Nevertheless, Augustine in some passages undoubtedly indicates human sexual difference to be physical rather than spiritual *(De ag. Chr.* 11.12; *Serm.* 280.1; *GL* 3.22.34; *De Trin.* 12.7.10; *C. Faust.* 24.2). But the notion of sexual differentiation conveyed by these passages is a subtle one. When he says that in the martyrs Perpetua and Felicity their courage was one thing (a virtue), their femaleness another (a physical, exterior matter), the primary contrast is not between two features of their nature, but between their spiritual condition and one feature of their nature—women can have a courage more conventionally associated with men *(Serm.* 280.1). Neither one's moral condition nor even one's area of moral development is determined by one's sex.

Still, Augustine complicates the matter by saying that those two women were neither male nor female "in respect of their interior humanity" *(secundum interiorem hominem).* Here it is not quite clear whether he is distinguishing between one's sex and one's inner being in which one's humanity resides (implying that in the core of our humanity we are completely sexless), or merely isolating humanity's moral aspect while prescinding from its sexual aspect. In *Contra Faustum* he is more precise on the subject, and his choice of words at one point is particularly significant. Men and women, he says, are equally made in God's image, and in either case there is one human being both externally and internally:

hunc unum hominem ad imaginem suam fecit, non secundum id quod habet corpus corporalemque vitam, sed secundum id quod habet rationalem mentem, qua cognoscat Deum.

This single human entity He made in His own image, not in respect of the fact that that being has a body and physical life, but in respect of the fact that it has a rational mind designed for coming to know God. (*C. Faust.* 24.2.1)

Regarding sexuality also, therefore, Augustine's distinction is not between a physical and a nonphysical human nature, but between two different aspects of one human nature. His point is not that sexual difference has nothing to do with the soul, but that sexual difference is not the aspect of a human being in respect of which that being is made in the image of God.

This still does not quite establish the place of sexual difference in human nature. But two passages from *De Trinitate*, taken together, give positive information on the subject (*De Trin.* 12.3.3, 12.7.10). In the earlier one (already discussed in this chapter), Augustine says that some of the soul's (naturally rational) being is "drawn off," "delegated" for involvement with the exterior world. This passage shows in general that there are not mental and sensory parts to the human soul, but mental and sensory (primary and secondary) functions of the same mental nature. In the other passage, four chapters later, Augustine describes sexual differentiation specifically as an instance of such "drawing-off": the reason why the woman must remain veiled in Church, he says, is that

she with her husband is the image of God, so that the entire substance is one image; but when it is distributed for the purpose of providing assistance [*ad adiutorium*], which applies to her alone, it is not the image of God. As to what applies to the man alone, it is the image of God as fully and completely as when the woman is joined to him to make one. As we said about the nature of the human mind, whenever it entirely contemplates the Truth it is the image of God; and when something of it is distributed, and by a certain attention [*intentione*] is drawn off to the administration of temporal matters, nevertheless in the part with which it still attends to the Truth that it has seen it is the image of God.

Insofar as a woman is simply a human being, as distinct from being a woman as opposed to a man, the image of God is evinced without qualification in her. Insofar as a woman is a woman as opposed to a man, her contemplative, God-imaging mind is in that respect drawn off from contemplation, which also happens in other ways in every human being regardless of sex; and in that respect the image of God is not evinced without qualification in her.

The central issue here is the nature of this inequality between men and women. The passage describes sexuality in entirely mental terms, for although sexuality can rightly be described as primarily physical, the physical itself is, in this final analysis, primarily mental. Sexual difference is a difference in the soul. Augustine has complicated his application of this principle by excepting the male, but not the female, from the rule that the "delegation" that is sexual difference is a distraction from being the divine image. The fact of being that image is an established fact for both sexes. There is, therefore, no respect in which a man as a human being is in the image of God whereas a woman is not. Rather, a woman differs from a man in having, together with the other characteristics in respect of which neither man nor woman is in the image of God, an additional characteristic in respect of which woman alone is not the image of God: the function of being helper to the man.

This, however, brings to the fore the idea, for which Augustine is notorious, that Eve was created for reproduction, that necessity being the only reason for the creation of woman as distinct from man.[20] But the main passage on which scholars rely for evidence of this view does not quite say that. "If woman," he says, "was not made to provide this assistance [*ad hoc adiutorium*] of producing children, to provide what assistance was she made?" (*GL* 9.5.9). He adds that another man, for example, would have been more suitable as a fellow laborer or as a friend. Augustine's assertion is not that the only purpose of

20. See ibid., 114; Soennecken, 293.

Eve's creation as a woman was one of assistance to Adam, but that such assistance, insofar as it was intended in that creation, was intended to take the form of reproduction. In other words, Eve's purpose as providing assistance delimits what Augustine says. To the question: What assistance to Adam was purposed in Eve's creation? he concludes that the only answer is: reproductive assistance. He does not ask, though he might have, what else, outside such assistance, was the divine purpose of Eve's femaleness. That would have been a different question. But later in his life Augustine does in effect consider it. Near the end of the *City of God* he speculates that in eternity the blessed will still be men and women, the purpose of their bodily sexual characteristics, and of all their bodily characteristics, being to have beauty and dignity, to manifest the greatness of their souls (*CD* 22.24). Even in this world, he says, nothing in the human body is restrictedly practical in function; every part of it has an aesthetic purpose as well—and in the end, with the sexual characteristics as with every other, all practical function will be superseded. And woman will still be woman then, he says, when she is God's perfected image in heaven; but she will no longer be an assistant to man, that cause of subordination having been a practical one, now superseded—proving, therefore, to be not fundamental to sexual difference after all. According to Augustine, then, women will reflect God's glory in their uniquely womanly way, thus fulfilling the ultimate purpose of their femaleness.

Though Augustine's idea of the eternal survival of the sexes has been described as anomalous and unconvincing on the grounds that in his view one's sex does not affect one's soul, effect on the soul is, as we have seen, not the point.[21] His view is that in the end, in all its characteristics, eternally, the body is an expression of the soul, without any functional subordination of one sex to the other. Although K. Børresen correctly observes that Augustine "backdated" to Cre-

21. For the view contested here, see Rist, 120.

ation the subordination of woman to man—that subordination being the material for the traditional simile of God's male relationship with his female church—it is important to add that that traditional imagery is taken from our temporal experience of sexual difference (in this world and its prelude—the Garden), and not from the difference between the sexes in itself, or in what is for Augustine the ultimate significance of that difference.[22]

It remains to be shown, however, whether this notion of ultimate equality in every respect between man and woman is compatible with his notion of their original inequality (which has moral consequences) in the Garden of Eden. Satan, he says in the *City of God*, chose to attack Eve as the more gullible, intellectually weak, of our first parents (*CD* 14.11). Does this prelapsarian difference imply simply that women are naturally inferior to men (which would make the heavenly abolition of that inferiority a partial abolition of human nature)? Augustine had explicitly denied this in *De Genesi ad Litteram* precisely in connection with the prelapsarian difference (*GL* 11.42.58). There he is concerned not simply with our being in God's image, but, more specifically, with our mental capacity to be imprinted with that image. His position is that a woman's mind has as much capacity as a man's to receive that impress, but that it was perhaps God's purpose for Eve "to live for a while yet [*adhuc*] according to the fleshly awareness rather than according to the spirit of the mind." That, however, "was perhaps because she had not yet assumed this reality [that of evincing God's image], which takes place in the recognizing of God, and had been intended to do so little by little, under the rule and dispensation of the man."

Thus Eve's inferiority to Adam is one not of nature but of condition: by temporary dispensation. This cannot, however, quite correctly be called an effect of the body on the soul. Rather, since sexual dif-

22. Kari Elisabeth Børresen, "In Defence of Augustine: How *Femina* is *Homo*," in *Collectanea Augustiniana: Mélanges T. J. van Bavel*, ed. B. Bruning, M. Lamberigts, and J. van Houtem (Leuven: Leuven University Press, 1990), 418–19.

ferentiation, like all human physicality, is in the final analysis mental (not adequately definable in contradistinction from the soul, though for some purposes conveniently characterizable in that way), Eve's designedly temporary inferiority is provisional. This provisionality will always attend the physical life of the soul until the final consummation.

Our final question concerns the nature of human individuality. As we have seen, the two primary divisions of the human race are into sexes and into individuals, and one of the consequences of the sexual division was a temporary natural conditioning (not determination) of one's morality. Augustine's way of putting this, following St. Paul, is to say that Eve was seducible, Adam not (though of course he was corruptible), and that that constituted, for the time being, a lesser moral vulnerability in Adam, though not greater moral merit (*CD* 14.11; cf. 1 Tm 2.14). This notion has a considerable indirect bearing on Augustine's theory of salvation; for when one turns from sexual to individual differentiation, the principle that people can differ from each other—in a sense naturally—in susceptibility to sin without any difference in moral merit raises the possibility that God might give or withhold grace in accordance with innate human individuality, even though not in response to independent merit in individuals. Although, according to Augustine, God does not will the damnation of any individual, he gives or withholds salvation individual by individual, and in each case the reason for giving or withholding is, according to Augustine, known only to God (e.g., *De pecc. mer.* 1.21.29). The main theological danger is of implying that the choice is arbitrary. This problem will be broached in a later chapter, where Augustine's conception of the human condition will be discussed directly. Here the question at issue is simply whether Augustine has a conception of innate human individuality that leaves logical room for divine grace to be, humanly speaking, anything other than arbitrary.

Natural, as opposed to acquired, individuality is most obviously to be sought in infants, in whom, however, it is for practical reasons difficult to detect. Augustine points out in the *Confessions* that seen from the outside infants can seem much alike (*Conf.* 1.6.8–9). But even while pointing that out he refers to a secluded depth of infantine life, about the individualities of which nothing can be said:

> As for the period of life, O Lord, in which I have no memory of having lived, about which I have had to rely on what others have told me, and which, from other infants, I have conjectured that I myself lived, though the conjecture is very plausible, I am reluctant to count that period of my life as part of the life I live in this world; for it is as much covered with the darkness of oblivion as is the life I lived in my mother's womb. But if "in iniquity I was conceived and in sins my mother nurtured me in her womb," where, I beseech you, O my God, where or when was I, your servant, ever innocent? But I put aside that entire period. What attention can I give something of which I have no traces left? (*Conf.* 1.7.12)

This passage distinguishes between what one can say about babies in general, from observation, and any given baby's individual experience. One can, for example, state a general truth about their inner lives: that an inherited sinfulness characterizes them; but the remainder of an infant's experience is in every case incommunicable by the infant at the time and shrouded in permanent forgetfulness later. That remainder is what is individual, for to treat of it properly one would have to remember one's own experience of it, and one does not. On the other hand, Augustine is far from dismissing that lost information as unimportant. On the contrary, those lost facts are so crucial that their loss closes the door on that period of a person's life. Moreover, his concern here is not with trivial matters but with moral and spiritual ones: we know that that hidden infant life was tainted with original sin; what we cannot get is knowledge of the individual dynamics of that spiritual effect. An individual's interior life before the time of conscious moral choices is already, therefore, a life caught up in the drama of salvation and damnation. Nevertheless, the crucial individual details are lost.

Fourteen years later Augustine still took essentially the same position. In *On the Merits and Remission of Sins* he again contrasts a general truth that can be known about infants with the great depth of unattainable truth about each one (*De pecc. mer.* 1.17.22). The one truth we know about an infant's experience, he argues, is that it is free of actual wrongdoing. (Therefore the remission wrought by infant baptism is of original sin.) Beyond that, the facts necessary for discussion of an individual infant's life are obscured from us.

Neither here nor in the passage from the *Confessions* does Augustine give examples; but at one point in the *City of God*, in the course of showing how absurd astrology is, he takes an actual case: twins, a boy and a girl, physically as similar as is possible given the difference of sex (*CD* 5.6). They are, he says, utterly different in temperament (far more than their difference in sex would explain): the girl reclusive, the boy gregarious; that difference has greatly influenced the respective paths they have taken in life. Though Augustine tacitly accepts the idea that in general a temperamental difference might well be connected with a physical one (he assumes that his readers have such an opinion and does not contradict it), he assures us that beyond the difference in sex, there was no outward, detectable physical difference in this case: in other words, one would not be able to point to some difference, isolable as physical, that would by itself sufficiently explain the enormous temperamental difference. But though that temperamental difference does not constitute a difference in moral merit, it patently has a bearing on one's spiritual path in life: the woman was a nun, never leaving her native area; the man married, had many children, and was a soldier.

A number of important convictions about human nature are asserted or implied here: people have temperamental individualities that are innate, not circumstantial or acquired; these have a vast effect on the lives of those people, and that effect is not restricted to superficialities; although such differences no doubt have a physical dimension, that consideration must not blind us to the reality of their mental basis and their spiritual significance; and although it is reasonable to expect a difference in sex to be associated with a difference in temperament, innate temperamental differences can also be completely individual in character. Thus Augustine's anthropology has ample room for innate, individual spiritual differences that are not matters of merit or demerit.

For Augustine human nature, though it bestrides the two radically different orders of being—the spiritual and the physical—is one nature. This is so by virtue of the perfect primacy of the soul, by which the body is an aspect of the soul. This primacy extends both to sexual difference, which though it is in the body is so because it is in the soul, and to individuality, for from the start, with eternal consequences, we are individuals in the mysterious roots of our being, in our souls.

We must turn from the primary features of the soul, as constituting human nature, to the primary features of the mind, which according to Augustine constitute human personality.

CHAPTER 2

THE FACULTIES OF PERSONALITY

Alasdair MacIntyre in *Whose Justice? Which Rationality?* says that according to Augustine: "The rationality of right action . . . is not its primary determinant, but a secondary consequence of right willing. Hence faith which initially moves and informs the will is prior to understanding. . . . This . . . is something to which Augustine was necessarily committed by his psychology of the will."[1] These remarks presuppose an idea of the human mind as divided into separate, independently operating faculties. We have already noticed (in the introduction) some of the criticisms, and theological doctrines, to which this very old interpretation of Augustine's psychology has given rise. Some parts of it have, however, been disputed: for example, Etienne Gilson forty years ago challenged the Jansenistic idea that Augustine thought emotion to be separate from the will.[2] The separatist view of Augustine's psychology has persisted nevertheless and has led to some reservations about the coherency of his thought in this matter; as we have seen, the possibility has been raised that in this connection he mixes categories and that he contradicts himself on the subject of the human mind as the divine image. These considerations have continued to cause some doubt whether the conception of the human

1. Alasdair MacIntyre, *Whose Justice? Which Rationality?* (Notre Dame, Ind.: University of Notre Dame Press, 1988), 158.
2. Gilson, 321–22 nn. 81–82. Cf. James J. O'Donnell, *Augustine: Confessions,* 3 vols. (Oxford: Clarendon Press, 1992), 2:12.

mind on which he bases his doctrine of morality, and consequently much of his theology, is tenable.[3]

Because of the ways in which he describes the mind's operations, this general question devolves into three specific ones: On what basis are the mental faculties related to one another and distinguished? What is the relationship between the higher levels of human awareness and those lower ones that, in some fashion at least, are also exercised by the beasts? (As will emerge later, it has been argued that for Augustine the human cognitive dependence on the senses results from the Fall, and is not intrinsic to the human mind.) And how can the mental faculties of a human being not only sufficiently constitute a single mind but also be sufficiently distinct to form, as Augustine claims it does, a human "trinity" analogous to the divine? (Here A. C. Lloyd's contention that Augustine's notion of person is based on a category mistake must be considered with particular care.)

Regarding the first question, two preliminary observations should be made. First, in a sense two modes of mental being are in question: the faculties, such as will and intellect, and their corresponding mental acts, such as volition and understanding. That distinction does not, however, need to be constantly applied here. One differentiates among mental faculties in virtue of a differentiation among mental acts. That is Augustine's own approach to the matter: what interested him, as E. Hill points out, was the functioning of the soul rather than its structure viewed in the abstract.[4] By *voluntas*, for instance, he commonly means "the act of willing" rather than "the faculty of will."[5] Second, in his mature analyses of the subject Augustine goes beyond his earlier division of the soul's activities into being, knowing, and willing, and eventually characterizes them either as willing, under-

3. Peter Brown, *Augustine of Hippo: A Biography* (London: Faber and Faber, 1967), 155; Lloyd, 203.

4. Hill, 258.

5. Ibid., 302 n. 23.

standing, and memory or as willing, understanding, and emotion, depending on the context (*Conf.* 13.11.12; *De Trin.* 9.2.2–9.4.4, 15.22.42–15.23.43; *CD* 14.6–9).

Because love, which Augustine treats as obviously an act of will, is for him the essence of morality—the "weight" that draws us to good or to harm—it is appropriate to begin the discussion with his approaches to the concept of the will (*Conf.* 13.8.9–13.9.10).[6]

In a passage from *De Trinitate* concerned directly with the question of opposition between volition and other activities of the mind, Augustine dissociates himself sharply from the Stoics (*De Trin.* 13.7.10–13.8.11). Having established that in order to be genuinely happy one has not only to have what one wants (or wills) but to want (or to will) rightly, he points out that this nevertheless is no easy matter. The Stoics, he says, are naïve enough to "invent for themselves happy lives of their own" based on the absurd assumption that by one's own power, by clearly and consistently willing the happiness one wishes, one can achieve it. Against this idea, with its implicit distinction between volition and emotion, willing and desiring, he sets a saying from Terence's *Andria*: "Since what you want cannot happen, you had better want [or "will"] what you can make happen": *quoniam non potest id fieri quod vis, id velis quod possis.* This capitalizes on the fact that the verb *velle* means both "to wish" and "to will" indifferently. The saying means either that one should simply will something more realistic than one desires, or that one should, by an act of the will, change one's desires. Either way, both the Terentian and the Stoic positions assume some sort of distinction between desire and will.

But Augustine greatly modifies the argument from his Terentian starting point. Terence has provided him with a perfectly good riposte to the Stoics, but not with an adequate account of the human mental reality. We all have an ineradicably deep desire (for happiness), he argues, which, though it may be unrealistic and therefore

6. See Dihle, 123–32.

ought according to secular suppositions to be changed, persists anyway, and inexorably, in everybody. Yet we cannot really be happy, whether in the obviously unrealistic Stoic way or even in the bluntly practical Terentian way, without immortality, for that, he says, is the only real happiness. Thus there is an unrealistic desire (the most basic and proper one) that nevertheless cannot be changed or replaced without absurdity; for inevitably (whatever the ultimate origin of this desire may be) one wants real happiness. In other words, if some theoretical conception of virtue were to direct us to stop wanting real happiness, we would instead stop wanting to have a virtue so conceived. Moreover, the universal human desire for happiness has, according to Augustine, a real (heavenly) object, although without the Christian revelation this would not as clearly be so. To a degree this desire connects us with heaven. It is, therefore, misunderstood if it is thought of merely as a desire: it is also, whether one realizes it or not, a piece of radically accurate, intuitive understanding: a primary awareness. No question is raised (at this deepest level) of its being originally an intuition and secondarily a feeling, or vice versa. Intellection and emotion are not presented as two different acts.

Here a piece of argument supposedly concerned with the will makes its clearest point about the relationship between desire and understanding, ultimately identifying the two. It leaves unresolved the issue it has initially raised: the relationship between will and desire.

That issue is addressed directly in a long section of the *City of God* written at roughly the same time (about 418) (*CD* 14.6–9). First Augustine spends a chapter arguing that all emotions are really acts of the will: proper emotions right acts of the will, disordered emotions wrong ones, though a good general volitional state is compatible with a wide variety of emotions because different circumstances appropriately call for different volitional responses.

What an act of the will is comes into question two chapters later, when he criticizes the Stoic insistence that volition is distinct from emotion. Specifically, he attacks three Stoic distinctions: between will and desire, between joy and elation, and between caution and fear (*CD* 14.8). His position is that here a philosophical school has invented a group of quasi-emotions and paraded them as pure judgments, and that in reality the judgments are merely versions of the emotions from which they are purportedly distinguished. "Both good and bad people," he says, "will, exercise caution, and rejoice; also both groups (and this is saying the same thing in different words) desire, fear, and are elated." His proof takes the form of a discussion of grief—a clear instance of a full-blown, spontaneous emotion, and admitted to be such by the Stoics, who have consequently rejected it as unacceptable, necessarily absent from the mind of a wise person. Augustine replies that on one occasion Alcibiades, having been brought by Socrates to realize that though he had thought himself happy, he was miserable, burst into tears. His grief was his realization of his misery. That is a clear instance of a good grief: one that was the onset of wisdom. The Stoics, as Augustine admits, had a kind of answer to this: they allowed that grief, though in itself something to be condemned and shunned, could be a temporarily desirable condition for lesser persons: something usefully felt by novices in wisdom when they became aware of their own inadequacy. Here Augustine completely parts company with the Stoics. He points out that the best and wisest, St. Paul, for example, and even Christ Himself, have experienced intense grief, and experienced it as the basis of their exercise of mercy. He relies on an argument of his own from five books earlier: to propose, as the Stoics did, that a virtuous will is an emotionless one is to deny the integrity of human experience in a radical way: it is to give an inhuman account of the will (*CD* 9.5). He concludes here that the Stoic distinction between volition and emotion is not a real one, and that to speak of emotionless human willing is mere verbal bombast. All acts of the will, then, are also emotions, though one does not refer to them as such in every context. If that is so and if, as he has said earlier, all emotions are acts of the will, emotions and acts of the will are the same thing (*De Trin.* 10.10.13; the will experiences delight).

Nevertheless, Augustine was conscious that one routinely experiences a division in the mind, which may reasonably be called a conflict between one's will and, say, the emotion of desire. Four chapters later, for example, he describes the human condition before the Fall as one "where desire did not yet resist the will": *ubi nondum voluntati cupiditas resistebat* (CD 14.12). As the context makes clear, however, what this refers to in current human experience is not a conflict between different faculties but a conflict, in each person, between different volitional tendencies: a natural inclination to obey God and an unnatural, though inborn, inclination to disobey him. It is therefore still convenient for Augustine to describe concupiscence in the very Stoic language the philosophical basis of which he has just rejected: one experiences concupiscence as if will and emotion were separate faculties. More turbulent mental experiences tend to be described as emotions; those more obviously characterized by discretion tend to be described as acts of the will. Strictly speaking, however, as he has already argued, will and emotion are convertible, and this philosophically stricter account of the matter absolves him from the philosophical objection that, like the Stoics, he based his ethics and theology on an untenable psychology of pure volition.

As for the relationship of will and intellect, A. Dihle has pointed out that "in the view of St. Augustine, will indeed partakes in the very act of cognition and is by no means restricted to preliminary and subsequent activities," for the faculties of memory, will, and intellect "are inseparably linked and cannot work independently of each other."[7] Though love, for example, may be described as the primary action of the will, we cannot love without knowing (*De Trin.* 8.4.6, 10.1.1); and conversely, coming to know in a sense entails loving. Augustine describes the process in *De Trinitate*:

That desire [*appetitus*] which exists in the act of internal inquiring originates in the person inquiring. . . . This desire, that is the inquiring itself, although it

7. Ibid., 125–26.

may not seem to be love (for one loves what is already known to one, whereas the inquiring we are talking about is exercised with a view to knowing), nevertheless is in the same general category as love; for it is clearly a willing, since everyone who seeks to find wills to do so. (*De Trin.* 9.12.18)

At this deepest level of motivation, one has to know in order to love, and one has (in a general sense) to love in order to know (though here, too, on a less deep level it remains possible to know without loving) (*De Trin.* 8.3.4). The faculties of will and understanding do not, therefore, operate independently.

It does not, of course, immediately follow that willing and understanding are ultimately the same act (as we have seen emotion and willing to be). Rist, however, takes us deeper into the matter by citing a section of *Ad Simplicianum* where Augustine describes cupidity as a disorder in the soul's desires themselves, not as mere misdirectedness of desires perfectly normal in themselves (*Ad Simpl.* 1.1.10).[8] In Augustine's view desires, says Rist, "vary qualitatively with their objects": in book II of the *City of God* Augustine talks of being led by a rightly ordered love to hate a disordered love that one also has in oneself (*CD* 11.28). One's soul's shape, as it were, is changed not in a restrictedly intellectual way (Augustine explicitly rejects that idea in this passage) but according to the love that it directs to objects. These passages correct Arendt's view that Augustine regarded *caritas* and *cupiditas* as exactly the same emotion differently directed, for they imply that each love is made what it is precisely by its object.[9] By virtue of its object each kind of love differently informs the soul. The difference concerned is one of apprehensional effect on the soul.

The relationship between willing and understanding is made clearer again near the end of *De Trinitate,* where Augustine considers the nature of the will itself (*De Trin.* 15.21.41). When is the will more itself (*valentior*) than at other times? As love, he says, for we make our most characteristically human moral choices when the will is attracted or

8. Rist, 158, 174.
9. Arendt, 18.

repelled. At such times the will experiences various emotions *(varias affectiones habet)*. Again, volition and emotion are identified. Then Augustine goes further. Having asked, "What is the will?" he defines it entirely in relation to the other faculties. "When a person has a right will we are surely not going to say that the will does not know what to seek, what to avoid. But if it has knowledge, the knowledge it has is certainly its own knowledge, and it has it within itself [*inest ei sua quaedam scientia*], and that could not be the case without memory and intelligence." The will may, therefore, also be called the understanding. It does not respond to some understanding seated elsewhere in the mind. Nor is this intellection by the will an intellection of some specialized, restricted sort, for, as we have seen, the deepest understanding is emotional. But emotion and will are convertible. Will and intellect are therefore one faculty and are each the entire mind.

Here again, as with will and emotion, it remains the case that it is sometimes useful to describe knowing and willing as different actions. For example, in an anti-Pelagian text Augustine, following St. Paul, says that charity can be said to exceed knowledge *(De gr. et lib. arb.* 19.40; cf. 1 Cor. 8.1). Yet he says this polemically (against the Pelagians who make knowledge the divine gift, love the human contribution); he then proceeds to quote Scriptural passages that tell against the very Pelagian disjunction that, for the sake of argument, he accepts and inverts. Moreover, the argument, on both sides, is concerned with the changing state of the already disrupted human mind. In *De Trinitate,* on the other hand, his interest is in the very nature of motivation, and there, as we have seen, loving and knowing are in essence the same action. Furthermore, on occasion, even in the anti-Pelagian works, where he explicitly describes the power exercised by God over the human will, what he in fact describes is in one case an emotional effect (God's throwing the Israelites into cowardly panic as a punishment) and in another (in the same list, without differentiation in kind) an intellectual one (God's deluding people into believing a lie) *(De gr. et lib. arb.* 20.41–21.42).

Internal mental oppositions notwithstanding, then, Augustine does not ultimately take the view that there are distinct operations of will, emotion, and intellect in the human mind. The notion of a pure, isolable will, attributed to Augustine with disapproval by Ryle, with approval by the Jansenists, is not in fact his view of the matter.[10] Although his psychology does not necessarily rule out the suitability of, say, describing concupiscence as if it were an emotional condition primarily, a moral condition secondarily, or divine grace as manifested morally at first, emotionally later, it implies that these are ways of describing how we experience things; but that in reality an emotional effect, for example, is an effect on the whole mind, for the whole mind is rightly characterized as emotional. Again, one might at this point in our discussion still argue that Augustine thought of divine grace as irresistible, but it would not be correct to say that he thought of God as intervening in one area of a person's motivation to the exclusion of another.

Augustine has successfully presented the three faculties so far discussed as fully mental, peculiarly human, in the forms they take. His presentation of the faculty of memory, however, raises a different problem (our second main one): the relationship between human and bestial awareness.

Memory, rather than emotion, is the faculty that together with will and understanding forms what one author has called Augustine's "final draft" of the trinitarian human mind.[11] Memory of self, understanding of self, and willing of self are, Augustine argues, the primary activities of the three primary human potentialities for excellence (*De Trin.* 10.11.17). This is in startling contrast with his statement in the *City of God* (made at roughly the same period) that God has equipped irrational souls with "memory, sense, and appetite" and rational souls with "mind, intelligence, and will" (*CD* 5.11). Verbally at

10. Ryle, 62–82; Jansenius, 3.3.1; Pascal, 895.
11. See Hill, 270, 286.

least, memory, which in *De Trinitate* analogously holds the place in the human mental trinity that the Father holds in the divine, is here classified in the lower, bestial area of reality—impinging on humanity but not specifically human.

It is a partial solution to this problem to say (or to imply, as O'Daly does) that the word *memoria* is used in two different senses: in *De Trinitate* a specifically human mental faculty entailing reason, in the *City of God* the mere power, which beasts also have, to recall things.[12] Thus the presence of "memory" in both kinds of creature does not, for example, imply a simple overlap between the rational and the irrational kinds of soul. And the human mind does not merely recall with its memory but thinks with it: one's understanding and one's love are always present in one's memory, whether one adverts to the fact or not (*De Trin.* 15.22.42). An analogical indication that Augustine did not think in terms of any such combination of bestial and intellectual as forming the human mind is his notion that the mind itself "gives something of its own substance" to form the images of physical things (*De Trin.* 10.5.7). This solves the problem by reference to general principle.

If, however, one wishes to take a thorough view of his approach to this problem, and of his notion of the human memory specifically, one must look more closely at how he specifies and relates the levels of human awareness. There is an elaborate account of this in his disquisition on the "visions" in the final book of *De Genesi ad Litteram* (*GL* 12.6.15–12.31.59). He uses a hierarchy of three "seeings" *(visiones)* to make a complete division of human consciousness. The three, which may be translated as "sense," "judgment," and "knowledge," are all engaged when, for example, one sees a physical object. One senses it by corporal vision; one conceives the image of it by spiritual vision; and in this process one brings to bear the contemplation of entirely nonphysical reality that constitutes intellectual vision. These

12. See O'Daly, 97–99.

are not different faculties but degrees of awareness.[13] For example, the intellectual vision is, according to Augustine, infallible. This means not that generally we are intellectually infallible, but that at our highest level of mental activity we have knowledge. When, on the other hand, the human mind acts yet does not know, that is not because it is engaging in some activity other than the intellectual (in the ordinary sense), but because it falls short of perfect understanding (*GL* 12.25.52).[14] The necessary (not sufficient) condition of that practical falling short is our partial dependency on the lower visions for our understanding. This dependency implies not that the intellectual vision itself depends on the lower ones, but only that full human awareness necessarily extends through all three. Indeed, the dependency of one degree of awareness on another works in the opposite direction. The spiritual vision, for example, is required if the visual sense is to be converted to full visual perception, because the soul must distinguish between physical objects and, say, daydreams; such practical discernment, moreover, entails already knowing (intellectually) the difference in essence between the two. On the other hand the knowledge, in intellectual vision, of such incorporeal realities, which are its proper objects, is itself independent of the lower visions. That knowledge, however, is not a separate mental activity but a dimension of mental consciousness. We, therefore—but not our intellectual vision—are dependent on the lower visions for cognition. We are subjects, and the intellectual vision, like the others, is a feature of our subjectiveness.

It is not correct, therefore, to say, as one contemporary commentator does, "that the author regards not merely our moral enslavement to the senses but our cognitive dependence on them as a result of the Fall, not as a consequence of the kind of nature we have been created with; that this dependence is a kind of sickness—all this marks off the Augustinian view from the more genuinely humanistic

---

13. Agaësse and Solignac, 2:563.

14. See ibid., 2:577.

aristotelianism of Thomas Aquinas."[15] In Augustine's view our cognitive dependence on the senses is a consequence of our nature as created—part of the breadth of human awareness. In this regard, then, his view is not marked off from the humanism of the Aristotelian tradition. Memory occurs in the two upper visions in two different degrees: in the spiritual by its more familiar manifestation (as remembrance of things outside itself) and in the intellectual with knowledge (as its own self-remembrance) (*GL* 12.23.49).[16] In a human being, then, memory can be said to exist beneath the intellectual level only in a very nuanced sense: as reaching down to a region of consciousness below the level of full knowledge. In this notion of the memory's place in the human mind we again meet Augustine's conviction of the utter unity of the human mind.

The third main question is whether that conviction imperils his analogy, in *De Trinitate*, between the human mental faculties and the divine Trinity, for this requires real distinctions among those faculties.[17] Here his "first draft" of the mental "trinity" is of particular interest, for his categorical difficulties with it indicate the assumptions most relevant to this question. His universe of discourse in that part of the work is the mind's self-contemplation (for him the most fundamental form of human awareness, prerequisite to all others) (*De Trin.* 9.3.3). The division of such contemplation into mind, mind's self-knowledge, and mind's self-love immediately proves problematic for him, for it bases a philosophical theory of person on one's observation of one's own love and knowledge (*De Trin.* 9.2.2).

15. Hill, 318 n. 2.

16. See Agaësse and Solignac, 2:563.

17. For perceptive short studies on the human mind and the Trinity, see Rowan Williams, "*Sapientia* and the Trinity: Reflections on the *De Trinitate*," in *Collectanea Augustiniana: Mélanges T. J. van Bavel*, ed. B. Bruning, M. Lamberigts, and J. van Houtem (Leuven: Leuven University Press, 1990), 317–32; and "The Paradoxes of Self-Knowledge in the *De Trinitate*," in *Collectanea Augustiniana: Signum Pietatis*, ed. J. Lienhard, E. Muller, and R. Teske (New York: Peter Lang, 1993), 121–34.

Three decades ago A. C. Lloyd published a trenchant critique of
Augustine's concept of person, using the specifically Aristotelian logic to which Augustine himself appeals (cf. *De Trin.* 9.4.5).[18] One of the
criticisms (though not the only one important here) concerns precisely this introspective approach. Lloyd argues that to base the investigation of such a matter on psychological self-observation is futile: for
first, what one discovers might be merely oneself, rather than anything essential (and necessary) to a human person; and second, what
one discovers, even if it is of the very essence of human personality,
might still not establish anything about what necessarily constitutes a
person: one would have to know already what a person is before one
proceeded to classify as necessary to personality what one had discovered in one's introspection. This introspective approach, however, is
not a logical blunder on Augustine's part but a matter of what intuitive assumptions one is prepared to accept as premises. Lloyd insists
on beginning with formal analysis and consequently with a far more
limited range of premises than Augustine. Augustine's position is that
before constructing syllogisms, one is legitimately aware of numerous crucial features of one's humanity: that mind and body are the
two fundamental aspects of a human being, the mind being the higher; that by virtue of our mind we are substantiated as human, and we
intuitively know this to be the case even before we have reflected
philosophically on it; that the constitutive acts of the mind are knowing and loving; and, by revelation, that these highest acts of the mind
are those in which we are in the image of God.

Lloyd's main criticism, however, concerns the next stage in Augustine's argument. At this stage Augustine's main problem is disparity
of categories, mind being in that of substance, love and knowledge in
that of relation, the self-love constituting a volitional relationship, the
self-knowledge a cognitional relationship. (In a sense Augustine had
started in the category of action, since initially he had described the
mind in its operation; but his study of that operation has led him to

18. Lloyd, esp. 196–98.

leave that category aside.) In the event he neither simply accepts nor simply abandons the resultant category mixture. Before even attempting to solve that problem, however, he makes a point of permanent importance for his argument: the mind's self-love and its self-knowledge are in a sense relations in it, but each also constitutes the entire mind. They do not, says Augustine, exist in the mind as in a subject (*De Trin.* 9.4.5). The mind knows, for example, not merely with its entire self but as its entire self. Knowledge and love are not accidents of the mind in which they exist. Nor, however, are they substances distinct from it, or a transformative combination such that each of those faculties has ceased to be itself (*De Trin.* 9.5.8).

Although Augustine has not yet arrived at a categorically consistent human mental analogy for the divine Trinity (and although, as we shall see, there are serious questions about his proposed solution when he does), he has at least made clear that the faculties in that mental "trinity" neither make the human mind a multiplicity nor are mere synonyms for it. The former point implies, as we have seen, that the human mind is its love of itself and is its own self-knowledge. The latter point implies that the distinction among the faculties must be real. This position is already established, then, when Augustine begins his final "draft."

Given that each faculty constitutes the entire mind, the distinctions among them will have to be strictly according to their relationship itself, a distinction in any other category being inconsistent with their essential identity. The mind's love of itself and its knowledge of itself are not, for example, different acts (for what they constitute is the same) but different mental relationships. Both God and the human mind, then, are triply constituted. Only by corporeality is a human being prevented from being three persons (though this is not made clear until the last book of *De Trinitate*) (*De Trin.* 15.22.42–15.23.43). A person, at this point in the argument, is the complete self-constitution of a rational substance—that by which a rational being, as distinct from a being of any other class, is real. Each member of the divine Trinity, therefore, is a Person in that sense (differentiated by relation with each of the others), but each faculty of the human mind stops short of being a person because the operation of the human mind (in a restrictedly mental way) is not the operation of the entire human being.

First, therefore, when Augustine thinks of the human mind as acting in its primary way (which in his supposedly categorically consistent final draft he describes as memory of self, self-knowledge, and self-love), he does not see it as engaging in different acts. Second, however, he admits that when the mind proceeds beyond its own internal life, what is, as we have seen, primarily a single act can still take the form of acts different from each other in character. Each act is nevertheless an act of the entire mind, and simultaneously an act of remembering, willing, and understanding. Third, he allows that because of the distortions affecting the mind, a mental act may seem to be an act in only one of the areas of mental ability (of the will, for example, to the exclusion of the memory and of the understanding), and may conveniently be described as such. But although, as Wetzel points out, Augustine thought of sin as having temporarily driven a "wedge between knowing and willing" in human beings, he did not think of this as a wedge driven between two parts of the mind.[19] On the contrary, the mind's memory, knowledge, and love are each the entire mind, not its parts or its accidents. Fourth, they nevertheless constitute it triply, not singly (as synonyms, for example). Hence they are, in Augustine's view, related to the Persons of the divine Trinity analogously (in the scholastic sense), not metaphorically. His position is that the human mental faculties are in every respect the partial instance of the relationship the fulness of which is the divine Trinity. Hence it is not correct to say that for Augustine the intellect, as opposed, say, to the will, is where human beings characteristically resemble God.[20] Though he gives several accounts of the human mind,

19. See Wetzel, 192.
20. See Laplace and Daniélou, 94 n. 1.

in each of which God is represented with different degrees of adequacy, consistently in each the image of God is not in any one mental faculty rather than another, but in their relationship with each other.

It is here that Lloyd's main criticism becomes crucial: is Augustine's formulation of this analogy, and its consequent notion of person, valid and consistent?[21] The analogy relies on a notion of person conceived in the category of relation. A rational being (God or a human being) is personal by virtue of being relationally determined. A decade earlier than Lloyd, J. Mader had already argued that if one posits a being without accidents, one is inevitably speaking in the category of substance (the only one left); if, however, one also says (as Augustine does) that such a being is a person and as such is relationally constituted, one confuses relation and substance, violating the very Aristotelian logic to which Augustine has appealed.[22] Lloyd, who takes a similar view (though he also does not think Augustine to be completely consistent on the subject), argues further that by tacitly defining a person as the determination of a rational substance Augustine shies away from the main implication of placing person in the category of relation: that other beings must exist, with which the personal being stands in relation. Lloyd adds that Augustine would have done well to accept this implication and its further consequences, rather than concentrating on the soul's reflexive dispositions (self-love, self-knowledge)—a futile attempt to avoid those consequences. One of these would, of course, have been the theologically alarming one that God's being personal assumes the existence of other beings than God.[23]

Regarding the former point, Augustine certainly does not simply confuse substance and relation. Saying that rational substance entails relation is no more to confuse substance with relation than saying

21. Lloyd, 199–203.

22. Johann Mader, *Die logische Struktur des personalen Denkens aus der Methode der Gotteserkenntnis bei Aurelius Augustinus* (Vienna: Verlag Herder, 1965), 97–99.

23. Lloyd, 203.

that a physical substance must be somewhere is confusing substance with place. But this still leaves Lloyd's more important criticism. Augustine's formulation causes a crisis in his thought, as to how the idea of relation is applied. It is true that in *De Trinitate* Augustine eventually restricts his discussion of love to its reflexive aspect. Is he, as Lloyd argues, thereby reneging on the main implication of the relational category, or merely prescinding from it for the sake of the part of his analogy that concerns God's internal self-sufficiency?

This question requires a study of Augustine's notion of charity (for him the core of morality). It will be addressed in chapter 4. First, however, his notion of the human condition (the controlling environment of morality) must be discussed directly.

CHAPTER 3

THE STAGES IN THE HUMAN CONDITION

J. M. Rist has pointed out that as a result of the spiritual history of the human race Augustine gives "not one, but three accounts of the relationship between soul and body."[1] The reason is that in specifying human nature Augustine examines practical human experience rather than attempting definition in vacuo; yet he does not think our nature to be fully perceptible in its present condition, either, for that condition has thrown the nature itself into more or less violent disorder (e.g., *CD* 13.3, 14.13). Consequently, he brings into consideration (as therefore we must) the divine *administratio* of human life in its three main stages: the Garden, this world, and heaven (or its privation). He does not, for the most part, give his three accounts separately but pieces together his delineation of our nature by constant reference to these starkly different phases of our condition (e.g., *CD* 13.14–13.24, 14.1–6, 14.14–14.27). We must now consider what Augustine says of these phases, in particular of their two main turning points: the Fall and the action of divine grace.

Our most comprehensive questions are: What, then, does he regard as specifically human about each phase of the human condition, and in that context, what do the Fall and divine grace consist in?—a very disputed area of his thought. Three sets of questions have been especially controversial. The first set concerns sin: Augustine's gener-

---

1. Rist, 95.

al conception of that doctrine, in particular his notion of concupiscence (the Fall's most immediate manifestation) and its moral consequences—original sin, original guilt, the two degrees of death, and what he thinks is the relationship of all these with one another. Here the pertinent modern discussions will be those of John Burnaby (on Augustine's notion of desire and its relationship with reason as well as on whether Augustine thinks of God as positively punishing the damned) and of James Wetzel, K. E. Kirk, and Peter Brown (on the contentious Augustinian notion that even baptized Christians remain concupiscent).

In the second set the general question is whether his doctrine on the matters just mentioned is coherent and consistent. There are numerous more particular questions: Does it make sense to say, as Augustine does in his late works, that all humanity since the Fall begins life lumped together in condemnation for Adam's sin? (Does the idea imply, for example, that we all participated as agents in Adam's sin? Or that the divine grace that gratuitously removes some from that morass overrides their free will?) Does grace, in its mode of choice, take any account of differences between individuals, or is it in human terms arbitrary, and does its dependency on sacramental baptism imply that infants who die unbaptized are victims of sheer bad luck? Finally, why, given the complete absence of independent merit in the *massa damnata,* is everybody not saved? The relevant modern interpretations here will be those of J. N. D. Kelly, Christopher Kirwan, and N. P. Williams (on what is implied by the notion that we all participate in Adam's sin) and of John Rist (on infants who die unbaptized).

The third set of questions directly concerns what Augustine's doctrine of sin and grace implies about human nature. Does the notion that those in heaven cannot sin contradict the notion—also Augustinian—that the ability to sin is an essential part of our nature? If, on the other hand, the heavenly impeccability is rather the culmination of human nature, why were we not created thus perfect in the first place? Here the criticisms discussed in most detail are Heidegger's (on whether Augustine thinks fear extends into heaven) and Rist's (on the problem of original peccability).

Though the issue of consistency is prominent in this chapter, it remains important not to expect Augustine to write systematically (with strictly demarcated terminology, for example, or constant, explicit delimitation of one notion as against another). Rather, his context is usually polemical in some way. Yet his modern critics quite reasonably expect him not to contradict himself (except in the case of a change of mind) and that one group of notions should make sense in terms of another. It is with these expectations that we must approach this area of his thought.

On our first set of questions (on Augustine's doctrine of sin), the first issue is concupiscence, which in his view is the Fall's primary manifestation in this world. It may be provisionally defined as the universal, morally destabilizing dislocation in human desires, incurred first by Adam and Eve and then inherited by their descendants (*De nupt. et conc.* 1.6.7; *CD* 14.15). In our first parents this was evil's first symptom; and in regenerate people in this world it is evil's last vestige before death. The notion of concupiscence is, therefore, a suitable starting point for discussion.

In his most developed accounts of the subject (the works of his anti-Pelagian period), Augustine repeatedly asserts that as long as we live in this world, a deep instability of the mind is a reality and a force for moral harm. To some extent even in virtuous people it stands in the way of every good aspiration (e.g., *De perf. iust.* 11.28; *De gr. Chr. et pecc. or.* 2.39.44). It takes away not free will, but the ability to exercise it with perfect purity (*CD* 19.25). He describes it, especially in its sexual manifestation, as emotion so strong as to be insusceptible to control (*CD* 14.16). The initial question, then, is whether he regards it as a primarily moral state that causes troublesome emotions, or as a primarily emotional state that impairs moral stability. In the treatise *On*

Marriage and Concupiscence he describes it first as one ("a certain affection of an evil kind") and then, five chapters later, as the other (the Pauline "sin that dwells in me: that is, in my flesh") (*De nupt. et conc.* 1.25.28, 1.30.34; Rom 7.18). Does this apparent ambiguity on the subject justify Burnaby's criticism that Augustine fails to distinguish between a mere nonrational desire and an unruly one?[2]

Although, as we have seen, his notion of the essential unity of the mental faculties ultimately precludes the idea of a completely nonrational natural desire, nevertheless in his *Against Two Letters of the Pelagians* Augustine himself directly confronts the possibility that such a distinction might after all be correct and applicable to human experience (*C. duas ep. Pel.* 1.17.34–35). His question is whether Adam and Eve experienced sexual libido in the Garden. There are, he says, four possibilities: that they would have had sexual intercourse whenever they felt like it (that is, reason would not have had anything to do with the matter); that "they would have reined in their lust" (*frenarent libidinem*) whenever sexual intercourse was not required; that "lust would have arisen at the will's direction when chaste prudence had sensed that sexual intercourse was necessary"; and finally, that "without there being any lust at all, just as the other parts of the body do service, each in the performance of its own work, so the genitals would without any difficulty have obeyed instructions, as willed." (The will is conceived of here as entirely rational.) Augustine ultimately rejects the first two possibilities, but allows both the third and the fourth. The distinction between the second and third is the one that Burnaby accuses him of not making: between unruly desire and desire *simpliciter dictum*. Between the third and fourth, on the other hand, there is a closeness amounting to fusion; for in the third Augustine mentions no "reining in" of desire such as in the second, and says that in this instance desire would not "outstrip, retard, or exceed the command of the will." A desire by nature so modest, so sensitive,

2. Burnaby, 59.

and so compliant to reason's commands can hardly be called even a nonrational desire. Rather, it is a rational one defined in prescindment from its rational aspect. The third and fourth possibilities, then, are essentially the same possibility. In this disquisition, therefore, Augustine, having initially accepted for the sake of argument the same distinction as Burnaby makes, in effect proceeds to show it to be wrongly formulated, for there is no such thing as a morally neutral desire; although it is easy, even common, to think of desire and reason as clearly distinct psychological functions, Augustine indicates such an idea to be mistaken. A desire is either unruly or rational.

This both confirms what we have seen to be Augustine's conviction of the fundamental unity of reason, will, and emotion, and shows that concupiscence works even at that most fundamental level. Though he distinguishes between wayward desire and the decision to obey it, he concomitantly acknowledges that desire is a moral as well as an emotional matter: "it is good not to desire waywardly" *(bonum est non concupiscere) (De perf. iust.* 11.28). Also, as we have seen, Augustine regards concupiscence as more deep-seated even than the distinction between body and soul.

That until we die concupiscence persists in us, even in those who are baptized and persevering, is another indication of its deep-seatedness (e.g., *C. Iul.* 3.26.62). The idea of this persistence (which is particularly associated with Augustine) has been much criticized but in starkly different ways: Wetzel argues that Augustine's theological contortions have drained it of definite moral content; Brown (with many others) asserts that on the contrary the general acceptance of this idea amounted to a definitive change in the moral theology of Western Christianity.[3]

Wetzel's criticism is that Augustine, in order to avoid implying that St. Paul's "I do the evil that I do not want" is a confession to being corrupted with unrestrained desire, interprets the statement in a

3. Wetzel, 175–86; P. Brown, *Religion,* 183–207; Peter Brown, *The Body and Society* (London: Faber and Faber, 1990), 426.

purely emotional sense, leaving the evildoing interpretable as mere "inoperative perversity," and taking Paul to mean that actually he does the good that he wants, but not with the accompanying emotion that he would like. Augustine's position is not open to that interpretation. In the passage cited (from *Against Two Letters of the Pelagians*) he indeed absolves St. Paul from admitting that he wilfully consents to evil; yet he still takes him to be admitting that his actions are morally impaired (*C. duas ep. Pel.* 1.10.18). He has already concluded that Paul was referring to himself as he was at the time of writing. Two contrasting statements must therefore be balanced: that not he, but the sin dwelling in him does the evil, and that he does the evil that he does not want. The claim not to be the doer shows that he does not admit to sinning with full consent. Yet the claim to be the doer rules out the suggestion that this concupiscence is empty of real moral significance. Augustine concludes that the two together imply impurity of motive, short of viciousness—virtue impaired, not destroyed. This conclusion entails the conviction that concupiscence's persistence rules out the practice of Christian moral perfection in this world. Such a notion of persistent concupiscence has, therefore, substantial moral significance.

The contrary contention, however, that Augustine by convincing the Church of this view seriously altered the Christian moral tradition, is practically a commonplace of Augustinian criticism. According to K. E. Kirk, for example, the usual assumption in earlier Christianity had been that a true Christian, once baptized, could be sinless, no longer morally feeble; and Brown calls "the Christianity of discontinuity" quite simply "the ancient Christianity."[4]

Earlier Christian writers (even Augustine himself) had certainly taken a more sanguine tone about the Christian moral life in this world than Augustine eventually did in the anti-Pelagian works. But

4. Kenneth E. Kirk, *The Vision of God: The Christian Doctrine of the Summum Bonum* (London: Longmans, 1932), 229–30, 146 n. 3; P. Brown, *Religion*, 194, 196, 200. Cf. P. Brown, *Body*, 426.

on this point it is particularly important to distinguish between rhetorical attitude and substantial moral theology. Kirk cites, for example, Justin's statement: "If someone is not found guilty of misbehavior, let that person be set free, for as a Christian he does not do injustice."[5] Although rhetorically this creates a division in one's mind between Christians and injustice, all it really asserts is that to be a Christian is not a moral offence. Another passage cited is the statement by Clement of Alexandria that the "true gnostic" (or Christian sage) is one who has successfully responded to the Lord's counsel of perfection, having been made perfect as our heavenly Father is perfect.[6] This certainly exemplifies Kirk's and Brown's contentions. But Clement's statement is part of an argument, Platonic in character, in which he (like Socrates in the *Republic*) uses idealistic portrayal to establish principles. His true gnostic is not a picture drawn from life but a mental construct, which has nothing to do with whether moral perfection can be achieved in this world. Moreover, Gregory of Nyssa provides a clear counterexample that after baptism the flesh still lusts against the spirit, even though the "snake bites" of desire are not deadly for the faithful who keep their eyes fixed on the Cross.[7] As far as it extends, this is the same position as Augustine's in his late works: baptism making the eternal moral and spiritual difference, but not moral discontinuity.

Nevertheless, the great emphasis on concupiscence in Augustine's late works, especially the sense he conveys of its radical character, raises our next question: What, according to Augustine, is original sin, which may be provisionally defined as the collapsed spiritual condition of the human nature shared by all with Adam? (*C. Iul. op. imp.* 3.57, 6.22; *Retract.* 1.13.5, 1.15.2). Augustine asserts that the concupis-

5. Justin, *Apology* 1.7.

6. Clement of Alexandria, *Stromateis* 6.12.

7. Gregory of Nyssa, *Life of Moses*, 271, 276. For a fuller treatment of the subject, see Peter Burnell, "Concupiscence and Moral Freedom in Augustine and before Augustine," *Augustinian Studies* 26 (1995): 49–63.

cence against which the baptized fight is not itself sin (*De pecc. mer.* 2.4.4). On the face of it, this might be taken to indicate a distinction in kind (concupiscence being a mere accompaniment of sin). In other texts, however, Augustine's position proves to be otherwise. In one anti-Pelagian text he says that the concupiscence of the flesh, passed on to us through our immediate parents' sexual concupiscence, is cured by baptism in such a way that it no longer harms (not "no longer troubles") the baptized (*C. duas ep. Pel.* 1.13.27; cf. *CD* 14.15). If it was parentally engendered in us, and it harmed us, then, in this context, it was original sin. Original sin, then, is in effect defined here as concupiscence that directly harms us. The underlying distinction is between essence and mode: original sin is one of the modes of concupiscence; residual post-baptismal cupidity another. The same passage also raises the subject of original guilt *(reatus)*. The reason, says Augustine, why carnal concupiscence in the baptized is not sin is that its guilt, passed on by generation, is abolished by baptism. This might be taken to refer to yet another liability (guilt, on top of sin), requiring such abolition. (One scholar has indeed commented that Augustine sees "nothing incongruous in saddling us with both.")[8] Again, however, that is not Augustine's position. In another text (arguably his clearest statement on the subject) he says: "Concupiscence is so harmful in those born but not reborn that unless they come to be reborn no advantage can possibly come to them from being born to reborn parents: the vice in our origin so remains in our children as to make them guilty" (*De gr. Chr. et pecc. or.* 2.39.44). Original guilt, therefore (as also original sin), is concupiscence in its spiritually catastrophic mode. The chapter in which this statement occurs is precisely about such difference in modes—between concupiscence that is damnable (or at least perilous) sin, and concupiscence that is not. In this context Augustine repeatedly says that what causes the defect in the soul to be sin is consent. (The chapter ends with one of his repeti-

8. Kelly, 364. Cf. N. P. Williams, 372.

tions of that point.) But as we have seen earlier in the present chapter, all concupiscence entails some consent. Moreover, in any case, as we saw in chapter 2, he takes the view that there is no such thing as a nonvolitional emotion. More precisely, then, his concern is with a decisive degree of consent. Furthermore, although actual sin is included in the generalities he states here, it is only a side issue, as it is also in the surrounding chapters. His main argument is that one inherits original sin even from baptized parents and that consequently one needs baptism. It is as part of that argument that Augustine describes consent of the will as the essence of sin. In an extended sense, therefore, we are born already committed to enmity with God—not, of course, consciously so, but by bearing the critically deep psychic imprint of distortion in our desires, which without grace remains a "vice in our origin" precluding adequately wholesome motivation. Actual sins done by adults are lapses or relapses into concupiscence's ordainment (CD 21.16).

Finally, it should be pointed out that Augustine shows the sheer comprehensiveness of concupiscence when he says here that at the end of time it will be through a regeneration of the flesh that baptism will free us of "distorted desires such as lead us, by consenting, to sins." Not only is the flesh the channel of our final regeneration (when it is eventually freed of concupiscence at the resurrection), but, as he implies in the *City of God*, it will have been the first of those dimensions of our being to die under concupiscence's power. It will not, however, in the case of the damned, be the last. In short, "there is no human wretchedness," he says, "other than this disobedience of oneself to oneself"; for not only is one's hold on this life fatally shaken by it; so is one's hold on Life itself. The final manifestation of our inward unruliness is eternal death (CD 14.15). In other words, even eternal punishment is conceived in Augustine's late works as the triumph of concupiscence.

To this economical summation of human disaster, however, Burnaby claims that Augustine gratuitously added the notion of a separate punishment, suffering inflicted by God upon the damned: "an eternal and as it were detachable consequence of sin."[9] This idea, he says, has led to a tendency in Western Christianity to attempt to avoid sin because of the suffering to which it leads rather than because of love for God. The principal text cited here is from the *Unfinished Work against Julian* (*C. Iul. op. imp.* 3.203). Isaiah, says Augustine, asserts that God creates evils; evils are of two kinds: suffering and sin. Since God does not create sin, he must create some suffering. But this is merely a logical move, not a developed theological position. The debate with Julian is about whether our condition is in God's hands. Julian has asserted that moral evil is the only evil. Augustine replies that sufferings also are evils, and some of them (as the text from Isaiah forces us to conclude) must be of God's creation. But in this context he is not concerned with discussing how that is the case. In the following book, however, he returns to the matter. Now he is very much concerned with the question of the exact sense in which God may be described as the source of evil for human beings. He is faced with the objection that if indeed the goodness or badness of our condition is in God's hands, God is gratuitously, and therefore unjustly, the source of evils for us. "It is shamelessness," Augustine replies, "to try to convince people . . . that God has judged unjustly in abandoning the wrongdoer with the result that one whose true happiness had been God now becomes his own punishment" (*C. Iul. op. imp.* 4.33). In other words, the sense in which God is the source of evil for us is simply that the divine perfection by its very existence unavoidably confirms that our sin is evil. Though it is acceptable, therefore, to say that God punishes us with suffering, what one means by this is that despite our sin, God simply remains himself, the only source of good for human beings, and agonizingly unapproachable by human delinquency. The suffering concerned is logically consequent, not additionally inflicted.

Again, in Epistle 184A (also cited by Burnaby) Augustine defines

9. Burnaby, 214.

the anger of God as "the punishment and vengeance owed by God in justice." Again, however, he identifies this (using *quippe,* which denotes explanatory corroboration of what has already been said) as concupiscence, giving a disquisition on that subject at this point: whatever is begotten, conceived, and born through this inherited disorder must, he says, be reborn to avoid punishment (damnation); and only spiritual regeneration can constitute this rebirth, just as a true olive is no more capable of producing, by itself, another true olive than a wild olive is. For the wrath of God, he argues, is not something that God inflicts on us by changing in response to our sin (God does not change); it consists in what we inherit from our ancestors. Here again, our liability to punishment consists in a mode of *concupiscentia carnalis,* and our punishment is the experience of that disorder in the face of God's unchanging goodness—not a divine action but a human condition. That condition is membership (whether full or vestigial) in the "condemned lump" of concupiscent humanity. Ultimately, then, damnation is simply that disorder, not a separate, positive infliction wreaked by God.

The second set of questions is concerned with whether this notion of the human condition is coherent. It has been argued on various grounds both that the notion itself is confused and that the doctrine of grace attaching to it is flawed.

First, it has been said that Augustine based his doctrine of original sin on the idea that we all actually participated in Adam's original sinful deed (this would in effect be a confusion of original with actual sin),[10] and in particular that Augustine's acceptance of the well-known Latin mistranslation of St. Paul's ἐφ' ᾧ πάντες ἥμαρτον as *in quo omnes peccaverunt* ("in whom all sinned") rather than, say, *eo quod* ("in that") distorted his entire theology of sin. Kelly describes this undoubted linguistic error (initiated before Augustine) as "the pivot of the doctrine of original sin."[11] Kirwan argues that Augustine confus-

10. N. P. Williams, 373; Kelly, 364.   11. Kelly, 354; Rom 5.12.

es the sense in which an action can be attributed to one part of a person (a blow attributed to a hand, for example, where blaming the part would be an absurdity) with that in which a person as a whole is said to do something—if each of us was in Adam, each of us could have acted only as a tiny bit of him.[12] Kirwan also argues that Augustine fails to distinguish between what one does unconsciously (for which one cannot reasonably be blamed and in which category our participation in the original sin must fall) and what one does consciously.[13] A partial reply to both criticisms is first, that part of a person can be harmed, even mutilated, as a result of some act committed by the whole person, even though it cannot be blamed for it; and second, that what one does unconsciously can be harmful to the doer, even though it does not make the doer culpable. These replies leave a residue of possible validity in both criticisms (the same in both): that it is absurd to blame a person for doing what that person has not actually done. This point is also the essence of N. P. Williams's criticism that Augustine confusedly attempts to establish the same basis of blame for original sin as for actual sin.

Certainly Augustine constantly used the text from Romans (always mistranslated) in argument to prove to the Pelagians the doctrine of original sin (*De pecc. mer.* 1.9.10, 3.7.14, 3.11.19; *De nat. et grat.* 8.9, 39.46; *De nupt. et conc.* 2.5.15). Frequently his purpose is little more than to show that by our natural participation in Adam we are all sinful from the start. Never does he come to the ridiculous conclusion that each of us, as a tiny part of Adam, assisted in the doing of his sin; and from some passages it is clear that he ruled that notion out. At one point in the *City of God,* for example, he connects the Pauline text with one from the book of Genesis: the soul of a male infant who has not been duly circumcised on the eighth day of his life "shall perish from among his people, for he has violated my covenant" (*CD* 16.27; Gn 17.14). It would be absurd, says Augustine, to regard the in-

12. Kirwan, 140.
13. Ibid., 135.

dividual child as a covenant breaker for his failure to do something at the age of eight days; therefore the violation must be Adam's original disobedience. This discussion is precisely about the difference between a coherent and an incoherent notion of blameworthiness. Augustine distinguishes between blame incurred by one's own action and that incurred through one's origin. Though both these notions are in themselves coherent, he bluntly discounts the idea that someone such as an eight-day-old infant could possibly be blameworthy in the former sense. The suggestion therefore that Augustine thought us responsible for having participated as individuals (*proprie*) in Adam's wrongful act is beyond serious consideration.

In *On Marriage and Concupiscence* he makes the same argument (with the same example) more explicitly: an eight-day-old boy is "an innocent baby, as far as he himself, as an individual, is concerned" (*quantum ad ipsum proprie attinet, innocens infans*). The respect in which such a child is not innocent, he says, is the corrupt condition of human nature inherited through the sexual concupiscence of one's parents (*De nupt. et conc.* 2.12.25). Adam's sin has become ours by our participation not in his act but in his nature (*De pecc. mer.* 3.8.15). Augustine's notion of our collective participation in Adam's sin is therefore a coherent one.

A number of much more serious problems arise, however, in his notion of the grace by which some are rescued from that condemned morass.

He clears the obvious pitfalls. Though, for example, there is absolute human dependency on gratuitous divine grace, there is no positive predestination of people to hell; for whereas grace is not at all a divine reward for independent human merit, damnation is a result of independent human demerit (e.g., *De gr. et lib. arb.* 21.43). Second (though here the matter is more complicated), he does not propound a notion of grace that overrides human free will, for as Rist points out, although the necessary virtuous impulse and perseverance are entirely God's grace, Augustine regards that grace as resistible but otherwise sufficient, motivating and enabling the exercise of virtue rather than forcing it.[14] It has, however, been argued that for Augustine, although in the end grace liberates rather than coerces the human will, it still operates irresistibly in the meantime, in this world.[15] But even in respect of that inchoate effect of grace, Augustine implies a crucial distinction: between what is irresistible and what, by divine Providence, is unresisted. (Saying that the universe is so arranged that a given person freely refrains from resisting an influence is not the same as saying that resistance of that influence is impossible.)

In itself, free will, he says in an early anti-Pelagian text, is a potentiality (*media vis*, "intermediate power") existing between the two alternative realizations of the human will—faith and unfaithfulness. Any inclination to good, starting from that given potentiality, is provided by God (*De sp. et litt.* 33.58). And he adds that God wishes all to be saved, but not at the expense of their free will. The question he is discussing is: Why is salvation not given to all? The single principle given in reply is that of the divine insistence on keeping human free will inviolate. The implication is that although in some cases the granting of grace does not violate human free will, in other cases it would. This was no passing notion of Augustine's: he confirms it, though in more general terms, in *On Grace and Free Will*. The Word of God, he says, "is not received by all; but what causes it to be received is both the gift of God and free will" (*De gr. et lib. arb.* 4.7; see also 15.31): not that the free will adds to the grace any further actual contribution to the achievement of salvation, but that the grace supplies that entire actuality without abolishing or short-circuiting the free will. Though (as Wetzel points out) Augustine thinks of free will as inseparable, in practice, from a context of prior motives and deci-

14. Rist, 133, 274. For a modern, general statement of the "irresistible grace" interpretation of Augustine, see G. R. Evans, *Augustine on Evil* (Cambridge: Cambridge University Press, 1982), 170.

15. Wetzel, 197–206.

sions, he nevertheless regards it as completely distinct from that context.[16]

At this point the first of the genuinely serious problems arises. It is fundamental to Augustine's argument that the divine choice, though it does not dissolve the potentiality that is human free will, is not a response to a prior disposition of that will. His most incontrovertible and poignant example of this is the case of dying babies at the point of baptism, their eternal destinies in the balance. He mentions them near the end of *On Grace and Free Will*—not, however, as exceptions to the rule he has mentioned earlier (that the principle of the withholding of divine grace is divine respect for human free will), but simply as the best example of the gratuitousness of divine grace (*De gr. et lib. arb.* 22.44). The baby is, for all eternity, saved if baptized before dying; otherwise, not. But babies a few days old lack a will already virtuously engaged. Augustine argues that completed baptism is a necessary precondition for salvation and, before the age of reason, in effect a sufficient one; but he does not indicate how in the latter class of case God could be thought of as withholding grace to avoid violating a particular child's free will. Because of this silence on what amounts to a test case for his doctrine of salvation, one may reasonably ask whether he implies God's choice to be arbitrary; whether the doctrine is sacramentally legalistic (implying that the eternal destinies of individuals can be determined by mere circumstances and chance); and, more generally, why God omnipotent would not have arranged things so that all except conscious and deliberate renegades might be saved.

The first two of these questions are in their different ways concerned with the possibility that according to Augustine an individual's damnation might be sheer bad luck. First, then, has Augustine so formulated his notion of grace as to imply that there are only two logically possible principles by which one infant is chosen over anoth-

16. Ibid., passim but, e.g., 216–17.

er: prior spiritual merit (or demerit) in the human beings concerned or arbitrariness on God's part? If so, since the former not only is patently inapplicable to infants but also contradicts Augustine's general position, one would have to conclude that his doctrine of grace is a doctrine of arbitrary divine choice.[17] But his notion that God saves except in cases where to do so would short-circuit a person's free will logically extricates him from this dilemma. It means that God chooses neither arbitrarily nor in response to independent human virtue. Though it is not clear how this principle is applicable specifically to newborn infants, the Augustinian notion of grace leaves the door open to such application. Moreover, as we have seen in chapter 1, there is ample room for precisely this application in his idea of innate individuality. A disastrous result of an individuality itself good is not an arbitrary act on God's part.

Second, is it narrow sacramental legalism to hold that a happy eternity can be irrevocably closed off to an infant because someone else does not happen to have that infant baptized? (*De pecc. mer.* 1.20.28; *De nupt. et conc.* 1.20.22). Rist describes Augustine's insistence on this point as "admittedly literalist" and as lacking "a substantive thesis about the baptism of desire."[18] But a thesis on that very subject, though in a sense not sufficiently comprehensive in scope, consistently formed part of Augustine's notion of sacramental grace. By using the example of the good thief to prove to the Donatists that faith and conversion gave "the power of baptism, without the visible sacrament" (outside the traditional channel of martyrdom in the strict sense), he had already distinguished between what is always necessary (the human disposition of faith) and what is usually necessary (the formalities) (*De bapt. c. Don.* 4.22.29). Later, in dispute with the Pelagians (in *On the Soul and Its Origin,* for example), he allows the same exception and gives the same example, the good thief, thus reaffirming that the essence of baptismal grace is faith in the heart (*De*

17. See Rist, 286.
18. Ibid., 285–86.

an. et eius or. 1.9.11): the thief's saving grace was his disposition, not his actions or circumstances. Augustine's theological position, then, is as it was before. But now he explicitly bars unbaptized infants from the possibility of grace in this form. When an infant is baptized, he says, the requisite faith is that of the sponsors, not of the infant.

Both the reason and the status of this limitation, however, lessen its importance. It is a matter not of theological principle but of practical psychology. His theological point is that there is baptism of desire. He does not, however, see a way in which that could work in newborn infants. But though he takes the notion of the sponsors' surrogate faith as a sign that it could not, that is only an assumption of his, whereas his consistent and fundamental position on this subject is that the practical psychology of newborn infants, whatever assumptions one might make about it along the way, is beyond our knowledge (See *Conf.* 1.6.8–9; *De pecc. mer.* 1.17.22). Moreover (and following from the point just made), the restriction of faith in infants to sponsorial surrogacy has the status of opinion rather than dogma in Augustine's argument. The reason why that surrogate faith is needed in the case of infants is, he says, "in order to prevent them all from passing from their common origin into condemnation, which is what would happen if that mystery were not fulfilled." His dogmatic point is not that a divine intervention, unknown to us, in infants' souls is impossible (that is merely his opinion), but that baptismal grace (essentially, faith in the human heart) is necessary for salvation. His Pelagian opponent Vincentius Victor had said that infants go straight to heaven even without baptism, original sin notwithstanding. Augustine's reply is that original sin cannot be so disregarded. In other words, "the mystery of faith in an infant's case is completely provided by the sponsors" means not "that mystery must be provided by the sponsors because in the case of an infant any other supernatural channel is categorically excluded," but "that mystery must be provided by the sponsors because any natural provision of faith by the child is, given original sin, categorically excluded." Augustine doubtless thinks the former to be the case also; but it is not implied in his argument concerning the essentials of the faith.

In a sense the third question raised here on the subject of grace (Why are not all saved?) has already been implicitly answered: given that initially we are all members of the *massa damnata,* the inalienable good that is our capacity to reject God must be in such circumstances allowed, even if tragically, to come between us and salvation. In another sense the question has not yet been answered, because, in our final consummation, the ability to reject God turns out not to be inalienable after all: God, according to Augustine, finally takes away our power to sin (*CD* 22.30). In this sense that question is subsumed into the first of the final ones to be considered here.

The final set of questions arises from Augustine's conception of heaven: will the ultimate inability to sin be a partial abolition of human nature? And if some human beings will eventually be endowed with that marvelous inability, why were we not all endowed with it from the start?

The first question is forcibly expressed by Heidegger, who regarded the heavenly *non posse peccare* as an idea always present in Augustine's thought, but as an aberration of his old age when it appears in the form of a steady conviction.[19] Heidegger's thesis (his interest in this matter specifically was early in his life) is twofold: theologically, that trouble (*cura; Bekümmerung*—in this context, fear of falling away from God) is properly irremediable (even the saints in heaven must fear they may reject God again) and interpretatively, that this idea is to be found in texts from Augustine's younger and middle life alongside the incompatible one of utterly secure heavenly contemplation, before the latter idea finally prevailed in his old age.

Heidegger's principal text purportedly showing the idea of eternal "care" in Augustine is from one of the *Tractates on St. John's First Epistle.* Fear, argues Augustine, is divided into unchaste and chaste. The

19. See Kisiel, 201–6.

former does not survive one's translation into heaven; it is like that of an adulterous wife—fear of the Bridegroom's presence. Chaste fear (fear of God's absence) lasts, he says, *in saeculum saeculi*; for like a virtuous wife, the pious soul will continue to be vigilant "for fear she may again sin . . . for fear she may be deserted by Him" (*Tr. in 1 ep. Ioh.* 9.5–8). This illustrates Heidegger's point. But in Augustine this chaste fear is fear in a very nuanced sense. He calls it "fear without insecurity." It may be described as desire for the continuance of God's presence. The heavenly perfection of such chaste fear, then, will be complete and unmixed desire for that continuance. But, as Augustine says near the end of the *Tractate,* "Love is God" (his converse of St. John's statement) and "all my good is to cleave to God freely" (*Tr. in 1 ep. Ioh.* 9.10). The desire for God, therefore, is God. The desire for the continuance of God's presence, then, effects that continuance, which only failure of the desire could threaten. Given clarity of vision, therefore, the more fear, thus defined, one perceived in oneself, the more security one would perceive. Such a fear, if pure and unadulterated, would be the experience of perfect security and permanent absence of sin: the will free but committed to good in a perfectly reliable way.

In essentials this is the same *non posse peccare* as in the preview of heaven at the end of the *City of God*: not, says Augustine, the taking away of the human power of free will (despite the words *non posse*) but liberation of the will from all delight in sinning "to the point of an inalienable delight in not sinning" *(usque ad delectationem non peccandi indeclinabilem)* (*CD* 22.30). Here too, then, heaven is the indefectibly efficacious desire to be with God.

This implicitly not only counters Heidegger's interpretation; it also answers his theological criticism, for though the inability to sin is a strictly divine attribute, human nature is nevertheless incomplete until completed by it (e.g., *Conf.* 1.1; but above all *CD* 12.1). The divine gifts constitute human nature's perfection and are not mere superadditions to it.

That implicit answer leads, however, to our final problem concerning the relationship of human nature with its condition: human beings, though not ultimately intended to be peccable, were created so—created without the presence of the grace that is nevertheless needed. "Why," says Rist, "did God create what seems to be a less than perfect Adam?"[20] The problem, as Augustine's conception of heaven shows, is not free will (logical peccability), which the saints in heaven have, but the fact that in this world, even in the Garden, the utterly sufficient heavenly grace is absent (practical peccability). Augustine's answer, argues Rist, is that God's redemptive Incarnation was providentially planned and that this divine plan required the original ability to sin. Rist regards this as, by itself, an unsatisfactory answer because it merely transfers the problem a stage back: it does not explain why our redemption from sin is a more satisfactory proceeding than our being endowed with the fulness of divine grace from the start would have been.

In his doctrine of grace itself Augustine goes no further toward solving this problem. And in a passage from the *City of God* he shows the inadequacy of a straightforwardly metaphysical approach to sin, taking the hypothetical case of two identical men seeing the same attractive woman. One lusts, the other does not (*CD* 12.6–7). Given their perfect similarity, the fact that one sins shows that sin was possible in both cases, but the same perfect similarity logically blocks any search for an efficient cause of the one's failure. The reason why sin was possible for both men was that in the final analysis both were created out of nothing. But this indicates merely that one necessary condition for sin in human beings is the general fact of creatureliness. It does not indicate that there is in them any specifically human necessary condition for it.

Two parts of the *Literal Commentary on Genesis*, however, taken together amount to a detailed exploration of sin in its specifically hu-

---

20. Rist, 278–86.

man origin. Augustine's general observation on the subject, in book 8, is that the prohibition on eating the fruit of the tree of knowledge was peculiarly suited to human beings because the reason for that prohibition was unclear (the fruit itself being wholesome). The specifically human morality implied is that of an obedience neither based on angelic knowledge nor blind (it being nevertheless clear that obedience to God, because it is to God, is appropriate) (GL 8.12.27–8.14.31). Obedience that is a rational act of faith, then, is the original human duty to God. To inquire further into the cause of the prohibition is pointless, Augustine says, for "in itself this is a great boon for a human being" *(haec ipsa magna est utilitas homini)*. He does not explain here to what aspect of human nature this morality is suitable.

Three books later, however, he analyses the temptation of Adam and Eve and treats directly as a problem the natural human difficulty in obeying God's command (GL 11.4.6–11.11.15). There is, he argues, a moral power unique and universal to human beings: that of withholding consent to evil persuasion. This logically entails susceptibility to temptation: such a clash of wills makes possible a uniquely human demonstration of God's power and grace. This essentially aesthetic explanation implies a heroic conception of human morality. Augustine's additional explanation, that Adam needed the sin and its effects in order to be humiliated, to be cured of a pride he had already conceived, transfers the problem to an earlier event, albeit a mental one (GL 11.5.7). The underlying cause of this mental fall is that our relationship with God entails our natural (not merely conditional) need to stumble and to be picked up by God. Human nature, then, had the original need not only to be susceptible to temptation, but to have succumbed to it. Both reasons are more readily adapted to explaining our fallen condition, given sin, than to explaining the genesis of sin in our originally good nature. Indeed, Augustine applies them to our fallen condition (for we, he points out, who are even more vulnerable to temptation than Adam and Eve were, have that same specifically human chance for moral heroism, and in counterbalance, as it were, the divinely granted benefit of becoming aware of our dependence on God through our enfeeblement by sin). But he has already established his reportation of these ideas into the less familiar context of our original state of nature.

In that context the first explanation is the assertion of a fundamental insight: that the opportunity (closed to an angel) of a successful struggle against evil is a good in itself, the specifically human moral good. The second (that we naturally need moral failure, not merely the possibility of such failure) demands a further explanation. The one he eventually gives is the closest he ever comes to a rational solution to the problem of evil (GL 11.10.13–11.11.15). The purpose of the damnation of some, he argues, is *pour encourager les autres*. Human nature is so created that people need to be chastened with the spectacle of others' punishment (specifically, eternal perdition: the *poena debita* of iniquity). Without that stage of mortal fear, human beings would be wise in their own conceit. In the case of human beings the spectacle of a definitive, irrevocable fact is needed. The mere threat of that disaster would have been inadequate (indeed, was so). Though this is close to implying that human beings were created prideful, it does not quite do that. Rather, it implies that we were created such that the humility that accords with our nature must be learned through our having lapsed into the lack of it, and in a fashion finally disastrous for some. In that way, the fall into pride, though unnatural, was providentially taken account of in the design of our nature. (This idea is the very contrary of that, incorrectly imputed to Augustine by J. Hick, of sin as a sheer catastrophe disrupting the divine plan for human beings.)[21] Man, says Augustine, is "the kind of good creature that guards against evil [*cavet malum*] by the comparison of evils" (GL 11.10.13).[22]

Augustine succeeds in resolving the apparent internal contradiction in this account, though not in mitigating its harshness. He im-

---

21. Hick, 214.

22. Or, with the reading *caret malo*, "lacks evil by the comparison of evils."

plies not that it is intrinsically natural for human beings to behave unnaturally but only that it is incidentally so: sin results not from human nature *simpliciter*, but from the experiences unavoidably entailed in having that nature. Hence he says in one chapter that the human creature "has it in its power to master illicit pleasure" (that is, in principle) and, in the following chapter, that even in the Garden that power could not (in practice) be successfully exercised (*GL* 11.7.9– 11.8.10). This means that for human beings sin was inevitable not absolutely but practically (divine providence having both arranged and taken account of this fact without, of course, positively predestinating any individual to damnation). Unlike angels, human beings are by nature the rational creatures that require discipline; part of our nature is brought into existence only through moral action in this world; its full actuation is therefore delayed till the end of this period of discipline; God might have created beings without that need (beings having the practical capacity, for instance, to respond favorably to the mere threat of eternal perdition: able, therefore, to have an adequate instantaneous, intellectual realization of sin's consequences), but in that case He would merely have created more angels. Without the existence of this comparatively stolid nature the variety of creation would, says Augustine, have been incomplete.

This idea, which is redolent of the *Timaeus,* is Augustine's implied answer to the question: "Why did God create what seems to be a less than perfect Adam?" The imperfection of created humanity in its initial state, as Augustine conceives of it, does not in itself constitute a disorder, but rather means that our entry into conscious experience initiates, rather than completes, the spiritual fashioning of a human being. That, in Augustine's view, is the moral difference in nature between us and the angels. We require a factual perception, not merely a conceptual awareness, of the eternal separation from God that sin has brought about. It remains the case, however, that this discipline entails not only an epic struggle and the chance for glory, but also the contemplation of an eternal tragedy.

This characterization of human morality does not reopen Augustine's notion of heaven to Heidegger's criticism that a heavenly inability to sin is inhuman. Heidegger's assumption is that from the moment of their creation human beings have had the full exercise of their nature. Augustine's position is that they have not, though some eventually will, but that in the case of these the additional gift of the divine inability to sin will not make them cease to be human, for it will not cancel the subangelic character of their relationship with God. In his speculative description of heaven at the end of the *City of God* Augustine includes abolition of all the temporarily requisite spiritual ineptitude of human beings, but not of the nature that had fostered it. We shall become sharers in God's peace "in accordance with our own mode" *(pro modo nostro)*, as the angels are sharers in the same peace according to theirs; and our peace with God and among ourselves will be the highest—"the highest human peace, that is" *(quantum nostrum summum est)* (CD 22.29); for in the human case the vision of that peace will still be "through the body," though how, says Augustine, is partly a matter for speculation. As it is in human nature to be temporarily subject to privation (though the privation itself is not in the nature), so it is a capacity of human nature to receive immunity from this possibility of such privation. Indeed, that is essential to human nature's purpose.

Hence, although Augustine distinguishes between the consequences of our nature and those of our condition, his attempts to solve the resultant problems lead him to find a principle of continuity between the two. This principle is in effect a refinement of his notion of concupiscence. In his view, as a result of our nature we have in us, in relation to God, some stolidity of mind, ranging from a certain prelapsarian moral rawness to permanent insusceptibility to divine influence. In catering for the complexities of human experience he distinguishes stages, both of degeneration and of regeneration, in the operation of this stolidity. The finest of these distinctions is between the human condition before the Fall and that after baptism but before any complication by renewed actual sin; for both are forms of insecurity from sin and neither is itself sin. The distinction is between latent moral vulnerability (which is not disorder) and active moral vulnerability (concupiscence, in the usual sense, which is disorder—an unnatural aggravation of the stolidity immediately resulting from human nature). But, as we have seen, in a different mode the concept of concupiscence is also applied at the bottommost region of human experience: the Fall is, in Augustine's view, a decisively more massive aggravation of that same, normal, ultimately dissoluble moral obstacle, causing it to become a fatal moral impediment. Here Augustine has conceptually extended the notion of concupiscence in the opposite (downward) direction, into being the principle of original sin, original guilt, actual sin, death (in the ordinary sense), and permanent inclusion in the *massa damnata*. (Because he refuses to specify evil, however, he does not isolate any principle by which normal human moral difficulty changes to abnormal moral depravity and helplessness.)

This elaborate, though economical, extension of the idea of concupiscence, and especially its implication that all human disorder originates in our initially proper, subangelic hebetude, is, up to a point, Neoplatonic in character. It has in common with Neoplatonism the idea that because our souls have a physical dimension they are spiritually inept compared with a higher, essentially nonphysical and in that sense purer, reflection of the divine reason, to which reflection they are, nevertheless, metaphysically related. Like Plotinus, Augustine both distinguishes between an orderly and a disorderly condition of the soul's relationship with the physical world, and maintains that nevertheless the physical world, even when the soul's relationship with it is orderly, causes a kind of prefiguration of disorder in the soul.[23] The peculiarly Augustinian development of this idea is the notion that disorderly concupiscence is the sine qua non of the

23. Plotinus, *Ennead* 6.4.14–16, 1.1.8.

divine pedagogy precisely because it has among its causes a specifically human weakness.

Thus Augustine provides a highly speculative, partial solution to the problems inherent in his notion of grace. That solution amounts to a considerable development of his notion of human nature.

We must return in the next chapter to the subject of personality—a characteristic common to the human and divine natures. But here, by way of preparation, we may ask: In the idea of salvation just described, what about the individuals whose damnation provides the spectacle by which the favored remnant are chastened? Augustine's solution has implied that God foreknew some individuals not to be susceptible to divine grace. As we have seen, taken in its theological context this implies neither divine purposing of their damnation nor arbitrariness in the choice of those to be saved. It does, however, leave a dilemma on the subject of divine love: unless further qualified, it means either that God's love is unintelligibly limited, which Rist takes to be Augustine's ultimate position, or that God's love is eternally frustrated, futile even while being infinite, in respect of those who are lost.[24] This matter must be considered in the discussion of charity; for Augustine's attempts to confront the problem in terms of justice and fairness constantly halt before the stark incommensurability of the human with the divine. *O altitudo,* he keeps quoting in such contexts (Rom 11.33; *C. duas ep. Pel.* 4.6.16; *De corr. et gr.* 8.17, 8.18; *De gr. et lib. arb.* 22.44; *De pecc. mer.* 1.21.30; *De sp. et litt.* 34.60).[25] In charity, however, as we shall see, he regards human morality and divine goodness as not merely akin to each other, but in the final analysis identical. In that context, therefore, the theological problem posed by the damned becomes more pressing.

24. For the former of these alternatives, see Rist, 288; for the latter (though not attributed to Augustine), see Albert Camus, *La chute* (Paris: Gallimard, 1956), 78.

25. Cf. Rist, 277.

CHAPTER 4

HUMANITAS

In *Sources of the Self* Charles Taylor reclaims an Augustinian conception of the structure of morality.[1] Both the similarities and the differences between Augustine and Taylor on this matter provide a useful approach to the problems of Augustine's ethics. Taylor proposes a hierarchy of three kinds of good: first, standards of propriety that differ from one culture to another (the privileges of a warrior, for example; the duties of a wife or a son); then the norms (courage; the wrongness of murder) with which people everywhere, ordinarily, successfully make some moral sense of experience—Taylor eventually calls these "life goods"; and finally norms of the highest order: the principles with reference to which, and as a result of which, all other goods are good. Taylor calls these "hypergoods," and in other contexts "constitutive goods" (divine wisdom, for example, or the principle that every being should reach its full potential).

In its general conceptual structure this resembles Augustine's account of morality in book 1 of the treatise *On Free Will* (*De lib. arb.* 1.5.11–1.7.16). First, Augustine argues that there are cultural variations in human morality, which he here describes in exclusively political terms. The choice between democracy and monarchy is not a matter of straight principle but of prudence. Democracy, for example, is a just form of government provided that people in large numbers are not in the habit of selling their votes. Second, this argument nevertheless implies an immovable basis: that selling one's vote is invari-

1. Taylor, 53–93.

ably wrong. In Augustine's example this is the controlling norm; the wrongness will therefore not change to rightness in other circumstances. (It should be noted that he has said—or rather Evodius in the dialogue has said, and Augustine does not contest—that a good law can be enacted by a bad man. This distinguishes between the intention and the externals of an act; the law concerned can still be good, but its enacting would have been a fully good act only if the intention had been good.) Thus, in this early text at least, Augustine balances natural law—practical rules as built into nature—with what is sometimes called "natural right"—principles of virtue as built into nature and not tied to any specific practical rules.[2] He does not choose one at the expense of the other: actions in one class are sometimes right and sometimes wrong; actions in the other are always right or always wrong. Third, such ineradicable practical norms, and the whole human moral life, depend, says Augustine, on supreme reason: the principle determining the rightness of action, the eternal source of moral awareness. By this one knows, beyond argument, what is good and beautiful and what is not (*De lib. arb.* 1.6.15). This is essentially what Taylor calls a "constitutive good." Augustine does not detail its content here, but, as Taylor himself points out, Augustine's moral theology as a whole asserts that there is one ultimate, constitutive human good, and this is (un-Platonically) God—divine charity.[3]

It is on the question of the ultimate singleness of the constitutive good that Taylor and Augustine part company. Taylor agrees that a constitutive good is real, not merely an invention of the mind, but his position is that there are more than one and that they are inconsistent with one another—indeed, often necessarily in conflict, though each indestructible.[4] (He typically thinks of religious principles, as opposed to deep-seated desires for natural self-fulfilment.) Augustine's

---

2. For the suggestion that in Aristotle, for example, there is such a disjunction ("right," but not "law") see, e.g., Leo Strauss, *Natural Right and History* (Chicago: Chicago University Press, 1953), 162–63.

3. Taylor, 93.   4. Ibid., 518–21.

position is that in the divine agape even the most deeply conflicting human loves are consummated and subsumed.[5] As we have noticed, he sees concupiscence, when fully actuated, as the essence of sin and death precisely because it is disorder at the basis of the soul's attitude—distorted love (e.g., *De gr. et lib. arb.* 16.32; *Conf.* 13.7.8).[6] Human motivations are all approximations (though some of them immensely remote) to the summative divine motivation. Hence, the master principle of Augustine's moral theology is his notion of charity, which may be provisionally defined as an ordered love whose motivation, whether working as a final or an efficient cause, is divine.

It has on occasion been denied that this ultimately single conception of morality is even his professed position: first on the general grounds that, in parts of the *City of God* at least, morality is centered not on the exercise of any virtue but on the fulfilment of obligations.[7] Yet the passages on which this view is based really indicate otherwise: it is true that Augustine gives much attention to Lucretia's fanatical discharge of her marital obligations; but he does not so much admire the act as suspect disorder in the moral disposition with which it was done (*CD* 1.19–20). And it is true that he praises Regulus—not, however, for keeping the oath sworn to the gods, but for the heroism *(virtus)* by which he rose above his misfortune (*CD* 1.15). So, even if certain kinds of action are typically virtuous, the virtue concerned is the crucial matter. Second, it has been argued that on the level of moral disposition itself Augustine holds both love of God and knowledge of good to be necessary and equally important, and that the two form a "double matrix" for his ethics (each real, each distinct from the other).[8] The notion of separation of faculties thus

5. Most obvious among the immense number of texts showing this are the entirety of the *Confessions* (most proverbially 1.1.1 and 13.9.10) and *Tr. in 1 ep. Ioh.* 7.8.

6. Cf. Dideberg, 370.

7. F. S. Carney, "The Structure of Augustine's Ethic," in *The Ethics of St. Augustine,* ed. W. S. Babcock (Atlanta: Scholars Press, 1991), 24–25.

8. Ibid., 11–37.

reemerges here. It is true that, most memorably in the first page or two of the *Confessions*, Augustine saw any human relationship with God as requiring at least some knowledge of God. The question, however, is what he thought the ultimate relationship between the knowledge and the relationship to be. In the seventh *Tractate on St. John's First Epistle* he addresses this matter directly. We know the Spirit of truth, he says, by exercising divine charity toward each other. Charity (which, he says, is God) is exercised by the human soul and can be known by a human being in that way only (*Tr. in 1 ep. Ioh.* 7.4). But that, he says, is what loving God amounts to (*Tr. in 1 ep. Ioh.* 7.9). Where this supreme Reality is concerned, therefore, our cognition is an act of loving. And in an earlier tractate he has said that one knows—or does not know—other people by the charity one has—or does not have—in one's heart. The deepest knowledge, then, is charity (*Tr. in 1 ep. Ioh.* 4.4).

Thus the radical unity that, as we have noticed, Augustine attributed to human mental acts reemerges in the context of ethics. It remains the case, however, that in this context by far his preferred way of describing the comprehensively formative human moral good is in volitional terms—as one divine love. Similarly, in another of the tractates he treats faith not as another virtue, alongside charity, but as being charity (taking the form of "desire to embrace" God) (*Tr. in 1 ep. Ioh.* 10.1). And in the *City of God* he argues at length that the greatest Roman "moral characteristics"—temperance, faithfulness, unselfishness—were morally hollow insofar as they had love of this world, not love of God, as their ultimate motive. Again, therefore, these are not other virtues, additional to love; and insofar as they are genuine virtues they are, at their core, charity.

Yet, as we shall see, the unity and integrity of his notion of love have been continually challenged by modern critics who have found it heterogeneous in character and in some cases have claimed to find major discrepancies or omissions in it. Arguably, then, the view that a single basis of love cannot adequately account for the whole range of authentic human motivation, which is Taylor's conclusion, also caused Augustine more difficulty in his ethics than he acknowledged. As a result, much of the discussion about Augustinian charity is concerned with the problems of its unity. Three questions have been especially controversial: Does Augustine regard charity as the only proper form of human love, or does he allow that there are other forms of love, also good in their different ways? What, according to him, is the nature of charity? And how can that virtue as he conceives it be exercised among the divine Persons, by God toward human beings, by human beings toward God, by human beings toward one another in this world, by the saints toward one another in heaven, and by oneself toward oneself, without some difference in its nature in each case, given the great differences in those relationships?

In the *Confessions*, when Augustine describes his first immeasurably intense emotional experience of evil, he describes it as an experience of love—this, he has later realized, is what his prostration with grief at a friend's death was. He also points out that there was something disordered, even idolatrous, about the mental attitude that led to that grief. Yet ultimately the event revealed more to him than his own inward distortion of mind: it made him realize that human experience was positively more profound than he had suspected. Its mystery is its love; the human heart is an immense deep: God alone fathoms its emotions and movements (*Conf.* 4.4.9–4.14.22).

But though human love as he describes it there is especially enigmatic in its depth, it is also puzzling in its apparent multiplicity. One can, of course, love a close friend; but quite outside friendship one can, he says, love people for their outstanding abilities. Again, one might even have merely heard of some person's brilliance, and in a way base a love on that. Such admiring loves, he says, often make one want to resemble the beloved, but not always—not in the case of a superb practitioner of some demeaning art such as chariot racing. Still, he allows that, in a fashion, one can be ardently loyal to such a person. Then again, there is the "frying pan" of voluptuous loves (themselves a multiplicity) in which he seethed as a youth in Carthage (*Conf.* 3.1.1). What, then, is the relationship of the different manifestations of human love with one another, and, in particular, of charity with the others?

Though he is acutely conscious of love's seeming multiplicity, Augustine, both late and early, asserts that love is one and is charity. In book 14 of the *City of God* he defines charity as love that is divine rather than worldly and then points out that love is good only if it is charity in this sense—only if it constitutes obedience to the two great Commands. When the word *amor* is used for this specifically theological virtue it is, quite simply, used in its good sense. In its bad sense the same word denotes "selfishness; love of money" (*CD* 14.7; see 2 Tm 3.2). Essentially the same division, he argues, applies to the word *dilectio.* Love, therefore, is in a sense divided, but its division is only into charity and that which wrongfully falls short of charity—charity and the (partial) privation of that virtue. He considerably elaborates this notion elsewhere. In the *Elucidations on the Psalms* he says: "it is charity that allows one to pray for one's enemies; does it, then, desert a friend, given that it wishes well to an enemy?" (*En. in Ps.* 31[2].5). Friendship, then, is not its own kind of love, distinct from charity: if benevolence to enemies can only be charity, benevolence to friends also is, a fortiori. Moreover, love of any kind, he says, is bound to be active. Even when it is idle it is active in a sense—in adulteries or violence. But where it is properly, rather than residually, active it acts as *caritas*: it "provides what it can" for others (cf. *Tr. in 1 ep. Ioh.* 2.14). This leaves no room for a positive love outside charity. And much earlier, in *Contra Faustum,* he had pointed out that to propound the existence of any positive love outside charity is an essentially Manichaean idea: when the Manichaeans said that the race of darkness was attracted to the Light and wanted to invade it, they were describing a love positive in itself; and to say that the spirit of light responded to that attraction with hatred is, Augustine argues, to imply that the offending love has an independent existence (*C. Faust.* 19.24). In reality, according to Augustine, loves that are not charity are dying fragments of what would have been charity if they had not been fragmented (*Conf.* 1.20.31).

It is at this point, however, that the most serious problems of unity begin. Both Catholic and Protestant commentators have maintained that he failed to resolve the great problem of the unity and integrity of human love.

The Catholic versions of this view are for the most part not directly pointed at Augustine, but brush him aside on certain points. Long ago P. Rousselot asserted that until Thomas Aquinas's great synthesis there had always been two conflicting notions of love in Christian thought: the "physical," which he also called the "unitive," in which natural self-interest and the desire for happiness are the central motives; and the "ecstatic," oblivious to self-interest, mystical, and uncompromisingly orientated to the transcendent. According to Rousselot (followed in this by M. C. D'Arcy), St. Thomas was the first to resolve the conflict between these two notions, and did so by pointing out that the part naturally seeks the good of the whole, and since God is the Good of all humanity, human beings naturally direct their love beyond themselves to that Good; furthermore, says Rousselot, because human beings are, most importantly, in God's image, the only way to foster that image is by seeking, beyond ourselves, the Reality of which we are the image: by the antithesis, then, of self-seeking.[9]

Though this argument simply dismisses Augustine in passing, it is worth pursuing somewhat further, as touching on distinctions that will be crucial here. St. Thomas indeed provides the solution referred to by Rousselot and D'Arcy: the individual, being part of the universe, has a natural affinity with the good of that whole. As the hand will naturally defend the head, and a good citizen will naturally face

9. P. Rousselot, *Pour l'histoire du problème de l'amour au moyen age* (Paris: Vrin, 1933), 8–11. Cf. D'Arcy, 89.

danger for the public safety, so every rational creature naturally loves God, the ultimate Good, both of the whole and of its parts, more than it loves itself.[10] This means not that it is natural to love God at one's own expense *simpliciter,* but that one loves oneself more truly by not distinguishing between loving God and loving oneself. (Without the head the hand would soon cease to be a hand, and one needs to preserve a public context if one is to continue being a citizen.) This solution is not, however, an innovation of Thomas's. It is already in St. John's Gospel, in a sacramental rather than philosophical mode: only by attachment to the Vine (an attachment by love, as R. E. Brown notes) do the human branches live and bear fruit. Yet they cannot do so out of self-interest in the restricted sense. Rather, the true actuation of the Vine's human branches is in their transcending of mere self-concern: severed from the Vine they wither and are burned and thrown away.[11]

Thomas's notion of charity of course goes further than that. If it did not, it would miss out much of what is familiar, known from general human experience to be good and essential to love: above all, friendship in its various modes, a direct affinity for another as a person, not in essence a desirous love at all (though desires may attach to it). That the relationship between human beings and God is, in its higher reaches, the perfection of friendship in this sense has of course been Christian doctrine from earliest times; for again, the love between the Vine and the branches in St. John is that kind of love also; and, as D'Arcy points out, this too has a place in Thomas's account of Christian love.[12]

D'Arcy's own position is that a bifurcation of love into the self-seeking and the self-transcending is to some extent inevitable, even appropriate, for human beings in this world, but he argues (as does

10. Thomas Aquinas, *Quodlibet* 1, Art. 8.

11. Jn 15.1–17; Raymond E. Brown, S.S., *The Gospel according to John (xiii–xxi)* (Garden City, N.Y.: Doubleday, 1970), 672.

12. Jn 15.12–15; D'Arcy, 115.

Burnaby) that nevertheless some mystics, such as St. Bernard, have approached a solution not really catered for by Augustine or even Thomas: a love for God treated as its own reward and thus purified of self-interest (if only inchoately in this world).[13] D'Arcy does not, however, make clear what, in his own metaphysical terms, the nature of this purification is—whether, that is, in saying "cupidity and Agape spring from the same stem" he means that the craving of a good for oneself is a valid but as yet impure part of agape (without which agape would be incomplete and which is destined to be corrected in heaven) or that it is a simple distortion of agape and destined, therefore, to disappear completely in heaven. (O. O'Donovan has cast some doubt on the second of these ideas by arguing that there is a certain absurdity in the notion of a love so "purified" that "Heaven is full of people not particularly concerned with being there."[14] Yet one could presumably have a transcendent, not self-centered, reason for wanting to be there.)

On this point, then, a number of Augustine's critics—broadly speaking, the Catholic ones—have tacitly assumed his thought to be, by the best medieval standards at least, undeveloped in its conception of charity.

His critics in the Protestant tradition have been more directly critical of him on the same point. Most famously A. Nygren, relying partly on K. Holl, argued that Augustine's notion of Christian love was internally inconsistent, as having two antithetical motives: an entirely human desire for God, Platonically erotic in character, and an exclusively Christian agape, divine in origin, lacking any cause in the human heart or any connection with human goodness. According to Nygren, Augustine did not acknowledge this division in his own thought, and Luther finally drew attention to it. This criticism (together with Burnaby's famous reply to it) has largely dominated the

13. D'Arcy, 95; Burnaby, 258–63.

14. Oliver O'Donovan, *The Problem of Self-Love in St. Augustine* (New Haven, Conn.: Yale University Press, 1980), 155.

twentieth-century debate on this subject. It has the obvious fault of imposing its own restrictedly doctrinaire notion of Christian charity on the discussion. Burnaby, having made this observation, counters by propounding, with a wealth of material from the Catholic tradition (the Platonic tradition included), the notion that charity is the reciprocal fellowship of persons arising from an ultimately spontaneous mutual response to what is good in the beloved.[15] He applies this to the central problem raised by Nygren—the notion that love defined as desire is essentially noncharitable—pointing out that desire is not essential to charity conceived according to his proposed Catholic definition, but merely universally attaches to our experience of that virtue in this world; such desire is "consummated in delight," though not, at least not fully, in this world. Most crucially, he attributes the essence of this doctrine to Augustine, citing the end of the *City of God,* book 14: "But in the latter City [the heavenly—specifically its members who are still in this world] there is no human wisdom except the devotion by which the true God is worshipped rightly, and which awaits the reward: 'that God be all in all' in the fellowship of the saints, human and angelic" (*CD* 14.28). And in this "analogy of love" what is now an imperfect, desirous, human participation in the divine delight will ultimately, according to Burnaby, be a perfect participation in it.

This, however, does not comprehensively answer Nygren. Where fellowship is so important, grief, as Augustine was aware, is in some cases inevitable, and where the bond of fellowship is deep, so will the grief be deep. And such grief, where it is pious, is caused—and intensified—by more than worldly considerations. The death of a friend naturally hurts us; news of a friend's willing moral or spiritual collapse hurts us much more deeply (*CD* 19.8). In this world, at least, such solicitude is a form of desire. And Burnaby himself points out

15. See Dideberg, 378–79; Nygren, 638–41; Karl Holl, "Augustins Innere Entwicklung," in *Gesammelte Aufsätze zur Kirchengeschichte* (Tübingen, 1928), 3:54–116. For the inadequate breadth of Nygren's argument, see Burnaby, 92–93.

how suspect is the notion of a love professedly indifferent to the beloved's response. But in the case of a beloved's final unrepentance, the heavenly culmination of charity, as he defines it, would have to entail precisely such indifference. Yet even if the beloved's goodness has been abandoned by the beloved, in a sense extinguished, it still has existed. And the beloved person still exists; so, in some degree, therefore, does that person's goodness. What, then, of the fellowship? And the same problem arises regarding the divine charity itself. Can the love consisting in fellowship toward that human being still be said to exist?

Thus, Burnaby's answer to Nygren, despite its richness, still leaves the impression that there is deep division in this area of Augustine's thought.[16] And Arendt, for example, argues that Augustine's *caritas* is a composite of three complementary but distinct notions: the first eudaemonistic and Platonic—love of God as desire for a future in heaven, the other two Christian in origin—love of God in the form of affinity for the absolute source of one's being and love of God as providing an entirely new principle of human society (that of redemption), which replaces our initial, now vitiated, society-in-Adam, but still leaves us with a common awareness of sin.[17] This complex of ideas raises questions about the inner nature of charity, which will be discussed later. Here it should be pointed out first that although, in Arendt's view, Augustine succeeds in combining these three loves into one system labelled (with reasonable appropriateness) *caritas,* he does so only by articular combination, not by integration: they are joined to one another but not traced to a single common principle; second, that all three are described by Arendt as loves for God directly, leaving love for neighbor as an indirect love; and third, that this account of Augustinian charity lacks the notion that the love between human beings and God is a friendship, or fellowship of persons.

A perceptive analysis of the rather various views we have now sur-

16. Compare Burnaby, 248 with 317.
17. Arendt, 22, 30–31, 111.

veyed is provided by O'Donovan: he concludes his study of Augustine's notion of love with the observation that Augustine and his critics (in particular the Protestant ones) diverge because of Augustine's acknowledgment that there are two modes in which God initiates love in human beings: love as divinely initiated polarly (our creation by divine charity at one pole, the pouring of divine charity into our undeserving hearts at the other), and love as divinely initiated immanently so as to bring about and to fulfil in us an appetite for God through our natural desire for happiness.[18] Such critics, says O'Donovan, applaud the polar but deplore the immanent. Yet really these two modes of love, he says, are on a continuum with each other, because a love that works partly through our eudaemonistic instincts, partly not, can still be regarded as one love rather than two, when it is understood as a divine action.

It remains unclear, however, whether when exercised on the human level such a divinely initiated love is seen by Augustine as taking the form of one love or of two; for one divine love might still have to take the form of two different human ones, with consequent problems of integration.

Among Augustine's Catholic critics, then, there is a general view that, in part by omitting some of the higher manifestations of charity, he failed to integrate the various forms of love with each other, where some of the greatest later theologians succeeded. The view of Nygren (which in essentials has had a greater persistence) and, to a limited extent, of Arendt is that Augustine should not even have tried to integrate them, for in reality human desire is different in nature from divine charity. And O'Donovan's observations, though having a bearing on these problems, still in a sense leave them standing. The crucial assumption common to both strains of criticism is that there is an unresolved opposition in Augustine's thought between divine love and the human desire for self-fulfilment.

18. O'Donovan, 157–59.

Our first question, then, is whether that assumption is correct. When, for example, Augustine says in book 14 of *De Trinitate* that those who love themselves but not God (or rather attempt to make that absurd activity love) really only harm themselves, this implies that God is ultimately the only source of human self-fulfilment (*De Trin.* 14.14.18).[19] Does it also imply, as, for example, Arendt argues, that to love God according to this principle is to love God out of self-interest, and that such a love is a kind of eros, quite different from, say, any disinterested love of God? This text, at least, does not justify that inference. Augustine explains that loving oneself in an unperverted way consists in loving God, because a human being is God's image not only by initial constitution but also by one's participation in the divine as one develops. This is in substance the partial solution noted earlier (eventually put systematically by Thomas Aquinas but, as we saw, already an early Christian idea) to the problem of self-interested love: God is the Reality of which a human being is the dependent, living image. There is no difference between fostering intimacy with that Reality and fostering the (ultimately external) self-fulfilment of the image that we are and that is so dependent. Hence, despite the distinction in nature between the Reality and its image, morally the human participates in the divine. Such a love can, of course, appropriately be called charity. This, in principle at least, removes the barrier between self-interested desire for God and gratuitous allegiance to God.

Similarly the context, before and after, is crucial in the following text from the *City of God* (also cited by Arendt):"That Being, however, who is happy not from another goodness but from that goodness that he himself is, cannot be unhappy, precisely because he cannot lose himself" (*CD* 12.1); for Augustine has just contrasted those who abide in the love (the *caritas*) of the Good common to all with those who, "delighting rather in their own power," have "flowed away" in differ-

19. Arendt, 30–31.

ent directions, seeking their private goods *(propria bona)*. This is a contrast both between religious and worldly motives and between private and public ones. The individuals in the latter group of people make self-fulfilment, delimited as such, their purpose in life. To condemn this motive, as Augustine does, is the very contrary of recommending trying to use God as an instrument to attain one's own benefit. Furthermore, later in the chapter, although he asserts that God alone can make a rational creature, such as a human being, happy, his argument runs quite counter to eudaemonistic pragmatism. We experience misery, he argues, in suffering the harm of self-withdrawal from our divine Good, for in human beings misery and harm, as also happiness and benefit, are convertible terms. This does not apply to lower beings. Only a very noble kind of being can suffer harm in this way. It is wrong that a being so noble should be so harmed. Therefore it is wrong for such a being to withdraw from God. Not "morality is for the sake of self-fulfilment," then, but "self-fulfilment is for the sake of morality"—for the sake of doing what befits so great a creature.

These passages both indicate and justify Augustine's view that all love that is good is love of God and must for that reason be classified as charity. Moreover, they imply that our attraction to the good that is human self-fulfilment and our attraction to the Good of which we are the image and dependents are not merely two different human loves with the same, divinely intended result, but are the same human motive.

What of that great remover of the barrier between self-interested and disinterested love, the Joannine doctrine that the love between human beings and God is, at its highest level, friendship—a personal bond created by a sense of fellowship and, again, not a craving? On this point Burnaby's account of Augustine's mature position is correct. Toward the end of the *City of God* Augustine specifies a divinely salutary love between human beings, a friendship rather than a search for happiness, motivated by compassion and extending beyond this world (*CD* 21.27). And in the *Confessions* he had mentioned a love that "is of friendship's very life-blood," that alone is so intensely a matter of personal fellowship as to make one willing to endure the evil of suffering in order for there to be the fellow suffering that is compassion. Yet this, he says, exists in its perfection only in God, to whom "suffering does no harm" (*Conf.* 3.2.3) The fact of divine consummation of this love shows it, too, to be a form of charity. Moreover, it is already clear from this that Augustine has a notion of charity that is direct love of neighbor for that neighbor's own sake.

The answer to our first question, then, is first that Augustine regards any good love as charity (love for God or from God), and second that the crucial forms of love that a number of modern critics attribute to other theologians and deny to him are in fact prominent in his notion of charity.

This, however, does not solve the fundamental problem of the unity of love, but transfers it to a different sphere. Our second main question, then, concerns the nature and, by implication, the unity of charity itself. Given that Augustinian charity is comprehensive, is it really one?

Here love for neighbor becomes a central issue: how is the second great Command the same charity as the first? Does Augustine successfully integrate the two? This has been a vexed question for decades and has not been resolved.[20] It is Arendt's starting point; her entire book is an attempt to determine Augustine's solution to this problem. She broaches some of the main issues raised here and clearly divides them into aspects, which she studies separately. Her discussion is therefore a rich (though idiosyncratic) exposition of the subject, and her exposition provides a serviceable framework for this part of our discussion.

20. For a detailed account of the history of this question, see Raymond Canning, *The Unity of Love for God and Neighbour in St. Augustine* (Heverlee-Leuven: Augustinian Historical Institute, 1993), 69–106.

The first form of charity she attributes to Augustine is desire to attain the "absolute future" that is heaven: a kind of religious or philosophical ardor not Christian in origin and precluding direct love of neighbor. Charity as defined in this way, she says, regards everything but heaven as valueless in itself.[21] As Arendt is aware, the idea that desire for God, as opposed to desire directed at any creature, has absolute primacy is an instance of Augustine's complete division of reality into the enjoyable and the usable: ultimately only God is to be enjoyed (adhered to for His own sake); one's desires concerning all other beings are to be subordinated to the purpose of achieving that fruition. Strictly, therefore, only God should be loved, in the sense of being desired for His own sake. Between God and beings merely to be used for the purpose of achieving intimacy with God there is admittedly a third class of beings (people, for example) that are properly to be both used for that purpose and also loved. But according to Arendt Augustine thinks that one loves these beings too for the same ultimate purpose: achieving intimacy with God. In her view, therefore, this division in human motives precludes loving people for their own sake.

The question of the rightness or wrongness of this reading hinges on the sense in which, according to Augustine, charity consists exclusively in desire for God. In the thirty-fifth of the *Eighty-Three Diverse Questions* Augustine, as Arendt notes, describes love as a desire: "to love is nothing other than to desire some being for its own sake": *nihil aliud est amare quam propter se ipsam rem aliquam appetere* (*De div. qu. 83*. 35.1). Here *propter* must mean "for the sake of" in the sense "with the purpose of possessing," and *se ipsam* implies "without ulterior motive." This description, which Augustine gives as if it were a definition, assumes that one can also desire some things for the sake of other things, but does not compare those two desires directly. It is the basis of the famous distinction (in *De Doctrina Christiana,* of a few years later) between love as use and love as enjoyment (*DC* 1.22.20–

21. Arendt, 39–44.

21). Use is desiring something (or otherwise exercising some affinity for it) out of the desire to possess something else; enjoyment is the satisfaction of the latter desire. It is already clear that, strictly speaking at least, love is not defined here as a desire, but that on occasion it takes that form. And neither use nor enjoyment is the same as love as described in the *Eighty-Three Diverse Questions* (desiring something for its own sake), for they are both logically secondary to it, being respectively its means and its fulfilment. This implies that the division of love into use and enjoyment is (unlike the division of reality into the usable and the enjoyable) not a complete one.

The crisis in Augustine's argument here is his consideration of what, within this ordering of charity, the charitable attitude to one's neighbor is. He starts with a blunt disjunction: if one had to choose between enjoyment of God and enjoyment of one's neighbor, one of course would choose enjoyment of God. It immediately becomes clear, however, that that was said only for the sake of argument; for properly speaking one does not have to make that choice—indeed, one is forbidden to do so; for he considers a sense in which one should not attempt to seek enjoyment; one should not attempt to have fruition of oneself. If one does, he says, then one's own condition, and consequently the attempted self-fulfilment, are impaired by the very attempt. Far from denying that self-fulfilment is a valid human end, he says that it cannot be achieved unless one directs one's desire to God. The distinction is between self-centeredness and immediate affinity for one's own well-being—an affinity stifled, thwarted except by orientation upon God. And, he adds, one should love others according to exactly the same principle. So it is right to be moved by an immediate sense of fellowship for one's neighbor, without ulterior motive. Thus other people are in themselves (though not by themselves) proper objects of enjoyment, because the affinity one has for them is fundamental.

This is a partial solution to the problem posed by Arendt. Far from implying that a proper love for God precludes desiring the good of human beings for their own sake, Augustine implies that it makes such a love possible. But Arendt's critique has also raised the general problem of the relationship between love that is conceived as a desire and love that is not. Her crucial assumption is that Augustine's "craving" for the "absolute future" of heaven must be not only described as a desire but defined as such. If it were indeed so defined, then the love for God experienced by the saints in heaven, for example, could not be charity in the same sense, for there any desire for heaven one may have had before is fulfilled. On these grounds alone Arendt would be right to regard Augustinian *caritas* as a group of distinct loves.

But as we have seen already, although in this part of *De Doctrina Christiana* Augustine treats charity as a desire, he neither explicitly nor implicitly defines it as such. Near the end of book 1 he makes explicit that he does not do so. In heaven, he says, the love we experience on earth as a desire, in the sense of a craving for something we do not have, finally becomes fully itself by entirely ceasing to be a desire in that sense (*DC* 1.38.42). Faced with the reality one has desired, one will simply find it to be the superabundant goodness that it is. That constant realization will be the fulness of the love that before was a desire. What was an admiration partly diminished by some removal from its object is finally an admiration so great that it could not be greater. (The exact relationship between this admiration and love of neighbor, and between love of neighbor as a reasoned desire for that person's good and love of neighbor based immediately on a sense of human fellowship, is still not clear at this stage of the present argument.)

The second form of charity in Augustine's thought, according to Arendt, arises from the awareness that we have an affinity with God as our origin; for in a sense each of us is produced by the universe, and at first we are inclined to think of our origin simply in that way; but, says Arendt, the prospect of annihilation in death causes human beings to shift their gaze to contemplation of God, our ultimate ori-

gin and our natural contact with immortality.[22] This notion of charity is not necessarily distinct from the preceding one. (The fact that
beings so remarkable as human beings are of God's creation is of
course regarded by Augustine as one of the *mirabilia Dei* (*CD* 22.24);
and an admiration than which no admiration could be greater will
readily embrace contemplation of that fact.) Nevertheless, Arendt's
second formulation of Augustinian charity also, like the first, has its
own way of appearing incapable of including love of neighbor. Here
the problem, as Arendt frames it, is that if one turns one's attention
to the divine source of one's being and away from this mutable
world, one inevitably turns away also from fellow human beings as
one encounters them in this world. The result is that one loves one's
neighbor only abstractly—as originating in the absolute stability of
God. This, argues Arendt, solves the problem posed by the prospect
of annihilation in death, for if one loves one's fellows with such a
charity as this, death will be a meaningless irrelevancy.[23] But the
price, she says, of this emotional and intellectual triumph over death
is a certain indifference to one's fellows as one meets them and likes
them in this world—one converts them into a generalized abstraction. Thus on this level, too, she claims to find in Augustine a kind of
opposition between the two great Commands.

Certainly some of Augustine's statements might be thought to imply this. In the principal passage cited by Arendt (one already mentioned here, from the *Confessions*), he remembers being engulfed with
grief at a friend's death and contrasts himself as he then was with a
(hypothetical) person so steeped in love for God as not to fall into
that morbid state. "The only person," he says, "who avoids losing a
dear one is the person to whom all are dear in the One who is not
lost" (*Conf.* 4.9.14). This illustrates Arendt's point and also touches on
the problem we have found with Burnaby's account of charity. The
crucial question is whether Augustine dismisses as an aberration (or

22. Ibid., 45–73.
23. Ibid., 94–96.

else as a temporary condition) all grief based on affection or personal loyalty or individual attachment. In this passage he does not pronounce on the matter, though he indicates that the particular form his grief then took was morbidly inflamed. He discusses the subject comprehensively, however, in the course of the celebrated disquisition on justice in book 19 of the *City of God*. There he eventually concludes that this virtue (defined in its classical sense: that of "distributing to each his own") consists in endeavoring to place every person in the presence of God, the Master of the universe—God, by whom each person has been created (*CD* 19.21–22). Earlier in the argument he discusses specifically what the just attitude is to a friend's death. He rejects philosophical ideas of autarky as shallow and argues that the just attitude in such circumstances is grief (*CD* 19.8). Though it is much more grievous, he says, to hear of a friend's moral defection (which is a death more profound), grief is still the right response to news of a friend's departure from this world. Here it is one's very duty not to reject or to minimize an agony centered in a personal affection; for not to respond to such news with grief that is real suffering is to show "a ruthless mental insensitivity" that would entail severing "the bonds of all natural human affections" (*humanarum omnium necessitudinum vincula*).

The human love implied here is a version of the spontaneous and disinterested fellowship of persons mentioned earlier. The crucial point, however, is the organic connection between this and the ordered love of God; for while a natural affection (*necessitudo*) is an emotionally potent bond of loyalty too fundamental to be dispensed with and emerging rightfully from the core and basis of things, yet a certain religious ordering of it characterizes even its spontaneous responses. For example, its grief, as we have just seen, is rightfully more horrific at news of a (presumed) spiritual death than of an ordinary death. In that way this notion of grief as a proper expression of *humanitas* proves also to be a special form of the general notion of justice in love, at which Augustine arrives thirteen chapters later: love cannot be just if it fails to desire and to rejoice in the intimacy of all human beings with God.

Although up to a point this conception of charity economically harmonizes the three orientations of love enjoined in the two great Commands (toward God, toward oneself, and toward one's neighbor), it still does not solve the problem, implicit in Burnaby's great synthesis, of a charity based on fellowship but finally indifferent to the fate of one's lost fellows. Here, however, Augustine is professing to give not a comprehensive account of the nature of charity, but a prescription (put negatively) of how that virtue must be ordered.

Third and last, Arendt finds in Augustine's thought a charity social in nature. Its background, she says, is the notion that among human beings there was originally a natural love based on interdependence; but that this, together with all other aspects of human goodness, has been universally ruptured by the sin inherited from Adam; the only vestige of the old, lost love, she says, is the acknowledgment of a universal community in sinfulness;[24] but this by itself cannot be charity; one cannot simply love one's neighbor as sinful. Nevertheless, the divine Incarnation has, she argues, built on this foundation: some individuals, severally conscious of their sin, when faced with the mysterious mercy of God participate in a form of charity granted through that Incarnation: love of one's neighbor as a member or potential member of the newly created community in divine grace; thus even here, she concludes, in his culminating notion of charity, Augustine sees love of neighbor as an indirect love.[25] To establish the point she cites a passage from the eighth *Tractate on St. John's First Epistle*:

You ask how we love our brothers. My answer is to ask why you love your enemy. . . . In order for him to be healthy in this life? But that may not be what he needs. . . . What you must desire for him is that he may have eternal life with you. Want him to be your brother. Then, when you love him you are loving . . . not what he is, but what you wish that he may be. (*Tr. in 1 ep. Ioh.* 8.10)

24. Ibid., 104–5.   25. Ibid., 110–12.

Although this illustrates Arendt's point, it does not establish it. Indeed, a few lines later Augustine says: "You see your enemy opposing you, . . . attacking you with lying accusations, pursuing you with hatred. In all this, advert to the fact that he is a human being." Thus the cardinal distinction is not, after all, between my enemy as enemy and my enemy as potential brother in God, but between my enemy as enemy and my enemy as human. The former distinction is the result of the latter. It is because I already love my enemy for being a fellow human being that I hope he will be converted and cease to be my enemy. In other words, the common humanity we inherit from Adam remains the basis of charity, even charity manifested as love of enemies. Here, then, an extreme form of agape, specifically Christian and exaltedly divine in character, is nevertheless described as the exercise of a natural human affinity—the bond of our common humanity. What makes this love of enemies a supernatural love, and stops it from being merely sentimental, is the desire for their conversion; loving one's enemies is inseparable from wanting them to be rescued from all spiritual evil.

It is important to note that this passage also adumbrates a notion of charity as mercy. This idea is one of the theses of the *Tractates*. It has already appeared, rather more clearly, in the fifth *Tractate* (*Tr. in 1 ep. Ioh.* 5.11–12; cf. *Tr. in 1 ep. Ioh.* 8.14). And there again Augustine marks out its highest and lowest terms—its ultimate divine perfection and its primal human motive; and although he is not giving a formal definition of charity (it cannot be formally defined since, as he says later, charity is God), he is nevertheless giving an account of its nature, not merely indicating one of its characteristics. He accepts the principle that if one wants to know what something is, one either contemplates it in its perfection, which in this case is the great Incarnational act of compassion for human beings—participation by God in human beings' sufferings, even to death—or one contemplates it in its most basic manifestation in human experience—one's own initial "piercing of the bowels" by compassion, the nascent merciful impulse toward a fellow sufferer. At either extreme, charity is compassion.

Moreover, what is essentially this doctrine emerges again in a passage of *De Trinitate* where Augustine once more informally defines charity (*De Trin.* 8.10.14).[26] "What," he says, "is the dearness or charity [*dilectio vel caritas*] praised and preached so much in sacred Scripture, except love of good [*amor boni*]." But what is love [*amor*]? Since where there is love there is also a lover and a beloved, he says, love is "a certain life" that joins the two. Love, then, is a relational term; and one cannot, of course, love what is evil for its evil's sake. This is part of an argument stretching back through the later chapters of book 8. Augustine has asked: "What is dearness" *(dilectio)*—true dearness, that is, as opposed to concupiscent desire *(cupiditas)?*" and has answered: "To live justly in adherence to truth, and therefore to despise all mortal things by comparison with love for human beings, by which we desire them to live justly. In that way we shall even be able to die for our brothers, which the Lord Jesus has taught by his own example" (*De Trin.* 8.7.10). Charity, then, is the self-sacrificing readiness, perfectly evinced in Christ's Passion, to extend God's mercy to fellow human beings who are afflicted (above all afflicted in the fundamental way: spiritually). Here too, therefore, charity is compassion for a fellow human being.

Arguably, this solution is open to the objection (raised in general terms by W. Schrage) that if charity is defined as an essentially human love, those who never receive it from a human being will never receive it at all. And T. J. van Bavel's reply—"when nobody loves us, we are none the less loved by God"—though accurate in itself and a reasonable riposte, does not entirely meet the objection.[27] Given that

26. For an assertion of the crucial importance of the analogy of love in *De Trin.*, book 8, see Lewis Ayres, "The Discipline of Self-Knowledge in Augustine's *De Trinitate* Book X," in *The Passionate Intellect: Essays on the Transformation of the Classical Traditions Presented to I. G. Kidd*, ed. Lewis Ayres (London: Transaction, 1995), 265.

27. W. Schrage, "Theologie und Christologie bei Paulus und Jesus auf dem Hintergrund der modernen Gottesfrage," *Evangelische Theologie* 36 (1976): 121–54; T. J. van

God, as unchanging, does not suffer, can the love exercised by that Being be the same as that of someone who suffers? Augustine's own implicit solution is that the love of God is primarily, not merely by extension, Incarnational, and so par excellence a love exercised by someone who suffers. This, according to him, is ultimately true even of the love operating within the Trinity. But charity is by nature outwardly directed: when we love charity itself, "we love her as loving something" *(aliquid diligentem diligimus) (De Trin.* 8.8.12). First, then, on the basis of this principle Augustine formulates a provisional human trinity constituted through charity alone: lover, love, beloved. The reason why it must, in that way, be constituted by more than one substance (and is, therefore, an imperfect human analogy for God) is that although love is, unproblematically, internal to the lover, the beloved must, by the very nature of charity, be someone else. By itself self-love within a human being leads only to a duality, for then although there is a distinction between love and lover, there is none between lover and beloved. (That is why he then proceeds, for his analogy of internal relationship, to add self-knowledge.) This crucial consequence of defining charity as compassion is fully accepted by Augustine. "If Charity loves herself, she must love something [something other than herself, then] in order to love herself as Charity" *(De Trin.* 8.8.12, cf. 9.2.2). Though charity can be reflexive, it cannot be merely reflexive and still be charity.

But how is it that charity can internally constitute God as the Trinity when (given its necessarily outward direction) it cannot so constitute a human being? This problem brings into question the definition of charity as compassion for one's human fellow sufferers, for by revelation we know that God is charity. Near the end of the work, having established that although each of the Persons of the Trinity can rightly be called charity it is particularly appropriate for the Holy

Bavel, O.S.A., "The Double Face of Love in St. Augustine: The Daring Inversion: Love Is God," in *Congresso internazionale su S. Agostino nel 16 centenario della conversione* (Rome, 1987), 76–78.

Spirit to be so called, Augustine extends the discussion to a related instance of such appropriation: the Holy Spirit is also called the gift of God, but in such a way as to come from the Son as well as from the Father. What causes this to be so, he says, is that the Holy Spirit as well as being God's gift to God (Father to Son) is also, through Christ, God's gift to man (*De Trin.* 15.17.28–31, 15.19.33). God's eternal begetting of the Son is accomplished with a view to the Holy Spirit's being Christ's gift to human beings. This giving of the Holy Spirit to human beings is an essentially Incarnational act. The crucial implication is that in this respect the eternal begetting of the Son is Incarnational in origin. The eternal begetting of the Son in charity by the Father, though of course it transcends time, has reference to this temporal event. When, therefore, the interrelationship among the Persons of God is understood as a Trinity of charity, the Incarnation is logically prior to the Trinity. The generation of the divine Persons has always had reference to this temporal event, and ultimately the charity that is God is compassion for fellow human beings, as is charity in a human being: for indeed it is charity in a human being. This implied aspect of the Incarnational mystery must not be taken to mean that according to Augustine there is change in God—that the temporal as such could be in any sense anterior to the eternal; rather, the relationships within the Trinity are precisely eternal in their reference to the Incarnation.

Essentially the same notion, in a different form, is already a main principle of the *Confessions,* for that is what leads Augustine to conclude there that even love erotic in character is properly an epiphenomenon of charity. The ravishing beauty of the universe, he says, is a gigantic laudation of God, which, however, is meant for human ears, and those ears are deaf to it except where "at a more profound level" *(altius)* God will have compassion on whoever is the object of His compassion: *altius autem tu miserebris cui misertus eris, et misericordiam praestabis cui misericors fueris (Conf.* 10.6.8). He has already developed at great length the thesis that the powerful erotic effect of physical beauty had acted on him as an inward divine influence toward conversion. Now it emerges that at a deeper level that influence was the action of divine compassion. He has made the same point in a different mode three chapters earlier. There it is his *Confessions* themselves that he thinks might fall on deaf ears; but where ears are opened to the real significance of what he is saying, they are opened by charity (*Conf.* 10.3.3–4). This, he says, is what he really wants: "that the readers' hearts may be excited out of the sleep of despair." And so that they may be, as his once was, he calls on God, "the physician of my intimate self," to provide that mercy. Thus the divine compassion that he once felt merely as erotic on the conscious level he now feels as compassion for his fellow human beings—that is, with clear consciousness of what it really is.

If love is ultimately compassion, this, as we have seen, implies the existence of other beings than the lover. By accepting this logical consequence of his concept of personality Augustine has in effect also solved the category problem raised by A. C. Lloyd (how can Augustine define God's personality purely reflexively when his notion of personhood itself implies relationship with other beings?). Augustine's notion of reflexive love (for example, within the Trinity), which he uses to show internal reciprocity, assumes a notion of outwardly directed love—its primary reality. Only by prescindment from this does Augustine speak exclusively of love as reflexive. What is decisive here is not merely that Augustine uses the category of relation to formulate the notion of personality—the Cappadocians had already done that[28]—nor even merely that he describes the relationship concerned as one of charity entailing community, as M. T. Clark is right to emphasize, but that the community concerned is primarily of the lover and other human beings.

---

28. For this and the following point, see M. T. Clark, R.S.C.J., *Augustinian Personalism* (Villanova: Villanova University Press, 1970), 13–16. Cf. M. Mellet, O.P., Th. Camelot, O.P., and E. Hendrikx, O.E.S.A., *La Trinité: 1–8. Bibliothèque augustinienne: Oeuvres de saint Augustin* (Paris: Desclée de Brouwer, 1955), 584–85.

In respect of charity, then, a person is for Augustine the complete self-constitution of a rational nature by compassion toward other human beings—a definition applicable to divine as well as to human persons and therefore entailing (as its last phrase indicates) the doctrine of the Incarnation. This is the main positive conclusion of the present chapter. It is an answer to our second main question and also readily absolves Augustine from Meyendorff's imputation that he was a theologian of the "Absolute Being" rather than of "the divine identity of the person of Jesus, as the first and fundamental Christian experience."[29] Quite the opposite is the case.

Nevertheless, this answer must face the set of objections that constitute our third and last question. Compassion is "a certain fellow suffering in our heart with the suffering of another, which in particular compels us to come to that person's help, if possible" (CD 9.5). Compassion then, though divine in origin, is peculiarly human in its seat of operation. Moreover, the circumstances that call for it are necessarily those of suffering. Is it, however, restricted within these confines? Although Augustine shows how compassion, albeit in essence human, is the charity uniting the Persons of the Trinity without violating the divine transcendence, the notion of charity as compassion still raises three main questions. Given that a human being cannot with sanity have compassion for God, or for Christ as He is now, how can the human love for God be charity (for as has repeatedly emerged, Augustine regards it as such)? If charity is compassion, which by nature is directed toward someone else, how can one have the charity toward oneself that is implied in the second great Command? And how can the charity that the saints have in heaven, where there is no suffering, be compassion, which, after all, is sharply distinguished from pity by the fact that it is a form of fellow suffering?

The problem posed by the first of these questions is the opposite

<hr>

29. John Meyendorff, *Catholicity and the Church* (Crestwood, N.Y.: St. Vladimir's Seminary Press, 1983), 41.

of the one that faced Arendt: no longer "Given that charity is essentially love for God, how does Augustine integrate love of neighbor with it?" but "Given that charity is essentially compassion for one's neighbor, how can human love for God be charity?"

Here the distinction between use and enjoyment in book 1 of *De Doctrina Christiana* is again important, because in that formulation of charity love for God is direct, and indeed the only absolutely direct love. Does it contradict what Augustine later says in the *Tractates on St. John's First Epistle*? O'Donovan points out that the distinction gets Augustine into difficulties.[30] Who, asks Augustine, are the proper recipients of charity? After adducing the parable of the Good Samaritan he concludes that the answer is: anyone for whom one perceives compassion to be appropriate—and that is any human being (*DC* 1.30.31–33). But then what of his distinction, earlier in the book, between use and enjoyment, which focuses on the desirous aspect of charity? In a sense Augustine's next point exacerbates the problem: he argues that the difference between the human compassion for human beings and God's compassion for human beings is logically dictated by difference in points of view; our compassion has our own enjoyment of God as its purpose, whereas the purpose of God's compassion is not His enjoyment of us, but, again, our enjoyment of Him. God has no possible advantage to gain, being already "Existence supreme and primary." He loves to our advantage; we, to our own (*DC* 1.32.35). This argument, on the surface of it, means that not any human being, but only oneself, is the proper object of charity. First, however, Augustine adds the further, crucial distinction between an individual's motive and the result, for an individual, of acting with that motive: "The person, however, upon whom we have compassion and to whose good we attend really is the person for whose benefit we act. That is our motive. But in some obscure way our own benefit is a consequence": *cuius autem nos miseremur et cui consulimus, ad eius*

---

30. O'Donovan, 27.

quidem utilitatem id facimus eamque intuemur; sed nescio quo modo etiam nostra fit consequens. (When he talks of "our own good" in this context he means, of course, what would lead to our enjoyment of God.) This text, then, though its central idea has been described as a "false start,"[31] which Augustine soon abandoned, in fact already adumbrates his mature doctrine of charity as one compassion, divine and human.

Second, his earlier distinction, between compassion as divine and compassion as human, was really between a purpose and an effect— the compassionate divine purpose and its effect on human beings. There, moreover, human beings were treated collectively, as a species. Regarded in that way, we are the recipients, not the givers, of compassion. The collective human reception of that compassion was treated by Augustine as having the human enjoyment of God as its purpose. The purpose concerned, however, is not ours, but God's. And another difference is that its effect from the human point of view comes about not consciously but, said Augustine, "in some obscure way" *(nescio quo modo)*. It is only after that, at this second stage of the argument, that Augustine discusses charity as the motive of an individual human being; and it is here that he indicates that motive to be compassion toward another individual, entailing desire, though incidentally, contingently on the circumstances of this world (the desire being to alleviate someone's suffering), and that this compassion is identical (except in respect of perfection) with the charity of God.

Augustine is, of course, still aware that a human being can experience charity as love for God directly. This he in particular associates with the Neoplatonic approach to God by ascent of an intellectual scale (e.g., *Conf.* 7.17.23). In an austerely intellectual account (in the *City of God*) of the relationship between that ascent and the fulness of Christian charity, he follows the Platonic path (conceived of here in a very restricted way) as far in God's direction as it will take him, which

31. Ibid., 29.

is not to the point of loving God with all one's being, nor of actually loving one's neighbor or even oneself, but only of knowing how to love oneself (*CD* 10.3). In order to attain that knowledge, says Augustine, one must properly direct one's desire for happiness (a given, constant and universal, in human beings) by referring it to another purpose again: that of cleaving to God.[32] Two of these three desires therefore lead to the fulfilment of the third. The desire to know how to love oneself brings one to the point immediately before one begins to keep the two great Commands (starting with the second). If all one's desire for happiness is properly aligned, by being directed at cleaving to God, one is correctly set in the direction of loving oneself. It is not the case, however, that in this series of desires fulfilment of one is prerequisite for fulfilment of the next. The desires themselves are causes and their mere sequence leads to the fulfilment of the last.

This achievement, taken by itself, is very modest compared with obeying the two great Commands, for one is not yet satisfying even the most basic of the duties that they enjoin; one is merely on the verge of doing so. Yet Augustine adds that at this point one receives the instruction to love one's neighbor. Here too, however, the instruction takes the form of a statement of how one goes about loving one's neighbor rather than a specification of that virtue in its inner nature: "When one is instructed to love one's neighbor as oneself, what is one's mandate, except to advise one's neighbor to hold God dear?" This is on the level of knowing the actions to be performed in exercising charity rather than of defining that virtue. The distinction is analogous to that between knowing how to play the violin (the manner of pressing the strings with one's left-hand fingers, for example, and of brushing the strings transversely, in both directions alternately, with a bow) and actually playing the violin (producing, by applying the bow to the violin, a series of sounds in accordance with what one perceives to be a composer's intentions or with one's own

---

32. On the desire for happiness as universal in human beings and as distinct from self-love, see ibid., 58.

musical sensibility). One comes to know how to love oneself by making God the goal of one's desire for happiness (for there is, of course, no division in the mental faculties); and the method of loving one's neighbor is to urge one's neighbor to love God. Here loving God is legitimately treated as a goal, merely aiming at which has a salutary effect. But, as he has said a few lines earlier, actually loving God consists in bringing others to divine grace or allowing oneself to be brought to it by others: not a methodological sequence by which one proceeds toward the exercise of charity, but the love of God immediately constituted by human mercy of the most crucial kind.

This distinction in Augustine's thought does not amount to a barrier (such as that proposed by Nygren) between the erotic moral activity of philosophy and the charitable moral activity of the Christian religion; for earlier again in the same chapter Augustine lists the most intimately Christian practices (sacramental actions, martyrdom, prayers of self-dedication) in the same description with striving to adhere to God by way of striving to satisfy one's appetite for happiness: all these are done so that oblivion may not quench charity's fire. In this way the intellectual "sequence of ends," which he then propounds, is an aspect of Christian charity.

It is still Augustine's view, however, that the more callow one is in respect of charity the more one's relationship with it will amount to a purely philosophical quest for the Good—a quest having no obvious connection with compassion at all. Correspondingly, the more one's quest for God is characterized by merciful Incarnational charity, the more mature one's love for God is. This point emerges dramatically in his account of the mystical ascent to God's proximity (shared with his mother in the window overlooking the garden at Ostia) and of the few succeeding minutes (*Conf.* 9.10.23–26). This ecstasy, as J. J. O'Donnell observes, is markedly superior to the earlier, more lonely one that Augustine had already narrated.[33] The earlier one, as of course Augustine indicated contextually, was Neoplatonic in charac-

33. O'Donnell, 3:122–37.

ter. This later one also is largely so, at least in its earlier stages; Augustine and Monica are, for example, lifting themselves upward *(erigentes nos)* early in the account. There comes, however, the crucial point where Monica, already a close participant in the experience, suddenly takes the lead and shifts the direction of thought as the sublime emotion fades. At the beginning, when they speculated about a human exaltation above the mutability of this world, they were both talking—*dicebamus*—then only Augustine—*dicebam*. Now in her turn Monica, the real spiritual guide, speaks alone.[34] She too talks still about being lifted above the changing events of the world. The difference is that she has abruptly ceased to echo her son's tone of soaring mental asceticism. The reason why the world and its distractions are now completely worthless to her is that her son's life finally evinces God's mercy. Her love for God is her cooperation with the divine mercy, and ultimately she describes its fulfilment not in terms of an intellectual ascent to ecstasy (though she has implicitly accepted that that is a legitimate approach to describing it, and there is no disjunction, no rejection of what her son—and she—have said), but as her participation in her son's rescue from fatal spiritual misery. Her love for God, therefore, is at its core her compassion for her son. Indeed, earlier in the work Augustine has said that the philosophical ardor for God, which he felt as a young man, was in reality Incarnational mercy—toward himself in the first instance. He even indicates that in an obscure way he himself sensed this fact at the time, for what slightly took the edge off that ardor, he says, was his awareness that the divine Incarnation was missing from the text that so excited him.

This, however, also touches on our second problem of integration, which arises from the essential outwardness of compassion. If

34. For the interesting suggestion that this passage is an account of "non-individuated, 'common' seeing," see Michel René Barnes, "The Visible Christ and the Invisible Trinity: Mt. 5:8 in Augustine's Trinitarian Theology of 400," *Modern Theology* 19, 3 (2003): 345–46. Barnes's suggestion does not, however, take account of the crucial, persistent individuality maintained by both Augustine and Monica in this conversation.

charity is compassion for another human being, how can one have charity toward oneself? Yet the second great Command implicitly requires this, and in the *City of God* Augustine accepts the consequence, repeatedly pointing out that sacred Scripture instructs us to have compassion on ourselves (*CD* 10.6, 21.27).[35] The problem is partially solved by the Socratic principle (which Augustine accepts) that to think of one person's real interests as clashing with another's is, as O'Donovan puts it, "simply a mistake."[36] Yet to lay down one's life for others as Christ did is a devotion to others at one's own expense too extreme to be so straightforwardly identified with self-love. In a chapter of the *City of God* largely devoted to self-compassion Augustine accordingly goes further. He identifies having compassion toward oneself, as toward others, with becoming a "true sacrifice" to God (*CD* 10.6). "Even compassion itself [*et ipsa misericordia*], which leads one to help a person, is not a sacrifice unless God is the basis of it [*si non propter Deum fit*]." Here *propter Deum* means not "for God's sake as opposed to that of a fellow human being," but "with God, as opposed to the world, as one's point of orientation," for that is his main thesis in this chapter. To say "even compassion itself" in this context is to imply that if anything could be expected to be a true sacrifice to God, compassion could. He then extends this to compassion toward oneself, quoting Sirach: "Having compassion for your own soul: be pleasing to God."

What is meant by compassion for oneself eventually emerges from the argument he then develops in support of this appeal to biblical authority. He mentions again (in a somewhat varied form) the sequence of referred ends (discussed here earlier) from three chapters before. The purpose of becoming a true sacrifice to God must be referred to another purpose: that of attaining intimacy with God; but this must in turn be referred to another purpose again: the attainment of true happiness. The series appears to present an essentially

35. In both passages Augustine quotes Eccl 30.24.
36. O'Donovan, 103; *De Trin.* 12.9.14.

eudaemonistic account of charity. When, however, Augustine considers the natures of the activities he has listed, he asserts that intimacy with God "in a holy society" is identical with resembling God by acts and attitudes of decency (for both amount to "referring oneself to God"); that this resembling God by one's decency is identical with "being a true sacrifice" to God, for one becomes acceptable to God by ridding oneself of what is alien to Him and retaining what is still inviolately divine in character; that such self-purification by human beings is also a divine action—the accomplishment of Incarnational compassion, culminating in our happiness; and that this divine action is identical with the human exercise of citizenship in God (for that exercise is God's mercy in action). In this context, again, therefore, mere eudaemonism proves not to be the essential motive of charity; for the notion of human happiness as an end, formulated earlier in the argument in a classically eudaemonistic way, now reappears in a thoroughly corrected form. The sense in which charity has human happiness as its purpose is not that one loves others in order to achieve one's own happiness, but that the divine care intends our translation from misery to joy. These formulations of charity are successively identified with each other on the principle that each is a human enactment of divine compassion. Since that compassion is Christ's for others than Himself, the charity one has toward oneself is indirect. This is the contrary of Arendt's interpretation.

The principle proposed here as the very essence of charity is not susceptible to the distinction, which O'Donovan accurately perceives in Augustine's thought, between self-love and the desire for happiness.[37] That distinction (based on practical human experience) is between a motive (desire for happiness) that is universal and, in the wide sense, an action (self-love) that is not universal. But in this passage Augustine describes a transformation in the universal human motive itself, in some cases brought about by the Incarnation. The

37. O'Donovan, 56–59.

motive, in such cases, is no longer desire for one's own happiness, but fellowship in the misery of another and the intention to relieve it. This disposition, since it is the essence of Christ's charity, is the culminating moral result of God's influence on human beings. Secondarily this same disposition is charity toward oneself: one loves oneself as loving others.

To a limited degree our final problem (how, given that there is no suffering in heaven, can a charity that is essentially compassion be exercised there?) is implicitly solved by Augustine in the same way. At the end of the *City of God* he considers what connection the saints in eternity will have with the sufferings of this world. They will remember them, he says, but no longer suffer them:

How will they "sing the mercies of the Lord eternally" (as the psalm puts it) if they do not know that they have been miserable? That company of heavenly citizens will find nothing more pleasant than that song to the glory of the grace of Christ, by whose blood we have been liberated. The saying "be still and know that I am God" will there be brought to perfect fulfilment. (*CD* 22.30)

Thus the saints will remember the miseries of this world in order that their contemplation of God may be of Him as merciful—as Incarnately human. Their love of God will, therefore, be a participation in that of the Father, for like Him they will love Christ as loving someone other than Himself, and in that way will participate in the divine love, which is primarily compassion. Here again, charity is indirect except insofar as it is compassion for suffering human beings. This is due to its divine character, the same being true even of the divine charity. This, then, is compassion in heaven for those who suffer in this world.

That answer, however, addresses only one side of our final question. The other is whether there is compassion in heaven for the damned. A parallel question is raised by Rist: "Even if *the condemned* have no right to complain, perhaps the saved could lodge an appeal on their behalf. The appeal, however, would still involve considerations of 'fairness' rather than of Augustinian 'justice,' and . . . Augustine brushes it aside."[38] This is true of such appeals to God on grounds of fairness: as Rist says, Augustine has no patience with those who would try to make God conform to human juridical rules. But what of such appeals on grounds of charity? The disquisitions on grief in the *Confessions* and the *City of God* indicate that a deep emotional engagement with another person (as opposed, say, to a generalized benevolence) causes grief when that person dies; that such grief, except where it is seriously morbid, is a genuine experience of reality; that it is inhuman not to care about the loss of a friend; and that such care is properly more intense when it is faced with eternal separation from the beloved (*Conf.* 4.4.9–4.7.12; *CD* 19.8). But in neither disquisition does Augustine discuss the implicit question: that of the eternity of such care.

Here, then, the Heideggerian idea of eternal, heavenly *cura, Bekümmerung,* has reappeared transmuted as compassion in heaven for the damned. The idea in this form is more difficult to dismiss as non-Augustinian. Indeed, in the *City of God* Augustine explicitly mentions the idea and does not dismiss it. It appears as one of the premises of an argument used by some of Augustine's opponents to prove that damnation is not necessarily eternal (*CD* 21.18, 21.24). In heaven (the argument goes) the saints will not cease to have "bowels of compassion" for their damned friends, because in heaven their own sanctity, and hence their compassion, will be perfect; so of course they will intercede for their lost fellows; nor is it to be believed that God will fail to hear them, for now there will be no obstacle between them and God; therefore, all those fortunate enough to be so prayed for will be saved in spite of their own unrepentance.

For our problem the important feature of Augustine's subsequent attack on this argument is that he does not attack the first section of it. Praying for those whom one knows to be damned not to be

38. Rist, 273.

damned would, he argues, be absurd: it would be asking for what has happened to desist from having happened. This point is logically sufficient for the rebuttal of the argument. He has not needed to attack the earlier part of it. But if he thought that nevertheless there was something wrong with this, it would be uncharacteristic of his argumentational style, in this context at least, to leave it standing. In the next chapter, for example, one of the arguments of his opponents is that the simple fact of ever having been Catholic is ineradicably salvific; some schismatic heretics, unlike others, began as Catholics and therefore they, unlike the others, are automatically saved despite their unrepentance. Augustine demolishes the first premise of this argument with a principle from Scripture: not only no fornicators or idolaters but also no fomenters of feuds or animosity will inherit the kingdom of God (Gal 5.19; CD 21.25). Here again, this is all that is necessary; but here Augustine also attacks the conclusion of the argument directly. Schismatic heresiarchs, he argues, far from being better off eternally than their theological victims born into schism, are more guilty. Logically this is irrelevant to his refutation, but he sees an idea wrong in itself and is unwilling to leave it intact. Similarly, in refuting the argument that the very fact of eating the Body of Christ till the end of one's life makes one a member of that Body to the end, that this automatically ensures salvation, and that therefore immoral communicants cannot finally be damned, he attacks both premises, even though his main attack (on the second) would have sufficed. If, then, he had regarded as mistaken the assertion that the saints in heaven have compassion for their lost fellows, he could still be expected to have rebutted it. His failure to do so, though not of course an implicit acceptance of this idea, leaves the question open to dispute and gives us no indication of his opinion on the subject. These chapters (16–27) are full of discussion about compassion, human and divine, in heaven, and nowhere here does Augustine suggest that any quashing, limiting, numbing, or abandonment of compassion, even for the damned, could possibly occur there. Moreover, in chapter 24 he positively accepts that the text "Surely even when angry He shall not in any way limit His compassion" may be taken to mean that God has eternal compassion toward the damned (Ps 77 [76] 10 [LXX]). Augustine explicitly takes care neither to support nor to rule out this interpretation. If one chooses to accept it, one must also accept its implication, that (according to the terms of Augustinian eschatology) there is such compassion on the part of the heavenly saints also—for, as we have seen, Augustine (in the same general part of the work) characterizes the human mind's state in heaven as participation in the divine, Incarnational compassion (CD 22.30). Augustine, then, allows, but does not take, the position that in heaven there is both divine and human "care" for the damned.

A problem posed by this position is that in such cases the compassion arguably could have no practical exercise: it could not be mercy—least of all infinite mercy. But mercy in some form is essential to compassion: Augustine's view, as we have seen, is that this virtue compels us to try, at least, to have mercy on the afflicted (CD 9.5). Where that avenue is blocked, all cannot possibly be well. Hence, what leads him in the Confessions to see tragic drama as a kind of pornography of commiseration is that the commiseration it arouses does not end in mercy but is itself enjoyed as an end; it is for this reason a travesty of compassion (Conf. 3.2.3). "Genuine compassion," he says, "would want the suffering not to be there." But practical mercy, this proper outcome, is precluded in the case of compassion for the damned.

Augustine minimally lightens the pressure of this enigma by suggesting that God in His infinite compassion might lighten the sufferings of hell. This suggestion addresses only the (vaguely conceived) accidents of damnation, leaving untouched its main theological problem: that infinite divine compassion would for the most part be eternally frustrated in such cases (CD 21.24). The corresponding problem, that the saints would eternally participate in that frustrated compassion, remains correspondingly unsolved. Not that this is reneging on a theological duty. Rather, Augustine has pursued his argument only to the point beyond which he would have had to abandon one of his fundamental presuppositions. One may be left wondering how such a frustrated compassion could be heavenly; but here, at least, he has not chosen to solve that problem either by saying that all are saved or by implying that the divine love is limited—that God's compassion, together with that of the saints in heaven, avoids frustration by withholding itself from the damned.

CHAPTER 5

CITIZENSHIP IN GOD

───────────

❧ In the treatise *On Free Will* Augustine, as we have seen, conceives of decency as practiced not only between individuals but in such a way as to form a developed society (his example is the choice of a political constitution) (*De lib. arb.* 1.5.11–1.7.16). Later, especially in the *City of God,* he continues to think of virtue in a context of structured relationships—of compassion itself as exercised by a paterfamilias toward the members of his family (*CD* 19.14; cf. 19.5). The thesis of the *City of God* is that human experience is, in the final analysis, the history of two complex, mutually opposed social organizations: the heavenly and the worldly. For this reason charity will not merely inform the soul with compassion; it will also be socially constituted. We must consider what sort of society it brings into being.

Eventually the controversies about this part of Augustine's thought devolve from three large questions. But if these are to be intelligibly asked, one must first trace the ideas that bring them to the fore. In summary, those ideas are: that the Incarnation, both before and after its initial accomplishment, is elaborated in human society; that peace, a social form of well-being, is the goal of all activity, and perfect peace the goal of human morality; that citizenship, in its fullness, is what constitutes the supreme form of peace, which, however, is exercised perfectly only in heaven; that citizenship consists in people's concordant devotion of themselves to a good; that that collective devotion or allegiance is always essentially religious, for the religious and the political are not ultimately distinct; that therefore all civil society is religious; and that hence, despite the persistent effects of original sin, even political life is in principle open to transformation, though not yet transfiguration, by Incarnational grace. The three large questions are: Why, then, does the *City of God* provide no comparative account of the various political forms of government, much less an ideal constitution? How can political life be essentially religious and susceptible to Christian decency if human society is still a victim of the Fall and particularly given that political life, unlike the other major forms of social activity, never had a chance to be exercised in the Garden, and has therefore been conditioned by sin from its inception? And, since citizenship is fully exercised only in heaven, what proper continuity is there between citizenship on earth and citizenship in heaven? Each of these questions challenges the notion of an Incarnational continuum between heavenly and earthly society implicit in the preceding chain of ideas. This notion must first be studied in some detail.

In the *City of God* Augustine makes clear that there is no division between his doctrine of human society and his doctrine of the Incarnation. He makes the point especially prominent by establishing it at the end of the final chapter of book 10—the apex of the work in respect of its construction. There Augustine compendiously lists the main divinely prophesied events of human history, the events with which the action of God in the world culminates. They begin with the Incarnation itself, then show an increasingly wide social character. Late in the list is the ban placed on public pagan sacrifices by the emperor Theodosius; next to the end is the damnation of the "society of the impious," and at the end the "eternal kingdom of the most glorious City of God." The stages in divine action are thus described as arising from the Incarnation and as accomplished socially (*CD* 10.32; cf. *CD* 17.16). Where proper order obtains in this regard, Augustine calls the resulting stability "peace"—the tranquillity that consists in orderly relationships. In some sense all beings in the universe (even a suspended corpse, says Augustine) desire peace (*Conf.* 13.35.50; but especially *CD* 19.12); but living human beings above all do so, because of the uniquely comprehensive character of human experience. Even a violent savage desires it when he is being violent, though the less extensive the form of it one desires, the further one is from being actively human. We have no choice but to desire it, but we can wickedly desire an insufficiently high degree of it (*CD* 19.12–13).

In his supreme account of this subject Augustine specifies nine modes of peace, severally occurring at nine levels of being listed ascendingly (*CD* 19.13): the peace of a body, of a soul in its irrational aspect, of a soul in its rational aspect, of a body and soul with each other (an entire animate being in all its natural aspects), of a human being with God, of human beings with each other, of a household *(domus)*, of a civil society *(civitas)*, and of the Heavenly Civil Society. (The tenth peace, mentioned after these, is not a higher one again, but the general principle applicable to all: "the peace of all things," which he defines as "the tranquillity of order.") A number of features of this intellectual vision are especially to be noted here.

This is a hierarchical list (from a single physical object to the Heavenly City) in which the degrees of peace are all degrees of the same thing. Both the peace of a body and the peace of the irrational soul, for example, are inevitably features of the peace of a body and soul with each other, which appears higher in the list.

Also it is a hierarchy of relationships. *Pax,* the word Augustine uses, is always in the category of relation. Where this word is used, one cannot be understood to be simply at peace; one has to be at peace with someone. (Hence the verb *pacisci,* "to strike a bargain.") Even the bottommost mode of it, that of a single body, Augustine describes as the peace of its parts with each other—an instance of proper, orderly relatedness, as are all the other modes of peace listed here. To be solipsistic, therefore, he regards as inhuman—a voluntary rejection of the most fundamental desire there is. It finally amounts to rejecting God (cf. *CD* 14.13).

Third, the wider the range of different relationships within a mode of peace, the higher that mode of peace is. This is axiomatic for Augustine. Hence, the reason why incest is against God's law is that it forces to be one relationship what might have been two or more different ones, by which the bonds of love might have been more widely distributed (*CD* 15.16). Hence, also, the peace between one human being and God is lower on Augustine's list than the peace of human beings with one another: this does not mean, of course, that God is less important than other human beings, but that in the latter case a greater range of relationships is entailed. One is, we may infer, moving closer to the great prize, the peace of the Heavenly City, when one proceeds from one's individual relationship with God to relationships with one's fellow human beings.

Furthermore, this ascent through peace is described only in terms of what is good. The peace of gangs, for example, is not included, nor, most important, is that of the earthly city (the society of the hell-bent).

Moreover, of the many possible forms of human society only two, citizenship and the family, figure in this list. One may conclude that they are its crucial forms, the peace of any other kind of society being somehow subsumed in theirs. But of these, citizenship has priority, because the two highest modes of peace, placed above the peace of the family at the supreme end of being, are two degrees of citizenship: citizenship *simpliciter dictum* (the giving and obeying of commands among citizens) and heavenly citizenship (whereby citizens in God enjoy God and each other in God). In exactly what sense citizenship, the same specific reality, occurs at both these levels is not clear from the passage taken by itself, and cannot be clear until the questions addressed here have been answered. What is clear, however, from this metaphysical ascent into citizenship is that this is the most important kind of human relationship—finally the only one: the heavenly society of citizens *(civitas caelestis)* is, for Augustine, the ultimate reality. Thus citizenship, whatever it is, is the human relationship that extends into eternity. (It should be noted that *civitas* denotes both citizenship and, by extension, the society constituted by it. As J. Ratzinger points out, one cannot speak of a sharp distinction, in Augustine, between these two meanings.)[1]

Finally, all the modes of peace are described in human terms (for example, the rational and irrational soul, the household, citizenship). Only human beings (though here Augustine does not say this explicitly) by nature run the gamut of all being, from physical objects to the civil society of heaven.

The passage raises but does not solve the problem of the relationship between the family and civil society. Since, however, they overlap only in this distorted world (after the Fall but before the final Judgment), the determining issues on this subject will emerge in connection with the second of our large questions. What is clear, however, in this passage and again three chapters later, is that human society par excellence is civil rather than familial (see *CD* 19.16). For Augustine, human beings are by nature not only social but designed to participate in an order both divine and civil. (Hence what makes his vast prayer, the *Confessions,* worthwhile, he says, is precisely that he utters it not only in God's presence but "in the ears of my fellow believers, fellow citizens, past, present, and future") (*Conf.* 10.4.6).

What, then, is civil society? There are four definitions of it in *The City of God.* They are working definitions, not fully definitive (*CD* 19.13, 15.8, 2.21, 19.21 [in the order in which the passages are discussed here]). Two are very loose: for to understand what is meant by "the giving and obeying of orders among citizens" (in the passage just mentioned), one would need to know what a citizen is, which would entail knowing what civil society is. The passage does, however, provide the information that citizenship is essentially subordinative, hierarchical. And in defining it as "a multitude of people tied together by some bond of fellowship," Augustine says little or nothing more than

1. Ratzinger, 225.

that it is a large society of people. The main piece of information is that it is large: a handful of people cannot make up a civil society. The other two definitions, however, are important. Strictly speaking, they define not civil society *(civitas)* but a people *(populus)* and, by extension, a people as sovereignly organized *(res publica)*; but neither Augustine nor, in the passages quoted, Cicero makes any clear distinction between *civitas* and *populus.*

The third definition, then, is "a cohering multitude whose principles of association are agreement as to right and commonality of practical interest." Only the former of these principles attracts Augustine's attention. He argues that right *(ius)* is impossible without rightness *(iustitia);* and rightness (justice, conceived in its classical sense: giving each being its proper place) is patently absent where proper place (absolute primacy) is not accorded to God. As R. A. Markus points out, Augustine here "converts the Ciceronian *ius* into 'righteousness' in the full, biblical sense."[2] By such an exacting criterion no pagan people is a people at all. The definition itself (taken from Cicero) is a retaining wall of the work; Augustine has noted it in book 2 and then returns to it, as promised, seventeen books later. It will be discussed here, by a common practice, in conjunction with the fourth definition.[3]

The fourth (Augustine's own) is "a rational, cohering multitude whose principle of association is commonality as to the things they agree in their hearts to love." This has the advantage of classifying as peoples the societies usually referred to as such, rather than propounding a species almost devoid of members.

The crucial words (absent from the third definition) are "rational" and "love" *(diligere)*. A civilization is essentially a shared love—it is chosen and is value-determined, rather than an automatic or unconscious feature of human behavior.

2. Markus, 65.

3. Rowan Williams, "Politics and the Soul: A Reading of the *City of God*," *Milltown Studies* 19–20 (1987): 58–60.

Moreover, in the final analysis this love has to be an ordered one, for the third and fourth definitions are not the incompatible alternatives that H. A. Deane asserts them to be; they illuminate contrasting sides of the subject but converge to the same conclusion.[4] From the third, which is Platonic in character, Augustine concludes that the only way one can know the nature of civil society is by intellectually contemplating it in its perfection (the community of those whose love is entirely as it should be—that is, the Heavenly City). From the fourth, which is Aristotelian in character, based on experience, he observes that although Rome can by this definition be classified as a civil society, it in fact started to break up during the late Republic, with numerous political factions and civil wars. Augustine does not need at this point to reestablish that the master principle of distributive justice is the accordance of absolute primacy to God, that by "God" Augustine means the God of Abraham, of Isaac, and of St. Peter (God as historically revealed), that the injustice of antique Rome consisted in not acknowledging this primacy (at least in the general, philosophically accessible way), and that Rome's other forms of immorality and her political shakiness were caused by this underlying injustice. For those foundations of his present argument he relies on the nineteen preceding books of discussion. Having merely alluded to those now, he points out that even in practice civil society, amoral definition notwithstanding, can be observed to be in principle just (or at least to have justice as an inseparable accident). Cohesion being any society's absolute sine qua non, justice proves in practical experience to be the basis even of a largely unjust society's cohesion; Rome failed to cohere, even in the mediocre way it intended, precisely for lack of that basis.

Furthermore, in saying that civil justice is a multitudinously shared love centered on God Augustine does not bypass his principle that charity (the only love) is compassion. The perfectly just civil society, he says, is so by being a perfect sacrifice to God. As we have seen,

4. Deane, 123.

what this expression means has been explained much earlier in the work: it is participation in the divine compassion (*CD* 10.6). He now relies on that entire earlier account: the reason for saying that we ourselves, God's civil society, are the best and most glorious sacrifice to God has, he says, been expounded "in earlier books." Love even on the civil stratum, then, is still in essence the Incarnational compassion, not some other love overlying that.

And these definitions do not distinguish in kind between an eschatologically significant civil society (the City of God or the earthly city) and a state (a sovereign society concerned with government in the practical order). This is most strikingly true of the fourth definition, which classifies both in the same species and which has the express purpose of including both the City of God and states, such as Rome. This is a large obstacle to any suggestion that Augustine regarded political action as different in kind from religious.

When one turns from essence to identity, the demarcations are quite different. In particular, every state is in identity distinct from the earthly city, the society of perversely and utterly self-devoted citizens, the lovers of an exclusively earthly peace, and worshippers, consequently, of what is not God (*CD* 14.28). What makes this distinction enigmatic is that, according to Augustine, states in this world commonly, even nearly universally, act as departments of the earthly city and historically originate in pursuance of that function. (Book 18 of the *City of God* is an attempted comprehensive account of both those processes.) This does not, however, mean that Augustine regarded any given state as ever perfectly identical with the earthly city or any part of it. The contradictory is true. The earthly city is unnatural. A sovereign society concerned with practical government is at its core natural. In book 2, for example, after his first devastating exposé of Rome's corrupt pagan background, Augustine does not tell that great city to cease to act as a state, but appeals to what is still naturally good in her (her *indoles*, or innate character) to wake up (*CD* 2.29): not to cease being Rome (it is the *indoles Romana* he addresses, largely admirable), but to cease being corrupt. And thirteen books later he says that although "the earthly city was first founded by Cain," many other cities were perhaps founded before that; we do not actually know; Scripture does not give us that information (*CD* 15.1–5 and 8). *Ex hypothesi* none of those could have been earlier foundations of the earthly city, and none could have been the City of God (founded not in this world but in heaven); they therefore stopped short of either ultimate loyalty, and they would, then, have been temporal cities, without being the earthly city.

If, as these passages suggest, a state is fluid as to its ultimate allegiance, though inauspicious in its circumstances of origin, the religious and the practical orders of civil society are not intrinsically divergent. In any such society, Christian or not, a separation of religion and state is, in Augustine's view, a sham. They cannot even be distinct, except in appearance. Though this is against what many regard as Augustine's view, his view is that it is in the nature of a civil society, however purportedly liberal, to require, or to tend to require, the total, the religious, allegiance of each citizen. Every city, in other words, tends toward one or the other of the ultimate cities.

He was, of course, aware that people sometimes theorized and proposed an entirely secular state, and at one point he vividly expounds that idea—but he does not take it seriously.

"Governors of provinces," they say, "are to be obeyed not as correctors of morals but as controllers of goods and resources and providers of pleasures. . . . The laws should be concerned with what harm one does to someone else's vines, not what harm one does to one's own life. One should not be brought before a judge except for damaging or threatening someone else's property, home, safety, or person against that person's will. But let each individual do what he likes with his own, in the company of his own, or with whomever he wishes, as long as it is with their consent."

Such people, he says, even recommend inventing a suitable religion to bolster up that system. This recommendation violates another of Augustine's axioms: that the transmission of truth by governmental authorities is of vital and unarguable importance (*CD* 2.20).[5] But also such people delude themselves, Augustine argues. They really are "the devotees of the gods whose imitators in crime and profligacy they rejoice to be"; they therefore are stupid to think that they can build a purely pragmatic state. They may think themselves the inventors of those gods, but actually they are disastrously worshipping them—gods that really, though covertly, exist. All civil society, therefore, even if it sees itself as secular, is ineradicably and primarily religious.

Here Augustine merely asserts that position. For its foundations one has to look in other areas of his thought. In the *Confessions*, describing how lust polluted his relationships when he was a juvenile delinquent, he cries, "Who was there at that time, to restrain my troubled life" (*Conf.* 2.2.3). The implicit suggestion is that it might have been appropriate for someone to. One's personal morals are not, therefore, merely one's own business. Moreover, his youthful lust was, without his realizing it, religious in its ultimate origin—an internal hunger for God, futilely directed outward; the mark of its spiritual genesis was that no extreme of profligate behavior, indeed no external action at all, even began to satisfy it (*Conf.* 3.1.1). Yet his waywardness was, he says, partly caused by the surrounding social mores: "Woe to you, river of human custom; who will resist you" he says, referring to salacious books commended to him as classics (*Conf.* 1.16.25; cf. 2.9.17). Irresistible metaphysical desires thus expressed themselves inadequately through lust further corrupted by social influence. And much of the first five books of the *City of God* is about that corrupting social milieu imposed by the religion originally imposed by the Roman state (e.g., *CD* 2.7–14, 2.19–29, 2.23, 3.6, 4.27, 4.30–32, 5.21).

But Augustine also implies a positive form of this doctrine. His idea that the impaired Roman goodness of the Roman state could

5. For the importance of public truth, see *CD* 4.27–29.

awake and throw off its pagan impairment has already been mentioned (*CD* 2.29). There is also, though one hesitates to mention it, the "mirror of princes" at the end of book 5—a passage that has been described as one of the work's shoddiest (*CD* 5.26).[6] The question is what relationship between the church and political society it implies. To praise the emperor, as Augustine does, for demolishing the pagan shrines might have been regarded as praise of cooperation between two independent social orders; but to praise him for his humiliating public self-abasement, insisted on by Ambrose, in penance for mass murder, is to praise him for recognizing the Church's moral authority on a matter of public policy.

Both passages are, however, early in the work (arguably, therefore, not Augustine's final verdict) and circumstantial in character. It might be argued that Theodosius's submissiveness, for example, was an act of purely personal piety, not a practical recognition that ecclesiastical authority subsumed the imperial institutionally. But much later in the work Augustine interprets biblical prophecy with the following statement about the Incarnation:

That people [the gentiles], whom Christ did not know by bodily presence, but who believed in Christ when he had been reported to them . . . are the City of God, having been added to the Israelites (the true ones, that is: Israelites not only by flesh but by faith). That City of God also gave birth to Christ himself physically, at a time when that City's existence was still only in those Israelites; for Mary was one of them, and it was from her that Christ took the flesh by which he became human. (*CD* 17.16)

The present believers in Christ on earth are the Church. That, materially, is what the word normally meant. They, living after the Incarnation, are substantially identified here with the "true Israelites" (the ancient children of Israel whose faith made them truly that). Those particular Israelites before Christ (actual people, of course) also were the City of God and not merely in the sense of symbolizing it, for the

6. P. Brown, *Religion*, 34.

passage is precisely about the very actualities that other biblical figures (Sion, Babylon) symbolize. And it was those Israelites that physically produced Christ. They emerge here, then, par excellence as the City of Christ. If the City of God in practice (rather than mere definition) is that society where those whose principle of unity is common agreement to make God the object of their love are placed in God's immediate presence, those Israelites were at that moment the City of God by the terms of Augustine's doctrine, and did not merely symbolize that City. The same, therefore, is true of the Church.

Moreover, the context of this passage implicitly extends that assertion to the Christian Roman Empire; for that empire, says Augustine, is a fulfilment of a biblical prophecy about the spread of God's worship to the gentiles in a psalm that also prophesies the Passion of Christ (Ps 21 [22].17, 19, 28–29 [16, 18, 27–28]; CD 17.17). Augustine does not idealize the Roman Empire here; he makes a religious claim about it: the Heavenly City is continuous not only with the Church (and even this is not visibly so) but also, in principle, even with political society—though as to the latter, in practice only fitfully and by conversion. An instance of the latter reach of this continuity has already been mentioned by Augustine: the prohibition, by law of the Christian empire, of marriage between cousins (CD 15.16). That prohibition, though entirely correct and divinely approved, was conveyed to us not, he says, through divine law in the strict sense, but through the Roman civil law of Christian times. What is especially important here is that Augustine presents this particular piece of legislation as the culmination of a development already precedented in the divine law strictly so called: at first there had existed so few people that brothers and sisters had had to marry each other; later, God's law had banned that practice (once such a ban had become possible) in order to create more kinds of human relationship—a fundamental good, for Augustine; that development in moral teaching has now been providentially extended, though long after biblical times, by the Christian Roman Empire. In this way the City of God has on occasion subsumed the practices of the polis. This is possible because there is essential continuity, though in this world never perfect identity, between any given state and the eschatological cities. Since God has by the Incarnation assumed historical actuality, political society, which is always religious anyway, can even be Incarnationally so: in other words, a given state can at least at times become practically an aspect of the Church, though (as with all human exercise of virtue in this world) not permanently or reliably. Thus a political society can occasionally tend to lose its distinction of identity from the Church. But in any case, that distinction itself is a result of the Fall (*CD* 15.1–5 and 8).

This thesis is sharply opposed by a number of other scholars. The important arguments against it will be discussed in connection with the first of the three large, final questions, to which we now come.

❧

If the City of God effectually reaches downward, and as a result the practices of political life can to an extent be turned upward so as to become an organ in the Divine City's actions, arguably some guidance on how to arrange society politically might not have been misplaced. (If Augustine's notion of that City had been exclusively otherworldly the matter would have been quite different.) The work baffles the searcher for such guidance. Book 3, for example, narrates at length how, over seven centuries, Rome changed from an inchoate dyarchy to a monarchy, then to an oligarchy, then to an unstable democracy, then to an informal dyarchy, then to a monarchy. In imposing monarchy Romulus usurped Remus's right to rule, says Augustine; yet the eventual overthrow of that monarchy was another presumptuous intrusion, this time a popular one, upon a ruler's power—this time the monarch's; he criticizes that revolution, however, for its undue haste, not for the fact that it was a revolution—the revolutionaries should have waited to see whether revolution was really necessary. He is sympathetic with Rome's first democratic revolutionaries, admitting the justice of their cause (to stop the wrongful possession by the rich of others' land) but deploring the bloodiness of the consequent events; he is contemptuous of the oligarchs who slaughtered those democrats; but then contemptuous of the later successful democratic revolutionaries who slaughtered the oligarchs —contemptuous of them as murderers, not as revolutionaries (*CD* 3.6, 15, 24, and 27); then he is equally contemptuous (on the same grounds) of the yet later oligarchs who slaughtered those later democrats. Points of justice are, of course, specified here, but there is no sense that any one of these forms of government has more justice intrinsic to it than any other.

The absence of an ideal constitution is understandable. One has to use political experience in making such a thing, and a philosopher who accepts that judges can have a duty to torture people—often (though incidentally) to death—in order not to kill them as a result of a miscarriage of justice, is not likely to think that any political constitution could be an image of justice (*CD* 19.6). Yet he shows some awareness that different aspects of justice come to the fore in different political milieux—that, for example, a republic can rise above catering to dynastic familial enmities (so Tarquinius Collatinus might have expected better than to be exiled merely for being named "Tarquinius"). Why, then, does Augustine's thought lack a reasoned account of the different forms of government that notes the different features of each as useful or obstructive in the quest for justice?

In book 19 of the *City of God* there is a celebrated discussion of plurality in political institutions (*CD* 19.17). The part of the Heavenly City that is on earth, says Augustine, is in temporary captivity to the earthly city. It therefore has to use and obey for its own purposes laws that the earthly city uses merely to attain earthly peace. Those laws vary considerably from one nation to another; but "that diversity," he says, "has one purpose: earthly peace." The diversity, then, is not innocent. It comes from the nations' having earthly peace as their exclusive purpose; and this is the mark of the earthly city, of evil in civil society. Here Augustine is referring philosophically to the point made historically by the whole preceding book: that states, though not parts of the earthly city by nature, have been, as it were, born into its service (as individual human beings, though not evil by nature, are born into original sin). But that diversity, says Augustine, evil though its origin is, does not deter the Heavenly City; for that City obeys whatever laws confront it except where this would endanger its relationship with God.

Yet if the diversity of institutions comes from the abnormality plaguing political life, this, if anything, exacerbates the problem of Augustine's abstention from guiding us as to political norms.

The most notable treatments of this problem tend to one or the other of two extremes. At one of these, Gustave Combès once argued that Augustine's constitutional indifference arose from his belief in a closed system of political causation: God will always simply provide a people with exactly the government it deserves. Worrying directly about methods of government is therefore pointless. Rulers are the spontaneous emanation of an entire civilization, says Combès. *Ils sont bons, si elle est bonne, mauvais, si elle est mauvaise.*[7]

Even taken in isolation, the text (from book 5 of the *City of God*) on which this idea is based does not have this simple meaning. Augustine says that even to such emperors as the unspeakable Nero, "the power to dominate is not given except according to the Providence of the highest God, when He judges human affairs worthy of such masters" (*CD* 5.19). To say that the condition of a people can be such that an evil emperor is suitable is not to say what Combès says; for Combès' statement in effect rules out other factors; Augustine's does not. And in Augustine the context of the statement in fact specifies other factors. Four chapters earlier he has ironically admitted that the great power and renown won by the Romans of the past was won under divine dispensation; God, he says, justly accorded them the booby prize of worldly glory, for which they gave so much. So in

7. Gustave Combès, *La doctrine politique de saint Augustin* (Paris: Plon, 1927), 85.

that passage it is the virtues, or rather quasi-virtues, of the rulers (in this case the Romans as a people) rather than the virtues or vices of the ruled (the non-Romans of the empire) that caused the rulers to rule. Then Augustine mentions another cause again: the historical spectacle, edifying to later generations if it is rightly understood, of Romans going to such heroic lengths for the sake of so little. And, humanly speaking, Augustine's position is that the allotment of political power in the world is determined not by the morality of the peoples ruled, but by the intensity of self-engagement in those who would rule—their degree of devotion, of allegiance to their cause (*CD* 5.15, 19.24). Thus a certain natural selection works in matters of political power: collective love, as we have seen, constitutes a civil society; intense collective love constitutes a powerful one.

Nevertheless, Combès is right to refer to divine providence in this connection. As these passages show, though states and empires are variable in form and personnel, Augustine certainly sees them as mysteriously guided by God's hand.

At the opposite extreme from Combès are R. A. Markus, J. Ratzinger, and H. A. Deane (all more recent writers). Markus argues that political institutions, far from being automatically generated from the ultimate loyalties of those ruled, are regarded by Augustine as a region of discretionary neutrality; the purpose of political institutions is only the establishment of a temporary, but quite necessary, earthly peace. They are therefore confined to a secular space between the two ultimate cities, neutral as to ultimate matters. Markus attributes this position to the *City of God* in particular, and above all to its later books.[8]

There are correct and important points in the argument leading to this conclusion. It is true that for Augustine any politically constituted society is, in both its rulers and its populace, an intermingling of individuals differing from one another in final loyalties, citizens of

8. Markus, 70–71.

one or the other ultimate city. As we have seen, however, such a society also as a unit moves variably in one or the other of the ultimate directions. In that way also it is completely run though by those ultimate loyalties. It can therefore be isolated from them only by abstraction. When it is, it is merely a potentiality, like free will. When, on the other hand, it actually exists, it is the opposite of an area of neutrality as to final loyalties; such neutrality cannot exist in it.

In this controversy much depends on how one interprets Augustine's discussion of plurality in worldly institutions, briefly mentioned already. That discussion conveys, as Markus says, Augustine's "most mature reflection on the secular components of human life" (CD 19.17).[9] For the purposes of the present study the first important question is whether, when Augustine says "the City of God uses the earthly city's peace," he is professing to define its political activity as such use or merely saying that its political activity entails such use. Markus assumes the former, but Augustine argues (in the most crucial passage concerned) not that the whole of political life is borrowed from the earthly city, but only that in this world there is no political life in which some tainted peace is not borrowed from the earthly city; for the Heavenly City's borrowing of the earthly city's peace is, he says, subject to "a proviso: that [such peace] does not impede the religion that teaches us the worship of the one, highest, true God," *si religionem qua unus summus et verus Deus colendus docetur non impedit.*

Furthermore, Augustine describes this borrowing not as a natural feature of human life but as a hard circumstantial fact that must be taken into account: this temporary accommodation between the two divergent cities is designed for the administration of those matters "that have been adapted to the sustaining of mortal life" *(quae sustentandae mortali vitae accommodata sunt)*. The perfect tense is crucial here: the earthly city has already established many procedures to pro-

---

9. Ibid., 71; cf. 101.

vide what is needful for mortality. It is not feasible to avoid making some use of them, for the City of God on earth is not now in a position to start from scratch—that point is long past. One finds oneself in the world as it is. And in saying that the City of God makes use of a given earthly peace Augustine implies not that all political life is independent of the Christian religion, but that the Christian religion is ultimately independent of worldly political life. It avails itself, but only as it sees fit, of the ready-made forms of such political life.

He moreover admits that such accommodation entails some compromise; when it comes to practical politics, he says, that city is in some sense a captive of the earthly one and uses the other's peace because it is "on foreign territory" *(peregrinans)*. But although this results in some temporary assimilation between the two cities, it is the Heavenly City that does the assimilating. Certainly this city often, as Augustine says, obeys the earthly city's laws, but its relationship with them is not passive, not a mere choice between obedience and disobedience. It is true, but not sufficient, to say, as H. A. Deane does, "only when their orders are contrary to the clear commands that God Himself has given to men must kings and rulers be refused obedience."[10] What Augustine says is that the City of God does not "tear down or destroy" the laws and institutions of the earthly city *(nihil eorum rescindens vel destruens)* if they do not impede true religion *(CD* 19.17). It is reasonable to conclude that if they do, it will. Though put in negative form, this is the language of intervention: the Divine City on earth does not make bold political reforms if it does not have to. Other passages, correctly understood, point to the same conclusion (e.g., *CD* 19.12).[11]

Here the problem of Augustine's abstention from guiding us as to the virtues and shortcomings of different forms of political institu-

10. Deane, 224.

11. On this, and for other passages, see Peter Burnell, "The Problem of Service to Unjust Regimes in Augustine's *City of God*," *Journal of the History of Ideas* 54 (1993): 177–88.

tion remains unsolved and more insistent. Some other arguments against the "Incarnational continuum," when analyzed, throw more light on the question. Deane denies the existence in Augustine's thought of that continuum at two of the connections: between the City of God and the Church, and between the City of God and the state.[12] Regarding the first his argument is that since Augustine includes in the City of God Jews who lived before the Church existed and excludes some, visibly members of the Church and born after the Incarnation, it is "absolutely impossible to identify the City of God . . . with the visible Christian Church in this world." The fallacy here is to define the institution exclusively by apparent membership. There could (to use a simile) be a hotel in two parts, one on land, the other a ship offering a proper hotel service, though less luxurious; it is under the same management and ferries people to the part on land. The temporary residents on the ship are as legitimately residents of the hotel as they will be when they have arrived at its safer, more luxurious section. If some criminals holding forged tickets are discovered, as they always are, that does not stop the ship from being part of the hotel. If it turns out that this ship has had a predecessor, now superannuated, and that in the past some people travelled to the luxurious part of the hotel on it, that does not stop the new ship from being part of the hotel. If one wished to recast the account purely in terms of people, one could speak of hotel residents, in transit and arrived, and distinguish them from impostors. That this simile gives a fair account of Augustine's position on this matter is clear from what has already been said.

The more difficult connection to describe, however, is the second, between the City of God and political society. Deane argues that a state's legal system "does not attempt to change the basic desires and attitudes of the men whose conduct it seeks to regulate." Positive arguments against this have already been given: the ultimately moral

12. Deane, 24 and 140, respectively.

and spiritual character of the Roman civil ban on consobrinal marriage, for example. It should be added that Augustine's decisive reason for recommending state persecution of the Donatists was that he had already seen many become sincere Catholics as a result (e.g., *Ep.* 93.5.17).

One passage cited by Deane, however, illustrates a point far beyond the immediate purpose for which it is cited. In the *Exposition of Certain Propositions from the Epistle to the Romans* Augustine explains the text "Let every soul be subject to the powers higher than itself; for all power is from God" to mean

regarding that part of us that has to do with this life, be subject to the powers: that is, to the human beings administering affairs "in some official capacity" [*cum aliquo honore*] . . . but not be subject to anyone "desiring specifically to subvert in us what God has seen fit to give us with a view to eternal life" [*idipsum in nobis evertere cupienti quod Deus ad vitam aeternam donare dignatus est*]. (*Exp. quar. prop. ex ep. Rom.* on Rom 13.1)

So, he concludes, one must pay one's taxes. Although this distinguishes between two levels, at both of which human life must be lived, it does not follow that even when the state demands obedience only at the level within its competence—that of this world's affairs—the obedience concerned could possibly be without effect on people's basic desires and attitudes. More important, the passage says not that political authority stops short of spiritually great matters, but that it stops short of them when the powers that be are gravely disordered—when they desire our spiritual destruction. It is also of particular importance in this passage that one must avoid treating as matters of stark principle matters that are not; for there are areas of legitimate human discretion, of prudence. Augustine is no liberal in respect of these, for he regards them as necessarily trammelled by rightful authority. They, or the ones he bothers to mention, are the purview of the individuals invested with political power. Hence, even something gravely important, if it is a matter of prudence as opposed to stark principle, falls, in principle, within the realm of politically constituted society.

But more light again is cast on this same matter in a passage cited by Ratzinger, who rightly points out that at one point in the *Tractates on St. John's Gospel* Augustine sharply distinguishes between divine law and imperial law. The Donatists (one of whose bishops he is addressing) must decide to which authority they wish to protest against the confiscation of some of their property. He poses a dilemma: they had held it, but now have lost it, by human law *(iure humano)*. By sheer divine law, on the other hand, it belongs to everyone in common. And in one of the *Elucidations on the Psalms,* says Ratzinger (again rightly), Augustine talks of a citizen of the kingdom of heaven engaging, in this world, in political administration: "He wears the purple, he is a magistrate, he is an aedile, a proconsul, an emperor, *he administers an earthly state [rem publicam gerit terrenam]" (Tr. in Ioh. Ev.* 6.25–26; *En. in Ps.* 51 [52].2).[13] Such passages, argues Ratzinger, show the state, including the Christian state, to be the *civitas terrena,* and that "in practice the entire doctrine of the two cities must be applied to the doctrine of the two laws" *(die ganze Zweistaatenlehre muß praktisch auf die Lehre von den zwei Rechten angewendet werden).*

Here the crucial issue is Ratzinger's claim that in Augustine's view a particular state is always, in practice, a particular instance of the earthly city, never of the Heavenly. But even allowing for the nuance "in practice," Augustine's position is more subtle than this. In the second passage he compares the Christian politician with Esther in Scripture; such a comparison with a servant of God exerting power in a pagan political world is with someone who in the process considerably changed and converted the pagan king's court. And Augustine's point in the first passage is again to insist on the distinction between simple principle and the rightful exercise of prudence. The Donatists have confused the two by claiming that their former possession was somehow by unchangeable right. They are mistaken, says Augustine: it was by human law. Again, however, this argument

13. Ratzinger, 313–14.

implies not excision of divine principle but discretionary application of it; for God's will, he argues, working through the emperors, was not that such a piece of property should be "held in possession by heretics."

Augustine's doctrine of political prudence becomes clearer again if we turn, for the third time, to Augustine's locus classicus on the use of the earthly peace, from book 19 of the *City of God* (*CD* 19.17). Although the Heavenly City uses the temporary peace of the earthly city, it refers it, says Augustine, to the heavenly peace. This implies that the religious goes beyond religion specifically: moral actions performed in an earthly civil context, indeed in the context of the earthly city itself, are placed on the same altar as what is more obviously religious. Augustine confirms this (in the last words of the chapter): the Heavenly City "refers to the attainment of that [heavenly] peace whatever good it does toward God and one's neighbor, because the life of a civil society is undoubtedly a social one" *(ad illam pacem adipiscendam refert quidquid bonarum actionum gerit erga Deum et proximum, quoniam vita civitatis utique socialis est)*. Hence, this prudential, constantly provisional activity is also a moral and even religious one. It can involve changing the political structure of society, as we have seen; but the terms on which that is so are elsewhere put implicitly but precisely by Augustine. He metaphorically refers to Virgil's monster, Cacus, as a city whose starving populace is rising up in desperation. For the metaphor to work, the revolution concerned must be a necessary one because Augustine's point is that without radically urgent action, Cacus would die (*CD* 19.12). Much earlier in the work Augustine has pointed out, as we saw earlier, that the founders of the Roman republic had leaped too hastily into revolution, not giving the king a chance to deal justly with the rape of Lucretia (*CD* 3.15). What made that particular revolution wrong, then, is that it might well not have been necessary. These passages imply two things: that having the right political structure is very important (even morally so), and that what is the right one varies circumstantially. The diversity of political institutions is not necessarily, therefore, a direct symptom of evil, but can also be a necessary diversity in ways of dealing with it.

Though this provides an answer (not, as we shall see, a fully adequate one) to our first large question (Why does Augustine in the *City of God* refrain from comparative evaluation of the different forms of political government?), it implicitly raises the second (How can politically constituted society be in its nature religious and morally reformable given the power that sin and brute practicality have always exercised over it?). Government in the practical order is always deeply influenced by evil; for according to Augustine political society, though ontologically senior to the family, originated after the Fall, and so, unlike the family, was from its inception conditioned by sin (*CD* 15.8). Since, as we have seen, Augustine accepts that evils commonly must be dealt with by evils, does he give a footing in his moral theology to what is by his own lights morally offensive?

John Milbank's recent statement of this criticism overtakes earlier ones and will be discussed here as representative.[14] He makes three arguments (the last of which is much the most important). First, comparing two of Augustine's letters, Milbank perceives a certain tension on the subject of punishment. In one (to Count Marcellinus) Augustine strongly argues against capital punishment or extreme torture (countenancing only the more schoolmasterly forms of torture and admitting that even these are undesirable in themselves) (*Ep.* 133). In the other (to Emeritus, written about seven years earlier) he regrets that some Catholic judges and governors have gone too far in their punishments of Donatists; but his regret is not going to stop him, he says, from recommending coercion (*Ep.* 87.8). Milbank argues that Augustine strays into moral ambiguity here, in effect approving what he knows, by his own admission, to be in some cases excessive. This criticism confuses ends with means: the recommendations to Marcellinus directly concern penal and investigative means; in the let-

14. Milbank, 417–20; R. Williams, *Politics*, 65–66.

ter to Emeritus he asserts the Pauline principle that the politically constituted powers have the purpose and duty of maintaining order. He does not say that in dealing with Donatists that end justifies means that are in themselves unjust, for he does not regard civil coercion in general as unjust, and he insists only on the continuance of that. He recommends, for coercion of the Donatists, the use of proper, moderate means. He does not, explicitly, implicitly, or tacitly, also recommend the use of means beyond these. A pharmacist who unambiguously recommends a particular dosage of a drug and knows from experience that some irresponsible patients will exceed it is not being ambiguous. One might think that he should try further methods of security or persuasion, but that is a different point.

Augustine comes closest to falling under Milbank's stricture when he shows some sympathy for a judge who, trying to do his duty, occasionally tortures people to death (*CD* 19.16). This patently goes beyond the limit he sets in his letter to Marcellinus and incidentally raises the question: What is one to do when mild punishment has not worked? Augustine's point (that such experience well illustrates the human condition) confirms that the judge is typical rather than hypothetical. Yet in the end Augustine is not ambiguous on the moral point. Though he does not explicitly condemn the actions of such a judge, he ironically says that the sort of person who does not classify them as sins is "our philosopher," a stereotype of a pagan luminary that has been the butt of his sarcasm earlier in the chapter. (The further question—extremely serious in its metaphysical implications—of whether such admitted immorality is nevertheless unavoidable, even by Christian judges, is beyond our present concern, but will be discussed in a later part of this study.)

Milbank's second criticism is based on Augustine's conviction that rule is for the benefit of the ruled; *imperant qui consulunt*, he says in the *City of God* (*CD* 19.14):[15] those who give orders have the right to do so insofar as they do so in the interests of those to whom they

15. Milbank, 419.

give them. From this, Milbank says, follows the paradoxical conclusion "that the good ruler must reduce the scope of the political precisely insofar as he is a good ruler," which leads to "virtually unsolvable dilemmas." This is true if what is meant is that a good ruler will not be motivated by the lust to dominate *(dominandi cupiditas, libido dominandi)* but that political rule tends very strongly to induce that motive. That, of course, would not mean that Augustine adulterates his governmental principles with the morally offensive. But if what is meant is that the better a Christian ruler is, the less he will exercise political power, *simpliciter*, so that he will tend to cease exercising governmental power altogether, Augustine neither states nor implies such a thing. The principle "rulers are those who consult the interests of the ruled" *(imperant qui consulunt)* concerns ends. It does not follow that such ends could be attained only by infinitesimally slight political action.

Milbank's third and most serious criticism is that by accepting even the moderate use of investigative or punitive torture Augustine breaks the continuity between the City of God and the practical political order; for in punitive torture, for example, there is no connection, intrinsic to the punishment, between the pain inflicted and the lesson intended. This creates an inconsistency, Milbank argues, "because in any coercion, however mild and benignly motivated, there is still present a moment of 'pure' violence, externally and arbitrarily related to the end one has in mind"; there is an "ontological" breach, then, between means and ends.

One must, however, take into account that actions have, as essential to their reality, manifold contexts, traditions of cultural understanding, conditioning circumstances, known and accepted purposes. When a schoolmaster inflicts physical punishment (in societies where that is permitted), the pupils, the schoolmaster, and the parents normally are all aware of the contextually ordered significance of the action. The matter would be different if a child who knew nothing of schools were suddenly put in one, immediately caned for not studying, and then informed of the purpose of that punishment. Then the caning certainly would be close to being a "moment of 'pure' violence."

Nevertheless, if the means and the ends of governmental coercion were, in Augustine's thinking, related to each other arbitrarily except in respect of external conditions, Milbank's criticism would still in the main be correct. Since the choice of coercive methods would not be limited by considerations attaching intrinsically to their purposes, the enlivening influence of Incarnational grace would then touch only the ends of government, not its means.

In one of the texts cited by Milbank (Epistle 133, mentioned earlier) Augustine not only begs Marcellinus to be restrained in punishing some violent Donatists; he indicates precisely the requisite relationship between mildness and severity in a ruler (*Ep.* 133.2). He allows a limited harshness to be used very frequently, even by judges with mild intentions, in order, first, for the details of the crime to be ascertained, and then for gentleness to be possible: *ut manifestato scelere sit ubi appareat mansuetudo.* This does not offer license as to the choice of paths by which to arrive at the goal of gentleness. As the context shows, savage punishment is not at all in the spirit of such mercifully intended investigation. It is because Marcellinus's zeal must be fatherly and diagnostic in intent that the infliction of extreme pain is forbidden (there must, for example, be no torture with fire). This implies that, whatever a perpetrator of savage torture might claim, such torture could not, in reality, but be motivated by the lust of punishment *(libido ulciscendi).* It is of the essence of this argument that for a ruler limited ranges of means are intrinsically commensurable with given ends. Given the horrible things that were often done, this principle transcends and bisects the conventions, circumstances, and practices of Augustine's time. Even extending, then, into the harsh life of the polis, morality is, for Augustine, of a piece.

The general effect of this is to imply that certain kinds of action are intrinsically brutal, uncivil. Like Agamemnon in Aeschylus's trag-

edy, a ruler may decide to perform an act beyond the canons of decency, even think that somehow he is doing the right thing; but because it really is an abomination, its disorder reaches past his ignorance, which anyway in such a case can only be partial ignorance,
and corrupts and destroys him nevertheless. Not only the motives,
then, but also the practices of government must be put in the transformative power of divine grace. For the middle-aged Augustine,
then, the norms of practical morality, in particular political morality,
remain an important tertium quid between the first principle of justice (devotion to God above all) and matters of pragmatic immediacy.

Behind Milbank's criticisms, however, is the larger problem of the
domination of one human being by another. Coercion is so ingrained
in governmental practice that one must ask whether the "giving and
obeying of commands between citizens" should be understood to
imply domination of citizen by citizen; and what, in any case, the basis of authority is for one human being to give orders to another.
Moreover, since both questions must, given Augustine's formulations, apply to family life as well as to civil, the relationship between
those two forms of society must be taken into account (see CD 19.16).

For Augustine all domination (any degree of enslavement) of one
human being by another is unnatural: at the Creation God did not in-
tend rational beings to dominate any but irrational (CD 19.15). The
fact that in the world as we know it human beings dominate each
other is a result of sin, not of nature. God, Augustine argues, guided
early human history so as to point this out: the earliest just human
beings dominated sheep, not people, for as yet there were no kings.
This implies neither that a complex, civil society is unnatural nor that
it is essentially coercive, but that the domination of human beings by
human beings is, though unnatural, so inherent in political practice
as to be characteristic of it. Similarly, such domination also characterizes the power of a paterfamilias over his wife; yet there Augustine
is quite clear that the institution of the family is natural (e.g., GL
11.37.50).

A suitable approach to the problem, as Markus points out, is to bring to bear on this context the distinction between natural and voluntary providence, which Augustine makes in two passages of the *Literal Commentary on Genesis* (GL 8.9.17, 8.23.44). In general, but only in general, the distinction is the same in both passages: between providence as a less immediate, and providence as a more immediate manifestation of the divine thought that guides the universe. Specifically, however, the two passages make quite different distinctions, referring to quite different levels of reality. In the earlier of the two passages he says that natural providence is that by which God causes the stars to shine, the waters to flow, and plants and animals to live and die; voluntary providence operates in the work of angels and in the human activities that are uniquely human, such as the administration of societies, the practice of arts and technology, and the rational provision of life's necessities, such as clothing. In the other passage, fourteen chapters later, he distinguishes quite differently: originally providence gives each being its natural place in respect of other beings— for example, subordinating the irrational to the rational, female to male, weaker to stronger, poorer to richer. Persons, however, it finally orders in quite another fashion: on volitional principles, placing the morally good over the morally evil, though under God.

If the two passages were read as being on the same plane, one would conclude that this is a single distinction that cuts between political and familial subordination, the "administration of societies" being voluntary, not natural (in the first passage), and the subjection of female to male being natural, not voluntary (in the second). That, however, is not so. Only the second passage is directly concerned with the principles of subordination. Moreover, the first passage is concerned with events, involuntary and voluntary, in this world in accordance with the order of creation; the second is concerned with the distinction between this world and eternity (between the temporal and the eternal modes of divine providence). What is part of voluntary providence according to one of these definitions is not necessarily part of voluntary providence according to the other. For example, all the providential events (both the natural and the voluntary) of the first passage would be restricted to natural providence if one applied the criterion of the second, since they are temporal. Hence affairs of state, although they are part of voluntary providence in the first passage, are (implicitly) part of natural providence in the second. (Furthermore, it is not clear on what side the family falls in the first passage, and the second does not help us on that point.) Moreover, the second distinction is between what is morally mixed (the natural here embracing all the subjection of some beings to others that happens in this world) and what is not (the eternally definitive). Thus it classifies some morally distorted subordinations, such as that of poorer to richer, as natural. They are natural not in the sense of being unperverted, but in the sense of not applying in eternity; whereas all the activities, both the natural and the voluntary, listed in the course of the first distinction could be classified as natural, in the sense of being referred to simply as they are by nature rather than in a fashion that includes distortion: the universe of discourse there is concerned solely with things as they are intrinsically. Hence, although Augustine classifies political authority as voluntary in the first distinction and the subjection of female to male as natural in the second, it does not at all follow that they are simply distinguished from each other as voluntary and natural, respectively.

Taken by themselves, then, these passages do not resolve the problem of coercion. In particular, in the second distinction Augustine points out a natural (that is, temporal) principle of subjection in the structure of the family, but none regarding political authority. But as has already been indicated, in the *City of God* he specifies precisely such a principle: that those whose ardor in public life is very intense are likely to rule over those whose ardor is less so (*CD* 5.15). This comes under voluntary providence by the first of Augustine's two distinctions in the *Literal Commentary* and under natural by the second, where it must be regarded as an instance of the subjection of weaker to stronger.

The matter of subjection is clarified by another passage from the same work (*GL* 11.37.50): though "your husband will dominate you" was a curse on the first woman, she was, says Augustine, even originally (before sin) made to be under his domination, but not such domination as has come to operate in families in this fallen world. Because of sin, woman's subordination has come to be a form of enslavement rather than a subordination according to affection—*dilectio*. On the other hand, in the "servitude of charity" mentioned by St. Paul there is no domination at all, even of the original, prelapsarian sort, this servitude being reciprocal. Under sin's effect, the originally nonenslaving domination of woman by man is replayed in this world without *dilectio* (replayed in the minor key, so to speak) as a real domination. (And if this were domination of man by woman, it would, says Augustine, be even worse.) At the other extreme, as a result of charity even the original, provisional, nonenslaving domination of woman by man, built into our first nature, has been resolved (though as yet partially). The servitude of which it was the counterpart has become reciprocal and so has ceased to entail even the provisionally natural subordination of woman to man. That subordination before it was corrupted had as its guiding principle not fully developed charity, but love in a less mature degree, an undistorted *dilectio*.

But in the *City of God,* as we have seen, *dilectio* is also the constitutive principle of civil society. The difference is that whereas any civil society is necessarily constituted by such love (possibly in a distorted form) on the part of its citizens, such love operates in a household only insofar as the motives of the people in it have not been distorted. The *dilectio* is not the single, constitutive principle of the household. First, therefore, the family can exist (albeit in a rather brutish form) without agreement in its members as to what they love. Civil society cannot. Second, the family attains some degree of appropriately human form only by its members' having the motive that is the very principle of civil society. In that way civil society provides the household with its rules (*CD* 19.16). It is in the nature of the family to point upward to the relationship whose essence (no longer merely manner) is its members' love.

In both degrees of human society, therefore, there are original principles of subordination (provisional in their initial forms), which sin has perverted into real domination. Coercion, though intrinsically not part of those principles, has as a result become necessary. This inevitable distortion in human social behavior requires and receives some counteraction by divine grace. Coercion, though unnatural, can as a result be exercised with a measure of justice. Only ultimately will civil society be transfigured, subsuming the family. Thus coercion of human beings by other human beings in the first instance is partly mitigated, then ultimately is brought to an end, in both instances by divine action.

This leads to the third and last of our main questions. Given the continuity operating downward, to what extent, if any, does citizenship, having been exerted in the practical order, survive the translation upward? Would we, in Augustine's view, if we were to attain heaven, still recognize ourselves there as citizens? To deny this (to regard Augustine's notion of heavenly citizenship as, for example, a metaphorical rather than analogical notion) would again be to deny that this theology has a fully Incarnational character—atonement would have failed to reclaim something whose place in human nature is absolutely fundamental.

Arendt starkly makes that denial. One of her main conclusions is that although on earth one should love one's neighbor, albeit only in certain oblique ways, one does not do so at all in heaven. "When Augustine frequently quotes Paul's words that love never fails, he means solely the love of God, or Christ, for which all human neighbourly love can only provide the impetus, and which we are commanded to have only to provide this impetus."[16] It has already been argued here that that is not an adequate account of Augustine's notion of charity. But what bearing would such an account have on his notion of society? Put in a more Augustinian manner, it would say that the human love of God, which in this world is a basis of social agreement and

16. Arendt, 111.

the principle of a civil society, survives in heaven, but in a form no longer humanly social. This opinion is expressed in the last two pages of Arendt's book, though no references to anything written by Augustine are given there in support of it.

One would not suppose that what is distorted by sin or specifically sinful (for example, judicial torture) would survive in the Heavenly City. What would remain? The characteristics of citizenship, either specified or implied by Augustine to be good, are its provision of the maximum range of relationships, that it is both large and subordinative, its basis in agreement as to what is loved, the decisive importance of the intensity with which that love is exercised, the origin of its cohesion in the justice of that love, the ultimately religious nature of that justice, its connection with the divine Incarnation, its vital interest in exercising correct human understanding, and the basis of its hierarchy in a selfless concern of citizens for each other.

Augustine's intellectually constructed description of heaven in the last two chapters of the *City of God* is of a social human condition (*CD* 22.29–30). Those in heaven will contemplate God but will do so as a socially organized multitude. Exactly how they will see God is a matter on which Augustine speculates, but he does not doubt that with their physical eyes they will see God Incarnate. There will be no circumstantial limits to the intensity with which their minds will be set on fire by gazing at God's glory; this will be an entirely accurate contemplation of reality, and included in it will be correct praise by human beings of each other's merits. Augustine speculates (and it seems to him most likely) that the blessed will see God by seeing the inward reality of each others' souls—that is, the love that other souls have for God (for now these will be perfectly open to view—the obverse of a judge's tragic ignorance in this world). As they will see God perfectly, but indirectly, by seeing the qualities of each other's souls, so they will observe this spiritual reality by physical means, for with their eyes they will see the qualities of souls expressed physically. Their rational minds will be caused to flare up into divine praise (in which, of course, they will be entirely agreed as to their object of love) by virtue of their delight in a physical beauty in others that appeals to the reason. The souls, thus contemplated, will vary in quality: they will have been set on fire by God's glory, and the souls will be related to each other in accordance with that variety. There will, therefore, be a great multifariousness of relationships which, moreover, will be hierarchical: there will be degrees of merit, though no envy (the lesser will selflessly rejoice, for example, in the greatness of the superior). There will therefore be perfect distributive justice. Thus the lower souls, though all happily stationed in their places, will see God more intensely loved in their superiors.

This doctrine implies a notion of leadership in eternal contemplation, by which the saints, in greater and lesser degrees of exaltation, demonstrate the divine mercy in their respective ways. Augustine describes this system of subordination not as a simple result of past evils but as a good in itself: alluding to St. Paul he says that the finger does not wish to be the eye; thus the subordination was always providentially intended—an essential part of the heavenly multifariousness. In that rightfully subordinative world there will be no possibility of injustice, of someone's losing their proper place or usurping another's, for throughout the hierarchy there will be a human partaking in the divine nature, entailing the impossibility of wrong. In the terms earlier established by Augustine, this is in all but evil a description of a civil society.

The two conclusions most important for our argument have been: that between civil life lived in heaven and civil life lived on earth there is a continuum unbreakable intrinsically but usually tenuous in practice (the decent and even the reprobate cities of this world—even the earthly city itself—receive from the heavenly the goodness that gives them their existence); and that any given civil society exists and has its place in that continuity as a result of its share in the divine compassion, which is the goodness specific to its being a human society. In the final analysis, then, the *dilectio* that constitutes the City of God, and in some degree of privation any city, is this compassion.

The latter conclusion, however, has not yet emerged here with the force and emphasis we might expect given that we have seen it to be correct. A more specific discussion is therefore needed on this point, and will form a coda to the present chapter.

Twice in the *City of God,* in books 5 and 19, Augustine specifies the different figurations of the love that constitutes a civil society. In book 5 he already assumes that the basis of a civil society is a love exercised by its citizens (though this is fourteen books before he clearly states his reasons for thinking so). The Romans, he says, gained world domination not by fate but because God brought a certain order to their (admittedly impure) motives (*CD* 5.1, 5.8–11). Augustine points to numerous such motives (love of liberty, of wealth, of praise, of the prosperity of one's fellow citizens) as having variously operated in Roman history (*CD* 5.12–18); then he classifies all the possible motives into three fundamental desires purporting to cover all civil motivation from its lowest to its highest forms (*CD* 5.19): desire to dominate others regardless of what people think; indiscriminate desire for human praise; and true virtue, which he describes as a cluster of closely related desires: for the eternal salvation of others, for deserved praise from others (not as an end in itself but with a view to the benefit of those praising), and for wielding civil power so that both those one rules—especially one's hostile subjects—and oneself may be brought to give due praise to God (again for the benefit of those praising). Here the motives comprised in the two inferior, impure forms of desire are also comprised in the highest, but unadulterated: the desire for power survives, but on this highest level its purpose is pointed away from its wielder toward the good of others, with a particular attention to the good of the hostile and alienated. What is missing is ephemeral self-aggrandizement, which merely makes an essentially social desire self-concentrated.

Similarly, the desire to be praised has a place in true civil virtue: Augustine admires the statesman immune to the vanities of public glory, but he does not admire what might have seemed inferable: a lonely and inconversible self-integrity, callousness to public opinion, insensibility to any view of oneself except what one supposes to be God's. Allowing that such a posture might have some virtue (that of not letting human respect keep one from God's good graces), Augustine nevertheless withholds full approval, and for a highly specific reason: a person trying to be orientated to God in such an isolated and idealistic way would indeed at some stage be presented by God with the chance for profound and comprehensive virtue, but only by being confronted with the source of all virtue, the Spirit of God; but this is the Spirit of love of enemies, the source for the human motive of mercy; realizing that one was under these auspices, one could no longer avoid having a merciful concern for what others thought: for in our present world, marred and racked by enmities, some people can repent, others be confirmed in goodness, by admiring decent people ruling over them; those so admired therefore have a very grave duty to make sure the admiration is justified—Augustine does not consider deception to be an act of mercy. This is why a certain love of praise is essential to the highest form of civil desire (cf. the much later *Ep.* 231.4). So, in practice, rulers who have complete contempt for human praise are tyrants. Such contempt is the perversion of immunity to vainglory, as vainglory itself is the perversion of an essentially merciful desire for public recognition. Because of the very structure of reality, then, the only way to achieve a decent immunity to vainglory is to exercise power and to court public opinion with the superhuman motive of divine mercy, of which the lower, improper desires of public life are merely the perversions.

This conclusion he illustrates with a series of examples from Roman history, ending with the notorious eulogy of Theodosius seven chapters later (*CD* 5.26); but that eulogy itself ends not (in the fashion so far followed) with yet another case of trite imperial benevolence, but with an account of that emperor's public, repentant self-prostration and the weeping it caused in the Thessalonians whom he had harshly ravaged after promising mercy. Thus the main conclusion of book 5 is that compassion—finally transposed as repentance for having practically violated it and as the consequent inspiring of it in others, even enemies—is the culminating civil virtue.

The work's other essay at specifying civil morality is book 19, where, as we have seen, the issue is set forth in terms of peace, the composedness of orderly relationships. Near the end of that book, in chapter 26, Augustine sets aside the morally distorted forms of civil peace, which have much concerned him up to now, and begins a summation of its proper forms: first, decent political practicality; even God's citizens on their earthly pilgrimage must pray for their worldly masters for the sake of earthly peace—their prototype being the captive Jews enjoined by Jeremiah to pray for Babylon because their earthly peace depended on it (Jer 29.7). Second, he distinguishes from that peace one peculiar to God's citizens, not shared with citizens of this world as the other is, and extending beyond the political; this is not yet "joyful blessedness," for in common with all peace in our present world it is experienced as consolation for our wretchedness *(miseria),* but it has its uniqueness nevertheless: the practical justice constituting it consists ultimately in the forgiveness of sins rather than in the other forms of decent behavior also required for it *(CD* 19.27). That, says Augustine, is why the prayer of God's City on earth is "Release us from our debts as we release those in debt to us"; but what makes that prayer efficacious is not its recitation but the practice of what it says, for "faith not practiced is dead," and "faith is put into practice through charity [*per dilectionem*]" (Jas 2.17; Gal 5.6). In this passage, then, what is meant by "the practice of faith" is the human exercise of divine mercy; in this world God's citizens characteristically experience their common *dilectio* as the impulse to forgive enemies, which, in this context, is an instance of bringing God's mercy to bear on others in the same condition of earthly *miseria* as oneself.

This notion of the highest duty of citizenship is presented as an advance on Jeremiah's injunction: there temporal peace, which can only be a modicum of peace, was sought, albeit justly; here, eternal peace. This distinction, however, is not in kind. As he has pointed out in chapter 26, the reason why worldly people will not have earthly peace forever is that they do not use it properly in this present life. We may conclude that God's citizens will have earthly peace forever in the sense that they will have heavenly peace: earthly peace is an inferior mode of heavenly. As we have just seen, he then points out what the employment of earthly peace for its rightful heavenly purpose is: the exercise of compassion in the corrupting and alienating conditions of this world; for although eternal peace is intrinsically perfect, one partakes in it only imperfectly on earth (hence the need for forgiveness on all sides and the futility of expecting to find this peace in ancillary forms of virtue). In the *pax finalis,* says Augustine, one will no longer meet anything offensive either in others or in oneself. That peace, then, is the mercy formerly practiced, now brought to fruition. So the conclusion of book 19 is that conferring on one's fellow sufferers a merciful forgiveness (whether prepared for, exercised, or fulfilled) is in the final analysis what constitutes the peace of civilization.

CHAPTER 6

HUMAN NATURE AND PERSON

———————

What, in sum, is Augustine's notion of humanity? More specifically, what does he think it means to say that human beings are made in God's image? In what sense does he think that human beings are ultimately deified? (In both patristic thought and modern scholarship on it, these are treated as aspects of one question and will be so treated here.)

Although the main purpose of this chapter is to draw positive conclusions, it will again be instructive to consider some modern criticisms. Louis Dupré has said that for the Greek Fathers redemption consists in the deification of a human being through "intrinsic participation of the image within its divine archetype"; for Augustine it is merely the extrinsic representation of that archetype by its human image.[1] Similarly, Vladimir Lossky has argued that Augustine's soteriology is characterized by a certain "static 'exemplarism'" (we are copies of God, further assimilable to the Original by divinely dispensed virtue), but that the soteriology of Greek Christianity has a "dynamic character" that excludes all such external notions of the relationship between the natural image and its supernatural archetype.[2] These contrasts use a version of the Alexandrian distinction between image and likeness (image the sempiternal, originally pre-creational, archetypal form of a human being in the thought of God; likeness

———————

1. Dupré, 32–33.

2. Lossky, 57, 130. Cf. Philip Sherrard, *The Greek East and the Latin West: A Study in the Christian Tradition* (London: Oxford University Press, 1959), 143–44.

the degree of similarity between a human being and God), and assert in effect that Augustine concerned himself with mere likeness, allowing it to condition and even to determine his notion of image, whereas for the Greek Fathers the notion of image, as independent of likeness, predominates. And although a number of studies in recent decades have demonstrated that Augustine conceives of salvation as deification, the idea has persisted that this is deification only in a limited, improper sense—not free participation, but some kind of programmed imitation, of God.[3]

One can readily find texts to support these assertions if one compares Augustine with the more extreme Neoplatonists among the Greek Fathers. According to Gregory of Nyssa, for example, the image of God in each of us has been hidden under dirt but not itself diminished; wash the dirt off by a virtuous life and the image will once more be visible; and such a divine radiance of soul is within our reach.[4] This notion implies that the most important part of a human being, one's spiritual core, is, like Plotinus's undescended soul, completely unfallen, even incapable of falling—that at the middle point of intelligible reality there is an unbreakable conjunction between the human soul and God. For Augustine, the divine beauty in us has been largely (of course not completely) lost, and Christ has restored it to us on the Cross by giving up His innate beauty in order to take upon Himself our lack of beauty (*Serm.* 27.6). He has removed from us our dissimilarity to God (*De Trin.* 4.2.4); still, we are so extensively damaged that the similarity is not quite restored as long as we are in this world (*De perf. iust.* 11.28). In Gregory's formulation, then, the vast core of a human being has remained ineradicably connected with

3. For Augustine on deification, see Gerhart B. Ladner, *The Idea of Reform: Its Impact on Christian Thought and Action in the Age of the Fathers* (Cambridge, Mass.: Harvard University Press, 1959); Gerald Bonner, "Augustine's Conception of Deification," *Journal of Theological Studies* n.s. 37 (1986); V. Capánaga, "La deificación en la soteriología agustiniana," in *Augustinus magister,* vol. 2, *Etudes augustiniennes* (Paris, 1954), pp. 745–754 (cited by Bonner).

4. Gregory of Nyssa, *Sermon on the Beatitudes,* 6.

God, inviolate, requiring merely to be uncovered; in Augustine's, no such notion is clear. If one seeks exactly that form of Neoplatonism in Augustine's mature theology, one does not find it.

From this, however, it follows not that Augustine's idea of divine image and human deification is extrinsic (a matter of sheer assimilation to a divine exemplar), but only that it is not intrinsic in exactly Gregory's sense. Furthermore, as we have already noticed, the complexity of Augustine's thought on this subject greatly exceeds the summary just given. In particular, for Augustine a human being is the image of God both by nature and by being a person (the determination of a rational nature by the relationship between one being with another of the same, rational nature); each of these approaches has different consequences. We must consider them separately. (In both, though in different ways, Augustine is concerned with the eternal significance of our present condition.) Thus our main questions are: How does he conceive human nature to be made and reclaimed in God's image? Then: how does he conceive the human person to be so made and reclaimed? There are two subsidiary questions: Does Augustine think of deification as the eventual dissolution of the human personality in the divine? And what does he consider to be the relationship, in this world, between Christ's human experience and everyone else's?

❧

On the subject of human nature, this is the place to review the Augustinian definitions of humanity either implied already in this study or more or less closely associated with what has been said here. It will be noticed that although these definitions are compatible with one another, none by itself is perfectly comprehensive, different definitions being suited to different anthropological or theological problems.

Augustine himself, near the end of *De Trinitate,* provides us with a good starting point for such a review. His main concern in that work is with the image of God as delineated in a human being personally;

but at one point in the final book he briefly discusses how that image is delineated in human nature (*De Trin.* 15.8.14). Having mentioned some relevant Pauline texts, he says that the meaning of the statement "Now we see through a glass darkly" (1 Cor 13.12) is that our only way of seeing God, at any rate as long as we are in this world, is by means of the reflection of God that human nature provides. That we are this reflection, Augustine argues, implies that we are ultimately God's glory, the image and the glory of God being ultimately the same thing. So we are primitively the image of God from the start but are also transformed into it.[5] Thus, having considered the possibility of a distinction between image and likeness, he in the end denies that there is a distinction in kind on this basis.

[We are] being transformed (as the Apostle puts it), changed from one form to another, moving from being an obscure form to being a lucid one; for even the obscure form is God's image, and if His image, then undoubtedly His glory, in which human beings have been created in superiority to other animals. The crucial point is that [*quippe*] when it was said "the man should not cover his head, because he is the image and glory of God," it was said about human nature itself. But this nature, already the most excellent of created beings, when its Creator changes it from wicked into virtuous is changed from a deformed form into a beautifully formed one. Again it is crucial to note that [*quippe*] even in wickedness itself [*et in ipsa impietate*], the more damnable the vice, the more certainly illustrious the nature; and this is why [*et propter hoc*] he has added "from glory into glory": from the glory of its creation into the glory of its being made fully virtuous [*iustificationis*].

As its context shows, this passage qualifies the notion that our sinfulness causes God's transformative intervention with the notion that our nature also causes it. There are three main assertions here (marked off by *quippe, quippe,* and *et propter hoc*): that what makes us superior to other animals is the dignity of our nature rather than anything adventitious; that our mutability from wickedness into moral beauty marks us as naturally more illustrious again—superior not

5. He cites 1 Cor 11.7 and 2 Cor 3.18.

only to other animals but, quite simply, to other creatures; and that the transformation thus made possible is the fulfilment of that superiority. These assertions imply two conceptions of human nature's specific excellence (of what makes it the image of God): that it is intrinsically transformable from impious to virtuous, and that this transformability enables human beings to be raised from incipient to perfect preeminence among creatures. In effect these conceptions are loose definitions of humanity, and since they are concerned with degrees of similarity to God rather than with inward relationship, as far as they go they illustrate Dupré's point; but they raise complications that prevent their meaning from being immediately clear. Above all, how can even an informal definition of human nature presuppose the Fall, as one of these does?

That problem is not Augustine's concern at this point in *De Trinitate*; but, as we have seen, in the *Literal Commentary on Genesis* he makes a serious attempt to solve it, and in the process implies another definition of a human being: as *the spiritual creature that, because it is intellectually more stolid than an angel, is consummated in its relationship with God only by having been brought to the edge of eternal damnation and terrified, chastened, with the knowledge that many of its own species either already are eternally damned or are going to be* (GL 11.10.13). This definition, unlike the two from *De Trinitate,* has the merit of showing a close connection between the human need for moral reformation and human nature as originally created; but correspondingly it is much less clearly the definition of the being made in the image of God. The contrast between Augustine's point here and a superficially similar one made by Plotinus makes this evident. "Immortality," says Plotinus, "by becoming an example through which justice is demonstrated, provides much that is useful, for it awakens people; it stirs up the minds, the understandings, of those set against the ways of wickedness."[6] Unlike Augustine, Plotinus does not say here either that the negative spiritual wake-up call is a necessity, as distinct from

6. Plotinus, *Ennead* 3.2.

a mere expedient, or that our susceptibility to it is specifically human. The chief difficulty, however, with this Augustinian notion of human nature (the difficulty Augustine himself mentions) is the ugliness of the motive that it implies is necessary to human salvation. As his (unidentified) philosophical opponents point out, "Could any being made by God [let alone, one might add, made in God's image] be the sort of being that would require its neighbor's ill for its own moral progress?" This objection has two references: to the morality of an individual—can a divinely made being naturally have such a twisted need?—and to social morality—can a divinely made being naturally have such a twisted relationship with its fellows? So Augustine's attempt to solve the problem of evil anthropologically has merely caused it to replicate into two, and he is now faced with attempting to find solutions to both.

The solution he offers in the *Literal Commentary* itself is not adequate on either count: "Could anyone," he says, "be so dense as not to have noticed that, all around us, the punishment of some deters others from crime" (*GL* 11.11.14).[7] As Agaësse and Solignac point out, this is an embarrassed reply—not surprisingly, because all he is (demonstrably) doing is to invite us to observe the human condition, whereas the objection is to his notion of human nature.[8] Moreover, a solution is all the more urgently required because what he has described as universally necessary to salvation is not mere temporary "inconvenience" designed "to break the evil practices" (the words are Rist's, not Augustine's), but serious moral disorder, evil motivation, of a kind condemned in Augustine's own moral theology.[9] Five chapters later, for example (in an advance summary of the *City of God*), he says that the difference between clean love (which builds the Divine City) and dirty love (which builds the earthly city) is the difference between the social and the private; the one devotes itself to the com-

7. Here brief paraphrases, not strict translations, are given.
8. Agaësse and Solignac, 2:544.
9. For the "inconveniences," see Rist, 274.

mon good, the other subordinates that good to what it regards as its own interests; indeed, this dirty love is so harmful that it even associates us with the bad angels (*GL* 11.15.20); it is therefore a satanic orientation of the soul. But the sort of fearful spiritual quest Augustine says we need to make, inspired by the awareness of others' damnation, must be classified as a manifestation of this dirty love; it is, after all, the attuning of one's mind to a divinely propounded economy in which one's own eternal interest is served by means of one's neighbor's eternal harm. Admittedly, there is a saving grace in the notion that now at least one's concerns are eternal (which puts the reformed motive at one remove from sheer worldliness); but the chief problem remains: the implication that the human soul is by nature so unlike God that in order for it to fulfil its proper potential a thoroughly selfish motive must be activated and exploited in it. Without further explanation, the spirituality implied here would indeed be definitively alien to Gregory Nyssen's idea that the human soul is transformed through an unbroken affinity with God.

Augustine does not, however, leave the issue there. He returns to the subject of the stolid soul in a number of later texts that imply further definitions of human nature; these, as we shall see, more closely address the problem of the necessity of evil, both individually and socially.

First, concerning the individual: Augustine argues (in book 14 of the *City of God*) that only in human beings can the distinction between a sinful disposition and its punishment become a separation (*CD* 14.3). His context is an assertion of the essential goodness of the human body. The corruption of that body, he says, is "not the cause, but the punishment, of the first sin"; in angels there is no such divergence: in them their sinful disposition is their punishment; in human beings these two evils are partially separated. Augustine has prepared us for this idea with a quotation from St. Paul: "For we groan in this body, yearning to put on the habitation that is from heaven" (2 Cor 5.1–4). So in human beings the punishment of sin is not only separated from the sin itself but also provides a possible circumstance of salutary piety. And in book 9 Augustine has contrasted the agonized moral turbulence of the fallen angels with the "steadiness of intent" with which "wise human beings resist mental perturbations of this kind, which nevertheless they must suffer, given the conditions of this life, where human weakness prevents us from being immune to them" (CD 9.3). Here a certain separation of suffering from culpable sinfulness is inherent in the fallen human condition, impossible to the fallen angelic condition, and the central prerequisite for the peculiarly human virtue of heroism.[10] Man, therefore, is *the spiritual creature uniquely capable of being heroically moral, by virtue of being able to suffer in some degree of innocence.*

Augustine still insists that this human separation of suffering from culpability is complete only in Christ; in the bulk of humanity it is merely partial (see CD 9.15, 14.3). For us, then, sin and suffering are still in part aspects of the same reality, as they are entirely for the angels; and in particular, as he says in our passage from book 14, the same human bodily corruption that is not the original cause of sin nevertheless causes further actual sin in us. But what function, if any, does this further sin have in the human moral economy? Augustine's answer (in two of the anti-Pelagian works) is that for salvation to be realized in us we need to be in some degree continually guilty of demonic pride (De nat. et grat. 27.31–29.33; C. duas ep. Pel. 3.7.18). His star text is from the second Epistle to the Corinthians—St. Paul's "thorn in the flesh, angel of Satan." This Augustine interprets as pride, used by God to cure the greater pride by which Paul would otherwise have been destroyed; thus even that great man kept finding this wickedness in himself—hating it, rejecting it, suffering in the process —and indeed such trials are necessary for us all, says Augustine, because in this life we fall short of the holy angels in spiritual exaltation: they already see God face-to-face.

These texts in effect yield a third definition of humanity: a human

10. For the angelic fallen condition, see CD 9.15.

being is *the spiritual creature that is unlike the fallen angels in being reclaimable by the partly innocent suffering of the effects of sin, and unlike the holy angels both in requiring such reclamation and in requiring this to entail the suffering of one's own wickedness, so that this wickedness may be rejected, in order that, in turn, the resultant suffering may be rendered in some degree innocent.* This inchoately Incarnational idea of human nature meets the objection that God would never have created a being that required evil, by tacitly pointing out that human beings are created in order for their suffering to tend toward that of Christ. But this proleptic referral of human nature to the Incarnation does not entirely acquit Augustine of dealing in extrinsic similarity, rather than in intrinsic connection, to God.

Moreover, the objection he has stopped short of answering in the *Literal Commentary* is not merely to the idea of a creature that naturally requires evil, but to that of a creature that specifically requires the harm of its fellows within its own species. We must now ask whether he deals with this social aspect of the objection. If human beings are so made that the chosen few must rush to spiritual safety at the expense of everyone else, does this indicate that (as Arendt implies) there is something shallow about Augustine's notion of human sociality?[11] In his mature theology he in effect confronts this problem on a number of levels.

First, he both asserts and greatly develops the notion that our origin in the single individual Adam is peculiar to humanity (no other animal having originated in this way) (*CD* 12.22; cf. 12.28, 13.3, 14.1). As we have seen, this does not mean that all human beings had a collective soul in Adam.[12] What he does infer (again in the *City of God*) is that although in practice most human behavior is more or less antisocial, there is a uniquely close social affection at the deepest level of human nature; our origin has therefore led not only to the *massa damnata* (because of sin), but also to a specifically human "shackle of

11. Arendt, 110–12.

12. For a recent assertion that Augustine espoused such a view, see Rist, 121–29.

concord" *(vinculum concordiae),* which is constituted "by the emotion that comes from lineal relationship" *(cognationis affectu)* *(CD* 12.22, 12.28). Augustine closely associates this human social unity with our creation in God's image *(CD* 12.28): in some (here unexplained) way, not exhaustive of the mystery concerned, human beings are like God in their unique kind of social unity.

Moreover, a sign that the positive social effect of this characteristic is more fundamentally important than the negative is that it subsumes the negative: it goes beyond familial affection to create a providentially decent society, in principle comprehending all human beings; for although sin, by involving us all, has in many ways made us more helpless than lower animals (human babies, for example, being feebler than the young of other species), even this decline in condition is a factor of superiority, "as though the energy natural to humanity were raising itself to a more exalted level, above other animate beings, in proportion as it has increased its momentum by being first dragged further back, as an arrow is when a bow is strained tight" *(CD* 13.3). Here the negative social effect of the Fall (involvement of us all in a degraded condition) is required to actuate our natural preeminence over other animals. And this positive effect, though grace works on us individual by individual, is nevertheless a social effect. Augustine's example here is the collective effect of death: if baptism brought immediate exemption from death, people would notice and rush to be baptized for that comparatively trivial reason; as it is, we have the greatness of the martyrs, struggle, victory, glory; without death, none of this would have been *(CD* 13.4). Thus he goes beyond the idea that given the Fall, death is a pastoral requirement to an idea of *felix culpa* put in entirely social terms; death, he argues, though an evil in itself, has so influenced the effect human beings have on each other as to make possible a moral splendor that is a good, even an unequalled good, in itself: if there had not been the Fall and death and the social effect of both, there would have been no struggle, no victory, no glory.

That this is Augustine's meaning is confirmed by several passages from his later theology. In *On Reproof and Grace* he applies the same idea to Adam (*De corr. et gr.* 10.28–11.29); and although Adam is an individual his experience preeminently extends beyond him; in the Garden Adam thought himself master of his own life and happiness; the grace he had (real as far as it went) fell fatally short of that now available to the saints on earth—the death of Christ, the blood of the Lamb, the strength to fight and overcome—and so brought with it the delusion of moral self-sufficiency and (for Augustine the core of sin) a private morality—Adam "had fruition of his own peace" (cf. *CD* 14.13, 14.28). In other texts the inference (that we need sin and death) is more explicitly extended to society—most clearly in *On the Merits and Remission of Sins*: again, if the Christian religion conferred instant immortality people's faith would be predictably jejune; so the collective effect of death (our seeing it "in all around") is required for the deepening of faith; but death, precisely because its purpose is in that sense social, will not always be necessary: at the end of time, says Augustine, the saved of the last generation will not need to die in order to inculcate heroism into any who might follow them, and can safely be rapt into immediate intimacy with God (*De pecc. mer.* 2.31.50). Another implicit definition, then, is: man is *the spiritual creature that, in order to actuate its potential, must learn heroic and generous motives from the collective experience of sin and death.* Thus the social aspect of our nature goes to our very core in this highly specific way.

Second, Augustine's general notion of society implies that the necessary separation of the chosen from their doomed fellows is not antisocial, though it may seem so. In the end the earthly city is not a society, because it does not exist in eternity (*CD* 15.4, 19.26; cf. 12.28). The earthly city's citizens will eventually be only a mass of ineluctably private beings. If, knowing this, one still remained socially connected with them on their terms, one would be accepting the ultimate abandonment, not exercise, of society with them (and, for that matter, with everyone). In the final analysis, then, the sort of individuality that leads one, as an individual, to abandon such society is the opposite of privacy; for in the end it is worldly citizenship that is private in the full, negative sense, whereas individuality has as its motive the great, socially formative principle: the love that builds the Divine City (*CD* 14.28, 15.1). Individuality, in this sense, is the assertion of society with anyone with whom it is ultimately possible to be in society.

Third, Augustine implicitly denies that in this world (where matters of social ethics are in question) by detaching oneself from the earthly city one mentally abandons its members to their fate; rather, one thereby fears for them as for oneself. His great example of this disposition, among the imperfect citizens of God, is St. Paul, who, he says, rejoiced with the joyful, wept with those who wept, had his own internal struggles, feared for the blatantly worldly Corinthians, ached with grief for the majority of his fellow Israelites, and mourned for the impenitent (*CD* 14.9). This evokes an exemplarily social attitude both to this world's citizens and to God's. To this great example Augustine adds the ultimate one, of which even St. Paul falls short: Christ, who of course does not in the same sense fear for Himself, but who weeps for His fellow Jews, is glad at a miracle because it would help the faith of His disciples, longs to eat the Passover with them—all charity in the context of a society and directed at both those who reject and those who accept. One may add that, although a certain "exemplarism" is at work here, the examples concerned do not clearly show a static relation of the human soul with its exemplar.

Fourth, in the *Literal Commentary* Augustine indicates a way in which even a society constricted by sin is a particular good—not merely in providing a terrible warning to the virtuous, but positively, in itself, as a glory of human nature (*GL* 9.9.14). The context is a vindication of the essential good of procreation. This good, he argues, has been that of making possible a human society; and the good of that is "to ornament the world." This purpose, he adds, has indeed been fulfilled, "even though only a few live rightly and praiseworthily." The divinely intended ornamentation, then, is moral in nature:

man is the animal whose purpose is to decorate the universe with its moral beauty. But this notion of humanity, like the Ciceronian definition of *populus* in the *City of God*, is in effect made to coexist here with a more practical one. Our natural superiority to the beasts, he argues, can be seen in "the great moral worth of the civil order by which even sinners are coerced into the shackles of a peace of a certain kind." Man, then, is *the animal providentially able, even while in a condition of moral degradation, to be coerced by civil society into providing moral beauty with which to decorate the world.* This implied definition makes a considerable concession to the immense majority who continue in sin, and even to the earthly city from which, as we have seen, methods of dealing with them are borrowed. Thus the extremely small number of just in the world are conceived by Augustine as being shackled by civil society to the enormous remainder, because in that way, sub specie aeternitatis, justice makes larger inroads into humanity.

But the four aspects of Augustine's social ethics listed so far are in one way or other concerned with human moral approximation to divine perfection; they might be thought to confirm that his notion of the divine image is restricted to such approximation. Fifth, however, a far richer notion of human nature's divine imagehood and deification is deducible from a series of connected ideas in books 11 and 12 of the *City of God*. These books are, among other things, a long disquisition on the relationship between the unity of God and the multiplicity of creation.[13] Augustine's general question is: How, given the infinite disparity in natures between God and us, can there be a divine civilization that includes us—a manifold society constituted by likemindedness between God and human beings?

In the two books concerned he approaches this question repeatedly and from numerous starting points (e.g., *CD* 11.2, 11.4, 12.1–8, 12.13–21). Speculating, in this context, on the possible theological

13. The issue emerges notably in *CD* 11.1–2, 11.4–5, 11.7–8, 11.13, 11.15, 11.21, 12.1, 12.19–21.

meanings of the word *light* at the beginning of the book of Genesis, he says that one possible meaning is "the supernal Jerusalem" where, as St. Paul puts it, "you, the children of the light and of the day," dwell (*CD* 11.7; Gn 1.3; Gal 4.26; 1 Thes 5.5). On this basis, says Augustine, the "evening" of the Creation account is the knowledge the created intellect has by its own powers, (a created light, then); and "morning" and "day" are the knowledge we have when, in company with the holy angels, "we come to know as we are known"—a knowledge far better than we have in this world (cf. 1 Cor 13.12). The former, merely creaturely, knowing is, he says, "discolored, so to speak, compared with that by which it [the creature] is known in God's wisdom—in the art, as it were, by which it was made." (A few years earlier Augustine had already asserted that God has always known each individual human being, even before Creation (*GL* 6.9.14); in this sense each of us has always existed in God's mind.) Here the uncreated light (the divine wisdom) is identified with the City of God; membership of human beings in that City is identified with seeing with that uncreated light. This same seeing is, moreover, deification, for in the last chapter of the work Augustine says that the blessed will truly "be like gods," by seeing with perfect clarity, with full divine assistance, "that God is God" (*CD* 22.30). In this sense, therefore, the City of God is not a created society; the Light in which humanity ultimately sees itself restored is the same light that was God's artistic conception of us before we were created.[14] Hence, not only is there deification of humanity but that deification, far from merely establishing external similarity, is humanity's regeneration in a society within the divine archetype. Moreover, as has been mentioned already, an aspect of this notion of the divine image is our origination in a single individual: "Man," says Augustine, "was made in God's image by being originally made as one individual" *(ad eius imaginem homo . . . factus est unus),* and he adds that this origin is the

14. For an account of the analogical place of the angels in this same system, see *CD* 11.29.

basis of the City of God (*CD* 12.28). He asserts three times, in this same context, that this origin has a mysterious significance, perceived only faintly by us but always clearly known by God; so in this respect, too, God's intellectual conception of us at our creation is the basis of the divine civilization: just as God's Wisdom is "multiplex in simplicity, multiform in uniformity," so the foundation of human nature is "a unity in what is multiple," beloved of God (*CD* 12.19, 12.23). In this way also our deification is by participation in the divine wisdom.

Finally, that participation is conceived by Augustine as dynamic, not static, in character. His argument for rejecting the theory of cyclically repeated human lives (as a way for human multiplicity to reflect God's unity) is precisely that no such interminable, stale repetition could adequately reflect God's unity: what is required is unprecedented, unique, spontaneously free human life; and this, he argues, is in fact the reality (*CD* 12.21).

But Augustine's notion of the human image of God goes beyond human nature, in that the human person is the image of the divine Persons. He summarizes the conceptual transition from nature to person near the end of *De Trinitate*: by nature we are made in God's image not physically, but in the soul; and not in the soul simply, but specifically in the mind; but when one looks inside the mind (which he has been doing for most of the work), one finds that it reflects the "inside" of God, because not only is the Son the divine image of God and every other human being in some degree like the Son, but also every human being is the image (not, he says, merely "in the image") of the entire Trinity, though the various aspects of a human mind constitute a human being as only one person, whereas the analogous divine mental activities constitute God as three Persons (*De Trin.* 15.7.11, 15.23.43).

The shift in conceptual focus depends on the distinction, which he has made in book 7, between "substance" and "person" (*De Trin.* 7.5.10–7.6.11): both words denote the determination of a rational nature as an existent being, but whereas "substance" denotes that determination in reference to the nature itself, "person" denotes it in reference to relation with other beings. So even if, for example, one talks about a being as having an innate relational principle, or as perfectible by the actuation of such a principle, one is talking about that being's nature; but if one talks about the determination of its nature in its relation with other beings, one is no longer referring to a relational characteristic (an aspect of its nature) but to a fact constituted by relationship. As we have seen, this notion, given certain other premises, leads Augustine to imply a radically Incarnational conception of both divine and human personality. Although in the last seven books of *De Trinitate* he eventually concentrates on merely reflexive relation and prescinds from the proper notion of relation (and hence of person), in book 8 he briefly stops short, before embarking on that disquisition, and reaffirms the proper sense of the word "person": a person cannot, properly, be the determination of a rational nature in a merely reflexive way, because in such a being love acts substantively, not accidentally. In other words, love is what causes the determination of a rational being to take place, but since love is nevertheless in the category of relation, it necessarily does its determining by relating that rational being to other such beings; for, properly, says Augustine, love can no more be merely self-love than a word can merely signify itself (*De Trin.* 8.7.10–9.4.5).

Moreover, as we have seen, he holds that in the final analysis love is compassion and compassion is intrinsically Incarnational (this is how charity is God).[15] And for Augustine the compassion of Christ is perfect compassion. Although because of it Christ is subject to death (the "first death," which for Augustine is a kind of failure within the soul—not exactly separation of soul and body, but failure of the internal principle of corporeity by which the soul is a human being), Christ can nevertheless experience that failure and still remain perfect because His human moral perfection is hypostatically established in

15. For "charity is God" in *De Trinitate*, see 8.8.12 and 13.10.13.

eternity (*C. serm. Ar.* 7.6; *CD* 21.15); but this is so because all the Incarnational relationships are entailed in Christ's Person. A person, as we have seen, is the determination-in-existence of a rational nature. In Christ the determination-in-existence both of that particular human being and of God is by all the Incarnational relationships. In other words, God has always been compassion for his fellow human beings.

It is not correct, then, to say as H. U. von Balthasar does that the idea of the Incarnation as the perfect expression of the Trinity is undeveloped in Augustine's thought.[16] Augustine's position is that the very Personality of the Trinity presupposes the Incarnation and is centered on it. And when K. Barth says that because of the Incarnation humanity is eternally enclosed in the Godhead, at the core of the divine compassion, he is in effect affirming what Augustine has already implied.[17]

A further implication (already briefly indicated) of this set of ideas is that because, human betrayals notwithstanding, Incarnational compassion constitutes all personality, so that each human being is a person by virtue of the Incarnation, on this personal level, too, Augustine conceives of the divine archetype as having an internal affinity to each human being. Though the unchanging God is of course not human by nature, he is personally so. On this level, where utter eternity takes eternal account of the temporal, the divine archetype is constituted by the same virtue by which human beings are persons; human participation in that archetype is therefore intrinsic both to the archetype and to every human being that is its image.

In this connection two final problems must be addressed, both concerned with the relationship between Christ's individuality and that of every other human being.

First, how can Augustine think that we are all constituted as persons by Christ's charity, given that we are imperfect—many of us cor-

16. Hans Urs von Balthasar, *Mysterium Paschale: The Mystery of Easter,* trans. Aidan Nichols, O.P. (Grand Rapids, Mich.: Eerdmans, 1993), 29.

17. Karl Barth, *The Humanity of God,* trans. J. N. Thomas and T. Wieser (Richmond, Va.: John Knox Press, 1960), 50.

rupt? One answer is obvious from what has already been said: although the divine compassion is the relational focus by which we are substantialized, that does not mean that we will act accordingly (fully as persons, that is). This, however, is only a partial answer. Augustine's position is that as persons we are not only founded but perfected in Christ's charity, and by virtue of the latter action our relationship with our fellow human beings becomes in some sense identical with His (*Tr. in 1 ep. Ioh.* 6.1). But identical in what sense? How does Augustine avoid concluding, given the principle that Christ's charity is that by which all personality is perfectly exercised, that other people's personalities, in their attainment of His perfection, are dissolved in His Personality?

The crucial point is Augustine's conviction that there is not only a human nature shared by everybody, but also individual human natures. We have already met the concept of these natures, expressed deficiently as the unique instantiations of original sin in individual infants (so that, in respect of one's ability to receive grace, original sin is not quite the same deficiency in each individual). But Augustine takes the same position concerning perfection in charity: he says that as the compassion of an imperfect person approaches the level of Christ's, "it must be nourished, and brought to its own peculiar perfection, with nourishments particular to itself": *nutrienda est et quibusdam suis nutrimentis ad perfectionem propriam perducenda* (*Tr. in 1 ep. Ioh.* 6.1). Thus each individual is perfected by compassion not merely in a manner generally applicable to all, but also in a manner uniquely applicable to each. ("Nourishments particular to itself" must mean "nourishments suited to one individual's capacity for compassion rather than to another's," not "nourishments for one's own compassion provided by oneself.") For Augustine, then, a human person is a uniquely individual determination of a uniquely individual form of human nature, by relation to other human individuals. In this sense, if one exercises compassion one has received one's own peculiar form of it (with this purpose) from God. It remains the case, however, that in each instance the provenance of that compassion (as well as its exemplar) is Christ, to whom each of us has always been divinely, providentially known. The perfection of one's person, then, is the transformative determination of one's individual being by a compassion that originates in Christ and even receives its individuality (its uniqueness to oneself) from Christ. That perfection is therefore not a dissolution of one's own person in the divine Person.

Second, how, according to Augustine, does Christ's compassion work in Christ? How does it connect Christ's experience with the suffering of other human individuals (as it must if it is to be compassion)?

In the *Literal Commentary*, during a discussion of some biblical texts problematically applicable to Christ, Augustine argues that the opening words of the Crucifixion Psalm, "My God, my God, turn back to me; why have you forsaken me? My words, which arise from my sins, are remote indeed from my salvation," apply to Christ "only in the sense that He transfigures us in Himself, fallen as we are shown to be by our bodily condition, for of His body too we are members": *non . . . nisi transfiguranti in se corpus humilitatis nostrae, quoniam membra sumus corporis eius* (GL 10.18.32; Ps 21 [22]). A number of parallel distinctions are implied here—in particular between the transfiguring Body of Christ and its individual members being transfigured, and between the sinless suffering of Christ and the sinful suffering of His Body's members. Christ transfigures in the totality of His Body, and suffers in its members by way of transfiguring them. Augustine cannot mean by this that the suffering in the members is merely vicarious (that only we do the suffering concerned), for the psalm he is expounding is about Christ's suffering on the Cross; the transforming and the suffering are different aspects of what Christ does on the Cross. So the members' suffering, though of course done by them, is not done by them only. Nor is Christ's share in their suffering a mere sampling—experience of the sort of suffering they experience; for, says Augustine, the way in which the problematic words of the psalm are suitable as a description of Christ is that on the Cross He transfigures our inadequacy. But precisely because He does it on the Cross He transfigures that inadequacy by suffering it, even though properly the inadequacy is only that of the individual members of His Body. What Augustine insists on subtracting from Christ, then, is the inadequacy (the sinful aspect of the "body of our lowliness"), not the suffering, which on the contrary he presents as essential to the transfiguring. But because nevertheless the suffering of the individual members is also done by them individually, what Christ on the Cross experiences is the suffering of each individual member of His Mystical Body.

And in the sixtieth *Tractate on St. John's Gospel* Augustine says that Christ "has even transfigured in Himself the emotional experience of our weakness, suffering with us in the emotional experience of His own soul": *tranfiguravit etiam in se affectum infirmitatis nostrae, compatiens nobis affectu animae suae* (*Tr. in Ioh. Ev.* 60.2). This is in an exposition of St. John's statement that Christ was "troubled in spirit" as the moment of Judas's betrayal approached. Though Augustine might have interpreted the phrase as denoting a victim's terror (and indeed for a while he entertains that possibility), or righteous anger, or even pity, his eventual, quite different, explanation is that somehow Christ was sharing Judas's own self-inflicted horror.

Strictly speaking, both passages are concerned with participation by Christ in another person's experience, rather than (our more central concern) participation by a human person in Christ; but our other passage, from the *Literal Commentary*, adds this soteriological obverse: that in Christ's Mystical Body His initiative suffering with His members transfiguratively joins their suffering to His; in this sense they participate in Him. Since this participation is through Christ's experience of their sufferings (this being of the essence of His compassion), and since His compassion is God, their sufferings are, in that personal sense, inherent in the divine original. Moreover, since those persons are transfigured through a divine Person's experience of their sufferings, and such transfiguration is, according to Augustine, the imparting of a charity proper to that divine Person, the individuals concerned are deified in this sense, too: by Christ's participation in the sufferings of each of them.

The general conclusions are: first, where Augustine thinks of human deification as the uniting of our nature with God's, he thinks this to be not merely the adhesion and assimilation of one unlike nature to the other, but the fulfilment in each individual of each unique, divinely conceived pattern. Admittedly, by a practical requirement of our nature the only way for us to be translated into God's presence is, in Augustine's view, by our being divinely extricated from sin by exercising the uniquely human characteristic of moral heroism; nevertheless, he conceives both that extrication, and the utter freedom it eventually brings, as citizenship in the divine society; and this citizenship consists in contemplating all reality in the same uncreated light that always was (even down to individualities) God's artistic concept of us.

Second, every human being is constituted as a person by God's compassion toward other human beings than Himself; the same is true of the constitution of the three divine Persons. The exercise of this divine compassion is the purpose of human personality. (So in this way too every human person is, by virtue of the Incarnation, comprehended in the divine archetype.) And in fulfilment of this purpose each individual's sufferings have also been suffered by Christ.

CHAPTER 7

THREE OPEN QUESTIONS

We have seen that Augustine's notion of humanity has at its every main declension the unity it needs to make the sort of sense he implicitly claims it makes: his general notion of human nature (that of a primarily mental soul of which the body is an aspect) is of a creature that with its own essence uniquely conjoins the two orders of being—the intellectual and the physical. This notion, together with that of the Fall (with which he closely connects it, for our nature has needed the various stages of our condition), is proleptically Incarnational, allowing the possibility of completely or partially innocent subjection to evil. On this level the principle of unity that makes the Incarnation possible is an expanded concept of concupiscence—that of failure in the soul's exercise of its own life; this concept extends from damnable sin to generous suffering and generous death; socially, there is a corresponding unity that again extends from perfection to abject privation; on this level the unity resides in the analogy between the Heavenly City and every other; on the level of individual morality, it resides in the principle that all human virtue is charity, which, despite variance and discord in its exercise, is either Christ's compassion itself or a devolvement from it; moreover, for Augustine this virtue, though seated in human nature, also transcends it, being the common principle of divine and human personality; and all acts, human or divine, and whether motivated by charity or by its privation, are acts of the entire mind, not different acts of different faculties.

Underlying his thinking on this subject is the conviction that ultimately the various human modes of unity resolve into one; all reality has a sole, supreme principle; good is in the final analysis one, not multiple; although there are lesser goods, they are good by participation in the one, divine Good; and although the lesser goods, at least as we experience them, can clash, they clash not in their natures but because of the intellectually misleading, temporal conditions under which they enter our consciousness.

It must finally be asked whether Augustine comprehensively solves the problems posed by this great thesis. These problems are more troublesome the more embroiled the argument becomes in the concerns of this world—the clashing lesser goods specifically. In book 7 of the *Confessions*, for instance, his statement of the thesis is not encumbered by such specifics. At the soul's focal center he observes the uncreated light, the absolute good transcending the created mind; in seeing it one knows that it is Being itself, but simultaneously one senses oneself to be separated from that Good: intellectually, morally distracted, scattered in pieces by conflicting impulses toward inferior, ill-integrated goods (*Conf.* 7.10.16). Thus Augustine mentions these goods but, here at least, only in general. In this respect the *City of God* is more ambitious—an attempt to analyze human history as an account of the relationship between those distractions and the Good. Here one of the many examples he cites is Lucius Junius Brutus, the proto-consul, who, when his sons supported a counterrevolution, executed them for the sake of the Roman republic. Following Virgil, Augustine indicates that this action unavoidably infringed another vital good—a father's love—but that the cause of the conflict of principles was Rome's partially corrupt condition (a characteristic of worldly sovereignties); the ultimate, Heavenly City will not place people in such circumstances, precisely because these are a direct or indirect result of evil (*CD* 5.17–18).[1]

How successfully such an example supports the thesis of a

1. Virgil, *Aeneid* 6.817–823.

supreme principle may be judged if we set against it the main, romantic counterview: that the truth is not ultimately one, that there is not merely one master principle but many, and that these are not integrable with one another in accordance with any principle higher than themselves but absolutes of their own, some of them incompatible with one another. Isaiah Berlin, the chief contemporary exponent of this view, both stresses its uncompromising character and indicates the general objection it poses to the doctrine of the preeminent Good. Even fundamental moral principles, he argues, can be stubbornly inconsistent with one another when one attempts to live by them in this world: justice and compassion, vigorously applied, eventually clash; so do liberty and equality, spontaneity and planned organization. "If we are told," he says, "that these contradictions will be solved in some perfect world in which all good things can be harmonized in principle . . . we must say that the world in which what we see as incompatible values are not in conflict is a world altogether beyond our ken. . . . The notion of the perfect whole, the ultimate solution . . . seems to me to be . . . conceptually incoherent. . . . Some among the Great Goods cannot live together."[2] This argument (a de facto attack on the whole Judaeo-Platonic tradition) fuses two different requirements: first, that a principle asserted to be the basis of human moral life must, if it is to be conceptually coherent, be articulated with reference to the problems of that life; and second, that such a principle must be shown, in detail, to resolve those problems in their particularity. Berlin, by brushing aside any merely general or purely theoretical solution, implicitly insists on the latter of these requirements; but Augustine's argument using the example of Brutus satisfies only the former.

2. Isaiah Berlin, "The Pursuit of the Ideal," in *The Crooked Timber of Humanity: Chapters in the History of Ideas*, ed. Henry Hardy (London: Fontana, 1991), 12–14 (see 13 for the quotation); cf. Isaiah Berlin, *The Roots of Romanticism*, ed. Henry Hardy (Princeton, N.J.: Princeton University Press, 1999), 63–67. For the preeminence of Berlin as an exponent of the view, see MacIntyre, 109.

Yet Augustine accepts the validity of both requirements. In the preface to the *City of God* he says that he will elucidate the supereminent Good not only "in the stability of its heavenly basis" but "in its present condition of temporal movement." In effect this is a claim to satisfy Berlin's second requirement as well as his former. But in order to do so, Augustine must at least indicate how a man in a position such as Brutus's, given the evils distorting his situation, might act so as to be morally at peace with himself. And there are two aspects to this: showing that the conditions of this present life are not such as to make nonsense of human moral practice, and detailing the subordinate principles (or a sizeable number of them) together with their varying applicability to circumstances.

Augustine finds the conditions of this life highly resistant to such a treatment, and in this respect he arguably does not successfully perform the task he has set himself in his preface. Albert Camus in effect made this point (more narrowly, more sharply, than Berlin) fifty years ago, in *L'homme révolté*, with the statement that "Augustinism supplies arguments in support of all revolt."[3] By "revolt" he means, as the context shows, unwillingness to accept the moral absurdity caused by evil in our present life. In Camus' view, then, the theological tradition that begins with Augustine reveals the futility of all attempts "to take away from suffering its injustice"; in other words, Augustinian theology so clearly and accurately characterizes the human condition that the reasonable human response is outrage.

From Camus' point of view this observation is, in effect, praise, not criticism, of Augustine; but much of Camus' life's work is devoted to showing the inadequacy of another, counterbalancing, Augustinian idea: that heaven, the final Good, offers a perfect solution to the problem of evil. "How great will that blessedness be where there will be no evil," says Augustine in the last chapter of the *City of God*.

3. Albert Camus, *L'homme révolté* (Paris: Gallimard, 1951), 51–55. The work's title is usually misleadingly translated as "The Rebel"; it is better translated as "The Human Condition of Revolt."

If this is taken to mean that every kind of evil will be resolved in heaven, Camus in one work after another dramatizes the notion that no such resolution could ever come about—that heaven, understood in that sense, is an impossibility. In *La peste (The Plague)* Dr. Rieux makes the point analogically: after the plague lifts, happy couples in their thousands walk about the town "with all the triumph and injustice of happiness," implicitly denying, "against all the evidence," that they had ever known a time when "the murder of a human being was as daily as that of flies."[4] In *La chute (The Fall)* Clamence says that Christ's passion and death were caused by an "incurable divine melancholy" at the Slaughter of the Innocents; like Rachel, God refuses to be comforted when, absurdly, hundreds of children are killed in the hope that one of them might be Christ.[5] In *L'homme révolté* itself Camus makes a similar assertion: that God in the Person of Christ has submitted to injustice "so that suffering may also reach heaven and snatch it from the curses of mankind."[6] Heaven, far from abolishing suffering, is invaded by it; in this sense a certain "despair" on God's part is the very essence of the Incarnation.

Such a notion of Incarnational compassion has, as we have seen, much in common with Augustine's. For Camus, however, as for Ivan Karamazov, this compassion would be entirely denatured if it were conceived as entirely fulfilled in our attainment of heavenly happiness. Even if heaven were to sweep away all our sufferings, that would not make the fact that, for example, the Holy Innocents suffered any less outrageous. On the terms asserted by Camus, to talk, as Augustine does, of heaven as comprehensively the cessation of evil is a bland oversimplification of a problem that Augustine himself often acutely pinpoints.

This is an implicit criticism and has evidence to support it, especially from the *City of God*, where Augustine details this world's evils

4. Albert Camus, *La peste* (Paris: Gallimard, 1947), 244.
5. Camus, *La chute*, 118–19.
6. Camus, *L'homme*, 145.

with particular care and vividness, expounding the problem posed by them more fully than Camus. Though evil in itself is of course insusceptible of formal definition, near the end of the work Augustine divides it into two modes: sin and punishment (*CD* 22.24). From its origin, he says, evil has been these two. The meaning of the division, and in particular of its second term *(supplicium)*, is not entirely clear, but if it is interpreted as a complete division into volitional evil (wickedness) and emotional evil (suffering), it is an inadequate summary of Augustine's own view of the matter; it omits intellectual evil, the crucial third mode to which large portions of the work are devoted. This mode of evil consists neither in wickedness nor in suffering, but in the apparent senselessness of much of human experience in this world (including some of the wickedness and some of the suffering)—in the realization, for example, that some suffering is an affront to reason. This is the subject of the work's first serious question: Why are infidels and ingrates frequently allowed by God to go through life unpunished? (*CD* 1.8). In a discussion of divine mercy the logical possibility has arisen that that mercy, at least as we now experience it, is cheapened by being conferred obliviously of its recipients' state of soul, so that our present life would make no moral sense. Here sin and suffering are data in a problem of intellectual evil. Augustine takes for granted that he has a duty to solve this problem—to obviate such violation of an elemental human theological intuition. He offers a highly intelligent answer—a series of suggested providential reasons for the absence of suffering in such cases. At this stage, then, he has no doubt that the problem is soluble, and is reasonably confident that his solution, or something like it, is the correct one.

In book 19 he is not so sure: in chapter 4, to show how silly it is to think that true happiness can be attained in our present life, he considers the phenomenon of extreme suffering. To this the Stoics think that suicide is a legitimate remedy. Augustine indignantly rejects this fatuous idea (such an act, he says, flies in the face of the most fundamental human instinct), but on one point he does not contradict the Stoics: that on occasion human suffering can be so terrible as to compel suicide. (Some suffering can be rationalized, but it is difficult to rationalize suffering as extreme as that.)

In the end Augustine somewhat mitigates this shocking idea by asserting that divine grace offers a means of tolerating what is otherwise humanly intolerable. Yet even this assertion must be understood in its larger Augustinian conceptual context. Such divine grace is a special instance of a Christian's privileged ability not to sin; but in formal terms, at least, it is still a potentiality—admittedly a potentiality that, as a Christian, one now has; but at this late stage of his thinking Augustine leaves unclear at what moment in a time of trial that ability might be relied upon to come to our moral assistance, for in his mature view all such ability not to sin is still, in this world, appreciably curtailed by residual concupiscence: so even honorable and devout people do not have the steady, practical ability to avoid sin (e.g., *CD* 14.16). Given these general conditions, it would not be correct to infer from this passage that he excepts Christians from the danger of suicide resulting from misery. The good and the bad alike, he says later, live "a condemned life" in this world (*CD* 22.23).

Thus Augustine has raised, and not quite then laid to rest, the suggestion that in this world even a Christian can be inescapably trapped in moral evil. That, indeed, is one of his chief points in this part of book 19. His description, two chapters later, of the hapless judge whose work typically includes torturing innocent witnesses to death is not merely an account of an unpleasant area of experience (*CD* 19.6); Augustine indicates that this apparent duty is extremely wicked. Of the many Latin words for moral evil he chooses *nefas*—by far the strongest—and greatly increases the horror of his disquisition by offering no serious alternative to this "unspeakable evil" that is not itself an unspeakable evil: the worldly philosopher, he says, absurdly "considers it unspeakable evil" to avoid such grisly obligations but not unspeakable evil to torture the innocent. Yet Augustine does not deny that to shirk one's public duty, even in such circumstances, is *ne-fas*. Indeed, acceptance of this point is one-half of his argument. But then he insists that in such circumstances, doing one's public duty is *nefas*, too. In this context, his curt statement of the philosopher's decision, "he will sit [as a judge]," has to be taken as ironic, not as the confident establishment of a moral position. A person in such a dilemma might, of course, attempt to resolve it by finding and then choosing the lesser evil (thus showing that this world, despite what Augustine says, is in this respect not such a bad place after all). And that is what Augustine's pompous philosopher is apparently satisfied that he has done. But Augustine by his implicit assertion that one commits *nefas* either way makes any such attempt look ridiculous—a calculation of which of two unspeakable evils is less unspeakable than the other. In such a case moral confidence is bound to be delusional.

Augustine is aware that his satire of the pompous philosopher is only one side of the matter. Which unspeakable evil is anyone, even a devout person in a Christian society, to choose? In the end Augustine admits that such a person can be in the same inescapable quandary as the pompous philosopher: "In such a necessity a pious and wise person shouts to God, 'Rescue me from my necessities.'" But in this world such a deus ex machina is a rarity. In other words, for resolution of such enormities Augustine puts the onus on heaven. To resolve them suitably, however, heaven would have to provide a revelation that would make moral sense of them; merely to bring them to an end would not be sufficient—and as we have seen, making moral sense of life in this world, in particular under the imperfect Christian administration of the time, is central to the work's original brief. (He was quite confident of making such sense when he was discussing torture—from the victim's point of view—in book 1 (*CD* 1.10)—not, however, in this later passage.)

But although Augustine has in that way prompted us to expect heaven to make sense of such moral absurdities, his speculative description of heaven, near the end of the work, holds in prospect the mere termination of wrongs, not a comprehensible resolution of their absurdity. He gives an enormous list of this life's evils, under the headings of moral weakness, corruption, wicked passions, delusions, stupidity, and mortality; and he points speculatively to the resolution of each by the translation of humanity to heaven (*CD* 22.22–24). Now, however, he entirely ignores the most poignant evil evoked in book 19, the failure of human life in this world to make adequate moral sense. He has good reason to ignore it; in book 19 he has shown the problem posed by it to be insoluble. Even if every tear will be wiped away, and sin, even its possibility, will be abolished, still, our present life's partial unintelligibility (which for an intellectual creature is an evil) must in the nature of things persist.

An analogous point can be made about the spectacle, evoked in one of the anti-Pelagian works, of a mother mourning the eternal loss of her dead unbaptized baby (*C. duas ep. Pel.* 2.6.11). Heavenly obliteration of this portion of that mother's consciousness is a logical possibility. In the *City of God,* at least, Augustine says explicitly that there will not be such oblivion (*CD* 22.30); but even if there were, that would not be a solution to the problem of moral and theological absurdity raised by the cause of such grief, for here, as in the case of the hapless judge, everything suggests that the absurdity of such a horror, even if not the mother's grief over it, is indissoluble.

Whether Augustine anywhere provides a solution to this set of problems, and whether indeed they are ultimately soluble (as for Camus they are not) may be regarded as open questions.

Augustine's task of temporal elucidation of the supreme Good has, as we have seen, a second aspect: that of positive practice. If this world is to make sense (even if only in terms of the next), the subordinate principles, the goods deriving from the highest Good, must be shown to work practically, in detail. Here again it is in the *City of God* that this task faces Augustine most starkly because of his position there that the Incarnation is the principle not only of relationships between individuals but of all human society, and preeminently of civil society. Though he admits that many political states are worldly in basis, he regards this as a cause of their eventual destruction; in the end civil society can exist only if it is just. For that principle to be comprehensible one needs to know how it applies to human experience—the content of civil justice. Though, as we have seen, Augustine clearly specifies its ultimate principle as the Christian faith and regards other principles as variably applicable according to circumstances, he is also aware that much of the content of human morality consists in principles intermediate between the two extremes—the Christian faith itself, and sheer practical prudence. For the most part, however, he does not reveal what that content is. Admittedly, he points out anecdotally that, for instance, democracy is a proper form of government only where the populace meets certain standards of responsible behavior; otherwise, some other form of government is appropriate. This indicates the sort of intermediate principle at issue here. But apart from such occasional instances Augustine leaves those principles unspecified.

E. L. Fortin in effect highlights this problem in a general criticism of Augustine's theory of human nature.[7] The criticism is that by emphasizing the incompleteness of human nature on earth Augustine neglects the scientific exposition of that nature; and that this shortcoming hampered the Augustinian tradition for centuries, relief arriving only with the medieval "rediscovery of an independent realm of nature." This general criticism depends on the philosophical assumption that there actually is such an independent realm. Even if one rejects that assumption, however, a more particular form of the problem still applies: Augustine's moral theology, though it asserts civil society to be natural, does not amply specify what is natural in it. On this subject Augustine's reticence (a result of his practice of stark-

---

7. Ernest L. Fortin, "Augustine and the Hermeneutics of Love: Some Preliminary Considerations," in *Augustine Today,* ed. Richard John Neuhaus (Grand Rapids, Mich.: Eerdmans, 1993), 35–59.

ly contrasting the absoluteness of heaven with the contingency of earthly life) leaves the false impression that he regards affairs of state as merely executive. We have seen that for him the *dilectio* constituting a civil society is either an instance or a thwarting of the virtue of compassion; but by what modes he conceives compassion to devolve into various forms of civil virtue is another open question.

BIBLIOGRAPHY

Agaësse, P., and A. Solignac. *La genèse au sens littéral: 1–7* and *8–12: Bibliothèque augustinienne: Oeuvres de saint Augustin en douze livres.* 2 vols. Paris: Desclée de Brouwer, 1972.

Arendt, Hannah. *Love and Saint Augustine.* Ed. Joanna Vecchiarelli Scott and Judith Chelius Stark. Chicago: University of Chicago Press, 1996.

Ayres, Lewis. "The Discipline of Self-Knowledge in Augustine's *De Trinitate* Book X." In *The Passionate Intellect: Essays on the Transformation of the Classical Traditions Presented to I. G. Kidd,* ed. Lewis Ayres. London: Transaction, 1995.

Balthasar, Hans Urs von. *Mysterium Paschale: The Mystery of Easter.* Trans. Aidan Nichols, O.P. Grand Rapids, Mich.: Eerdmans, 1993.

Barnes, Michel René. "The Visible Christ and the Invisible Trinity: Mt. 5:8 in Augustine's Trinitarian Theology of 400." *Modern Theology* 19, 3 (2003): 329–55.

Barth, Karl. *The Humanity of God.* Trans. J. N. Thomas and T. Wieser. Richmond, Va.: John Knox Press, 1960.

Berlin, Isaiah. "The Pursuit of the Ideal." In *The Crooked Timber of Humanity: Chapters in the History of Ideas,* ed. Henry Hardy, 1–19. London: Fontana, 1991.

———. *The Roots of Romanticism.* Ed. Henry Hardy. Princeton, N.J.: Princeton University Press, 1999.

Bonner, Gerald. "Augustine's Conception of Deification." *Journal of Theological Studies* n.s. 37 (1986): 369–86.

———. "Augustine's Doctrine of Man: Image of God and Sinner." *Augustinianum* 24 (1984): 495–514.

Børresen, Kari Elisabeth. "In Defence of Augustine: How *Femina* is *Homo.*" In *Collectanea Augustiniana: Mélanges T. J. van Bavel,* ed. B. Bruning, M. Lamberigts, and J. van Houtem, 411–28. Leuven: Leuven University Press, 1990.

———. *Subordination and Equivalence: The Nature and Rôle of Woman in Augustine and Thomas Aquinas.* Kampen: Kok Pharos, 1995.

Brown, Peter. *Augustine of Hippo: A Biography.* London: Faber and Faber, 1967.

———. *The Body and Society.* London: Faber and Faber, 1990.

———. *Religion and Society in the Age of Saint Augustine.* London: Faber and Faber, 1977.

Brown, Raymond E., S.S. *The Gospel according to John (xiii–xxi).* Garden City, N.Y.: Doubleday, 1970.

Burnaby, John. *Amor Dei: A Study in the Religion of St. Augustine.* Rev. ed. Norwich: Canterbury Press, 1991.

Burnell, Peter. "Concupiscence and Moral Freedom in Augustine and before Augustine." *Augustinian Studies* 26 (1995): 49–63.

———. "The Problem of Service to Unjust Regimes in Augustine's *City of God*." *Journal of the History of Ideas* 54 (1993): 177–88.

Camus, Albert. *La chute.* Paris: Gallimard, 1956.

———. *L'homme révolté.* Paris: Gallimard, 1951.

———. *La peste.* Paris: Gallimard, 1947.

Canning, Raymond. *The Unity of Love for God and Neighbour in St. Augustine.* Heverlee-Leuven: Augustinian Historical Institute, 1993.

Capánaga, V. "La deificación en la soteriología agustiniana." In *Augustinus magister.* Vol. 2, *Etudes augustiniennes,* 745–54. Paris, 1954. .

Carney, F. S. "The Structure of Augustine's Ethic." In *The Ethics of St. Augustine,* ed. W. S. Babcock, 11–37. Atlanta: Scholars Press, 1991.

Clark, M. T., R.S.C.J. *Augustinian Personalism.* Villanova: Villanova University Press, 1970.

Clarke, Thomas E., S.J. "St. Augustine and Cosmic Redemption." *Theological Studies* 19 (1958): 133–64.

Combès, Gustave. *La doctrine politique de saint Augustin.* Paris: Plon, 1927.

D'Arcy, M. C., S.J. *The Mind and Heart of Love: Lion and Unicorn: A Study in Eros and Agape.* 2nd ed. London: Faber and Faber, 1954.

Deane, Herbert A. *The Political and Social Ideas of Saint Augustine.* New York: Columbia University Press, 1963.

Dideberg, Dany, S.J. "Caritas: Prolégomènes à une étude de la théologie augustinienne de la charité." In *Signum Pietatis: Festgabe für Cornelius Petrus Mayer,* ed. Adolar Zumkeller, 369–81. Würzburg: Augustinus-Verlag, 1989.

Dihle, Albrecht. *The Theory of the Will in Classical Antiquity.* Berkeley: University of California Press, 1982.

Drobner, Hubertus R. *Person-Exegese und Christologie bei Augustinus: Zur Herkunft der Formel "una Persona."* Leiden: E. J. Brill, 1986.

Dupré, Louis. *Passage to Modernity: An Essay in the Hermeneutics of Nature and Culture.* New Haven, Conn.: Yale University Press, 1993.

Evans, G. R. *Augustine on Evil.* Cambridge: Cambridge University Press, 1982.

Fortin, Ernest L. "Augustine and the Hermeneutics of Love: Some Preliminary Considerations." In *Augustine Today,* ed. Richard John Neuhaus, 35–59. Grand Rapids, Mich.: Eerdmans, 1993.

Fredriksen, Paula. "Beyond the Body/Soul Dichotomy: Augustine on Paul against the Manichees and the Pelagians." *Recherches augustiniennes* 23 (1988): 87–114.

Gilson, Etienne. *The Christian Philosophy of St. Augustine.* Trans. L. G. M. Lynch. New York: Random House, 1960.

Hick, John. *Evil and the God of Love.* Rev. ed. San Francisco: Harper and Row, 1977.

Hill, Edmund, O.P., trans. *Augustine: "The Trinity": The Works of Saint Augustine: A Translation for the 21st Century.* Ed. John E. Rotelle, O.S.A. Brooklyn: New City Press, 1991.

Holl, Karl. "Augustins Innere Entwicklung." In *Gesammelte Aufsätze zur Kirchengeschichte*, 3: 54–116. Tübingen, 1928.

Jansenius, C. *Augustinus*. Rouen: J. Berthelin, 1643.

Kelly, J. N. D. *Early Christian Doctrines*. 4th ed. London: Adam and Charles Black, 1968.

Kirk, Kenneth E. *The Vision of God: The Christian Doctrine of the Summum Bonum*. London: Longmans, 1932.

Kirwan, Christopher. *Augustine*. London: Routledge, 1989.

Kisiel, Theodore. *The Genesis of Heidegger's "Being and Time."* Berkeley: University of California Press, 1993.

Ladner, Gerhart B. *The Idea of Reform: Its Impact on Christian Thought and Action in the Age of the Fathers*. Cambridge, Mass.: Harvard University Press, 1959.

Laplace, Jean, S.J., and Jean Daniélou, S.J. *La création de l'homme (Grégoire de Nysse)*. Paris: Editions du Cerf, 1943.

Lloyd, A. C. "On Augustine's Concept of a Person." In *Augustine: A Collection of Critical Essays*, ed. R. A. Markus, 191–205. Garden City, N.Y.: Anchor, 1972.

Lossky, Vladimir. *Orthodox Theology: An Introduction*. Trans. Ian and Ihita Kesarcodi-Watson. Crestwood, N.Y.: St. Vladimir's Seminary Press, 1978.

MacIntyre, Alasdair. *Whose Justice? Which Rationality?* Notre Dame, Ind.: University of Notre Dame Press, 1988.

Mader, Johann. *Die logische Struktur des personalen Denkens aus der Methode der Gotteserkenntnis bei Aurelius Augustinus*. Vienna: Verlag Herder, 1965.

Markus, R. A. *Saeculum: History and Society in the Theology of St. Augustine*. Rev. ed. Cambridge: Cambridge University Press, 1988.

Marrou, Henri-Irénée. *Saint Augustin et l'augustinisme*. Paris: Editions du Seuil, 1955.

Mellet, M., O.P., Th. Camelot, O.P., and E. Hendrikx, O.E.S.A. *La Trinité: 1–8: Bibliothèque augustinienne: Oeuvres de saint Augustin*. Paris: Desclée de Brouwer, 1955.

Meyendorff, John. *Catholicity and the Church*. Crestwood, N.Y.: St. Vladimir's Seminary Press, 1983.

Milbank, John. *Theology and Social Theory: Beyond Secular Reason*. Oxford: Blackwell's, 1990.

Nygren, Anders. *Agape and Eros*. Trans. Philip S. Watson. London: SPCK, 1953.

O'Connell, Robert J., S.J. *Art and the Christian Intelligence in St. Augustine*. Cambridge, Mass.: Harvard University Press, 1978.

———. *The Origin of the Soul in St. Augustine's Later Works*. New York: Fordham University Press, 1987.

O'Daly, Gerard. *Augustine's Philosophy of Mind*. London: Duckworth, 1987.

O'Donnell, James J. *Augustine: Confessions*. 3 vols. Oxford: Clarendon Press, 1992.

O'Donovan, Oliver. *The Problem of Self-Love in St. Augustine*. New Haven, Conn.: Yale University Press, 1980.

Pascal, Blaise. *Pensées*. Paris: Bibliothèque de la Pléiade, no. 267, n.d.

Portalié, Eugène, S.J. *A Guide to the Thought of Saint Augustine*. Trans. Ralph J. Bastian, S.J. London: Burns and Oates, 1960.

Ratzinger, J. *Volk und Haus Gottes in Augustins Lehren von der Kirche*. Munich: Münchener theol. stud. 11/7, 1954.

Ricoeur, Paul. "Original Sin: A Study in Meaning." In *The Conflict of Interpretations,* 269–86. Evanston, Ill.: Northwestern University Press, 1974.

———. *The Symbolism of Evil*. Trans. Emerson Buchanan. Boston: Beacon Press, 1969.

Rist, John M. *Augustine: Ancient Thought Baptized*. Cambridge: Cambridge University Press, 1994.

Rousselot, P. *Pour l'histoire du problème de l'amour au moyen age*. Paris: Vrin, 1933.

Ryle, Gilbert. *The Concept of Mind*. New York: Barnes and Noble, 1949.

Schrage, W. "Theologie und Christologie bei Paulus und Jesus auf dem Hintergrund der modernen Gottesfrage." *Evangelische Theologie* 36 (1976): 121–54.

Sherrard, Philip. *The Greek East and the Latin West: A Study in the Christian Tradition*. London: Oxford University Press, 1959.

Soennecken, Silvia. "Die Rolle der Frau in Augustins *De Genesi ad Litteram*." In *Signum Pietatis: Festgabe für Cornelius Petrus Mayer*, ed. Adolar Zumkeller, 289–300. Würzburg: Augustinus-Verlag, 1989.

Strauss, Leo. *Natural Right and History*. Chicago: Chicago University Press, 1953.

Taylor, Charles. *Sources of the Self: The Making of the Modern Identity*. Cambridge, Mass.: Harvard University Press, 1989.

van Bavel, T. J., O.S.A. "The Double Face of Love in St. Augustine: The Daring Inversion: Love Is God." In *Congresso internazionale su S. Agostino nel 16 centenario della conversione*. Rome, 1987.

Wetzel, James. *Augustine and the Limits of Virtue*. Cambridge: Cambridge University Press, 1992.

Williams, Norman Powell. *The Ideas of the Fall and of Original Sin: A Historical and Critical Study*. London: Longmans, Green, 1927.

Williams, Rowan. "The Paradoxes of Self-Knowledge in the *De Trinitate*." In *Collectanea Augustiniana: Signum Pietatis*, ed. J. Lienhard, E. Muller, and R. Teske, 121–34. New York: Peter Lang, 1993.

———. "Politics and the Soul: A Reading of the *City of God*." *Milltown Studies* 19-20 (1987): 55–72.

———. "*Sapientia* and the Trinity: Reflections on the *De Trinitate*." In *Collectanea Augustiniana: Mélanges T. J. van Bavel*, ed. B. Bruning, M. Lamberigts, and J. van Houtem, 317–32. Leuven: Leuven University Press, 1990.

INDEX

actual sin. *See* sin: actual

Adam, 118; and concupiscence, 11, 35, 72, 77, 81–83, 107, 117; and the human body, 24, 27; and human morality, 90, 91, 93; and individuality, 50, 181, 183; and the soul, 6, 7, 19, 24, 33, 34, 35, 38; and superiority of over Eve, 7, 44, 48, 49

Adam and Eve, 7, 8, 28, 31, 45, 73, 74, 91. *See also* Adam; Eve

administratio, the divine, 25, 38, 71; and dualism of body and soul, 26, 28, 30, 37, 39–40; and divine grace, 38–39

agape, 99, 105, 118. *See also caritas;* charity

amor, 102, 119

angels, 94, 163; and the created intellect, 21, 186; creation of, 20–21, 23; fallen, 180, 181; and the human soul, 39, 179; nature of vs. human nature, 21–22, 93, 179

Aquinas, Thomas, 65, 103,109

Arendt, H., criticism of Augustinian notions of: human sociality, 181; love, 14, 60, 107, 108, 109, 111–15, 117–18, 124, 130, 166–67

Aristotelian tradition, 65, 66, 69, 98n.2, 142

art, Augustinian theory of, 3–4

atonement, 166. *See also* divine grace

Augustinian anthropology, ix; central subjects of, 2–11, 14–16, 18; comprehensiveness of, 35, 36, 53; unity of, 36, 37, 38

Augustinian psychology, 10, 54, 59, 62, 87. *See also* human mind

autarky, 116

awareness: levels of human, 30, 31, 49, 55, 57, 63–65, 93, 114; moral, 98, 107, 128, 149, 179; relationship between human and bestial, 31, 55, 62–63

baptism, 39, 182; and concupiscence, 12, 13, 72, 78–79, 95; of desire, 85–87; of infants, 52, 72, 85–87

Barth, K., 189

beasts, 1, 21, 29, 30, 185; and relationship of bestial and human awareness, 31, 55, 62–63

Berlin, Isaiah, 17, 196, 197

blameworthiness, notion of, 32, 82–83. *See also* sin, actual

body. *See* human body

Bonner, G., 10

Brown, P., 12, 72, 75, 76, 77

Brown, R. E., 104

Burnaby, J., criticism of Augustinian notions of: concupiscence, 12; desire, 74, 75, 79–80; love, 14, 105, 106–7, 110, 115, 117; punishment, 12, 79. *See also caritas;* charity; concupiscence

Camus, Albert, 17, 197, 198, 199, 202

Cappadocians, the, 122. *See also* Greek Fathers; Gregory of Nyssa

caritas, 60, 102, 107, 109, 114, 119. *See also* agape; charity

carnal concupiscence, 78, 81. *See also* concupiscence

causal reason, 26, 27, 28

charity, 165; of Christ, 119, 121, 130, 131, 189–91, 194; and Christianity, 106, 107, 109, 118, 119, 123, 125, 127, 131; and civil society, 136, 166, 171, 184; as compassion, 118–25, 129, 142, 171; and death, 114–16, 118–19; and divine grace, 117, 127; as exercised by God, 14, 98, 99, 101, 104, 107, 108, 120–21, 123, 125, 131; as exercised by human beings, 14, 100, 101, 104, 106, 107, 111, 119–20, 122, 126–28; as exercised by saints, 101, 114, 123, 131, 132, 133, 134, 135, 168; and faith, 100, 171, 184; and human desire, 104, 106, 108, 112–13, 114, 117, 125; and human motivation, 110, 112, 118, 124, 125, 130–31; and human personality, 61,

❧ *The Augustinian Person* was designed and composed in Dante by Kachergis Book
Design of Pittsboro, North Carolina. It was printed on sixty-pound Natural Offset
and bound by McNaughton & Gunn, Inc., of Saline, Michigan.